CANARY

A VISUAL TRAVEL GUIDE THROUGH THE CANARIES

DISCOVER NATURAL BEAUTY, HIDDEN GEMS & HIKING TRAILS

ISLANDS

Lannoo

↳ Welcome to the Canary Islands. In this book we hope to dazzle you, trigger your senses, inspire you, and make you want to get out and explore the world. It is first and foremost an aesthetic object. We have worked with incredible designers and photographers to create a thing of beauty, showing the unique treasures the Canaries has to offer. Second, it's a visual travel guide. We will offer you tips and tricks, and show you the most beautiful places, hidden gems and must-sees across the seven islands. With a comprehensive palette, focusing on the islands' enduring nature and culture, we aim to cater to a wide profile of visitors. This book is indispensable for hikers and nature lovers, for culture seekers, and beach boys and girls. Besides selecting and curating places and activities, we have gathered useful information such as nearby facilities, access guide, and ideas for hikes and schedules. Third, it's an account of our journey through the Canary Islands. In April 2023 a group of eight exploratory runners covered the 560km (348-mile) GR131 in 14 days, crossing the Canary Islands from east to west. The GR131 is a marked trail that crosses the seven main islands plus Lobos, a small island north of Fuerteventura. This was no mean feat. We had to run more than a marathon per day, spiced up with 1,800-plus vertical metres. A professional photographer followed the runners and captured highlights on and off the course, of every island. The result of all this blood, sweat and tears lies in your hands. We hope this book and our journey is an invitation to wander, explore and get lost. There is intense beauty to be found in this world, both inside and outside. If anything, we hope this book inspires you to go out and live your life to the fullest.

CHARLES VAN HAVERBEKE,
AUTHOR

Canary Islands ↳ Credits

AUTHOR
Charles Van Haverbeke

PHOTOGRAPHY
Arthur Chambre

CREATIVE DIRECTION
Marcus Brown

DESIGNERS
Marcus Brown · Camille Liebaert
Els Lorié · Josephine Van Haverbeke

SUPPORT CREW
Hélène Corinne · Maeve Canning
Léo Chambre · Ben Stassijns

RUNNERS
Amélie Harvengt · Charles Van Haverbeke
Kasper Van Herpe · Matthias Valcke
Stephane Ficaja · Thomas Thewissen
Thomas Van Woensel · Thomas Van de Weghe

PARTNERS
Innerme · Oleus
On Running · RVE Compression

TO THE RUNNERS

To the crazy ones who joined us in this adventure. This is the first archipelago to cover and hopefully the first of many more. What a brutal challenge it was: 650km with 25,000 vertical metres on 14 days, or more than a marathon per day with 1,800m elevation on average. The cut-off times set by the ferries we had to catch added some extra spice to the Canarian sauce. What a team and what an adventure.
Las Palmas!

TO MARCUS

I'm honoured that you have led the design of this book. Thanks for breaking away from the conventional travel guide identity. Your design language is pure, without being boring. Bold, without being extravagant. Refreshing, without pushing too hard. Thanks for your genius mind and your generosity in effort.

TO ARTHUR

You will have to do your best to find a photographer more dedicated than Arthur. When the idea for this project was born, Arthur had to be in. Combining superior quality and sheer dedication, running up hills to get that one shot of the runners in the scenery. If I could give Arthur a rocket suit, I would. Thanks for spending hundreds of hours on not only shooting marvellous imagery but also editing them to sheer beauty.

TO MAEVE & BEN

To two of the most gentle souls on this planet. A lucky coincidence brought us together, a wild invite with an unexpected turn leading to a cheerful 'yes'. Willing to support us, they coped with our pains, our demands, our smell and our grumpiness. The drove and shopped relentlessly, they cooked for us like Michelin chefs and through all this effort, they were always smiling. We need more Bens and Maeves in this world.

TO MAX

For being an inspiration, a great friend and my soulmate and buddy on the 'Follow The Coast' project since its inception in 2019. Because Max focused on supporting runners along the shores of Galicia and Portugal with the goal to run the entire coast of Europe, there was time to bring 'Crossing the Canaries' to life. This 'archipelago spin-off' embodies the same spirit as the Follow The Coast project. We want to explore, connect and challenge ourselves through long collective endurance projects. Bolder, better, bigger.

TO ELS

Thanks for making a second book (!) together. The first was 400 pages long, this one is over 300 pages. It's a hell of a job and only possible with sheer positivity, patience, determination and precision. Thank you for all the hours and the sophisticated monk's work that led to this piece of beauty.

TO CICERONE

We are grateful to have found this incredible hiking guide to the GR131, complete with GPX files and detailed stage-per-stage descriptions.

Handed to us as manna from heaven this guide led us step by step into the wild. A must guide for all hikers.

TO THOMAS & STEPHANE

Every crazy idea needs early adopters for it to succeed. Thom and Steph were the first one to unconditionally love this baby from its very foetus form, when it was a vague friday idea, until it became a fully blown concept. Thank you for your love and support, in all the ways it was needed throughout the entire life of this project. Thanks for all the adventures we did together. I feel privileged to be part of this trio and hope to live many more adventures together.

TO EMMA

Thanks for your support during all the hours put in this book. For the daily calls after crossing the finish line and for your brilliant love, to me and everyone around you.

TO CAMILLE & JOSEPHINE

Editing a book is a hell of a job. The last stretches often tend to stretch endlessly in the unknown. That's why this time we didn't need one but four designers to bring this piece of work to the finish line. Just one more iteration? A few pages more. Oh, one more thing. Thank you for bearing with this one going the extra mile or millimetre of design.

TO KARIM

To one of the bravest, most joyful and inspiring people out there. You seemed to live life fully, in the moment, worryless yet passionate. You'll always inspire us to enjoy, to keep playing and to smile.

TO CELINE & MY FAMILY

Travel, challenges and dreams have the power to elevate us and to propel us forward, especially when times are tough. This book is dedicated to those who struggle and can't see the light sometimes. It's created in the hope it can inspire, move and trigger. Beauty and hope are everywhere. It's my dearest wish for everyone to find their spark.

TO MY PARENTS & MY SISTERS

For having raised me in a warm home where the superpower of marvel and wonder was key, for patiently yet consistently showing us art, books, nature and culture. Never too much, always on invitation.

Thank you for creating a herd of gentle people with big hearts. Thanks Jos, Carole and Pauline for always being on the sideline during those crazy adventures.

Canary Islands
↳ The Fortunate Isles

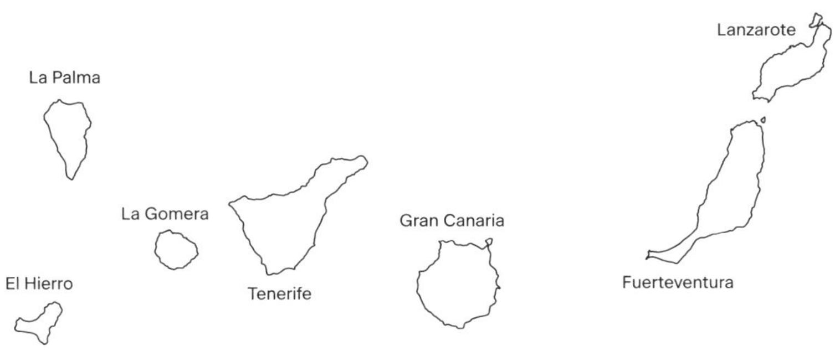

THE FORTUNATE ISLES

The Canary Islands, or Las Canarias, are a paradise of seven main islands plus a few smaller ones, 100km off the west coast of Africa.

Famous for offering all-year-round spring-like temperatures, the islands are often cited as one of the best places to live in the world.

Some 1,800km south of the capital Madrid, the archipelago is part of Spain and even hosts, at 3,718m, the country's highest peak, Mount Teide.

The islands' gentle climate and wealth of landscapes attract millions of holidaymakers from all around the world. They are considered one of the best places to relax and enjoy the sun. But the islands offer so much more than that ideal beach holiday.

The Canary Islands are often referred to as a micro-continent, encompassing an astonishing range of climates, the next one only a boat or car trip away.

A MICRO-CONTINENT

Golden dunes formed by the sands of the Sahara in Fuerteventura or Gran Canaria. Lush, humid jungles. damp with mist and moss, in Tenerife or La Gomera. A mountain summit – Mount Teide – higher than most Alpine peaks. Canyons, on Gran Canaria or La Gomera, seemingly straight out of a Western. Black and red volcanoes in Lanzarote or La Palma. Endless beaches. Natural turquoise pools. Some of the best stargazing or scuba-diving spots on Earth. Charming whitewashed villages.

The Canary Islands have it all, and it's not a question of one-size-fits-all. Surfers and windsurfers flock to the islands' shores for the constant wind and waves. They are a gathering place for triathletes and hikers from all over the world. Tenerife and Gran Canaria offer one of Europe's best-known nightlife holiday destinations. Hundreds of all-inclusive resorts offer the perfect spot for family holidays. You can pick what you want and leave the rest on the buffet.

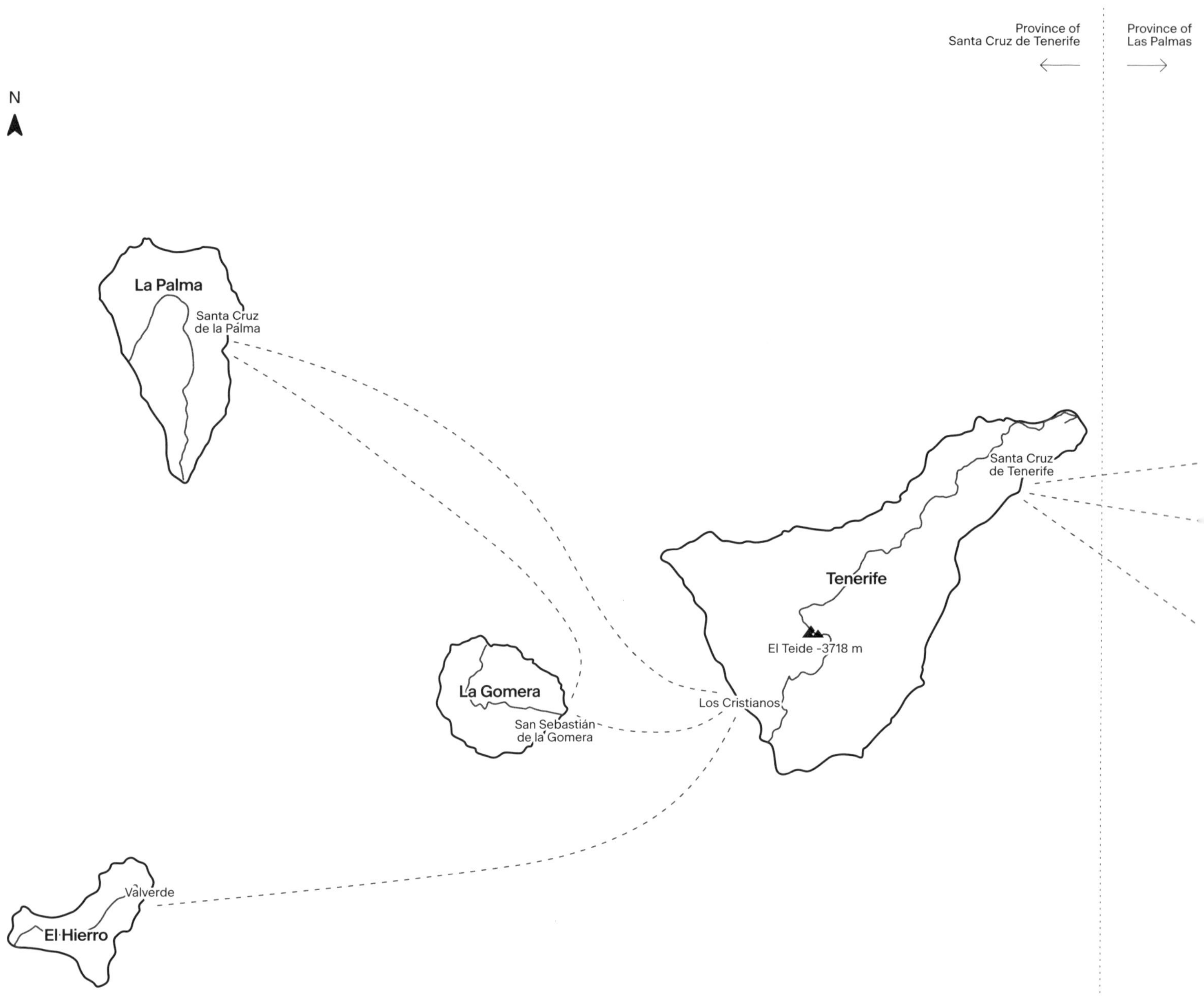
Province of
Santa Cruz de Tenerife
Province of
Las Palmas
N
La Palma
Santa Cruz
de la Palma
Tenerife
Santa Cruz
de Tenerife
El Teide -3718 m
La Gomera
San Sebastián
de la Gomera
Los Cristianos
El Hierro
Valverde

La Graciosa
Órzola
Lanzarote
Arrecife
Playa Blanca
Lobos
Corralejo
Puerto del Rosario
Fuerteventura
Morro Jable
Las Palmas de
Gran Canaria
Gran Canaria
Maspalomas
0
20 km

Canary Islands
↳ Get To Know

THE BIG TWO

Tenerife and Gran Canaria are the best-known islands of the archipelago. They have the widest offer of hotels, resorts and natural landscapes and attract the most tourists. Both islands are considered micro-continents, as they offer a bit of everything, from long sandy beaches to mountainous highlands. On those islands, Los Cristianos and Maspalomas, respectively, are the big tourist resorts where you can find the widest range of holiday activities, while Santa Cruz de Tenerife and Las Palmas are the biggest cities on the two islands.

Lanzarote and Fuerteventura are the runner-up islands, offering similar versatility but of a different magnitude. These two islands are the arid ones, lying to the east, closest to Africa. The three western islands, La Palma, La Gomera and El Hierro, attract considerably fewer tourists but offer sufficient accommodation options to make the journey pleasant and comfortable. These smaller islands are considerably greener, with more lush vegetation.

HOW TO GET THERE

International airports are found on all islands except for the two smaller ones, La Gomera and El Hierro, with most airports located conveniently next to the bigger cities or resorts. The commonest way to travel from one island to the other is by ferry. Fred Olsen and Naviera Armas are the two ferry operators and offer a multitude of connections. Check our map for more information. Travel on the island is mostly done by car or bus, and most journeys can be done within or around the hour.

ETERNAL SUNSHINE

The Canary Islands have a Mediterranean, sub-tropical climate, which means that temperatures are mild and stable throughout the year within the range 18–25 °C, offering 3,000 hours of sunshine. Summers are often extremely dry and winters gentle, with averages of 21 °C in January on Tenerife, making it a much-loved winter destination. Owing to elevation, wind and cloud, the climate – and therefore the amount of sunshine and rain – can vary tremendously from island to island and within each island. Tenerife, for example, has 20 micro-climates.

HIGHEST PEAK IN SPAIN

Mount Teide, 3,718m high, is the highest peak in Spain and the third highest volcano in the world measured from its base. It's home to the Teide Natural Park, one of the oldest and the most visited natural parks in Spain and among the most visited in the world. Mount Teide dominates the island of Tenerife and the surroundings, and can be seen from all neighbouring islands. All islands offer significant elevation, with Tenerife, La Palma and Gran Canaria (almost) beating the 2,000m threshold.

name	capital	highest peak	population	size rank
LANZAROTE	Arrecife	Peñas del Chache (670m)	152,289	4
FUERTEVENTURA	Puerto del Rosario	Pico de la Zarza (807m)	111,886	2
GRAN CANARIA	Las Palmas de Gran Canaria	Pico de las Nieves (1,949m)	851,231	3
TENERIFE	Santa Cruz de Tenerife	El Teide (3,718m)	917,841	1
LA PALMA	Santa Cruz de La Palma	Roque de los Muchachos (2,426m)	82,671	5
LA GOMERA	San Sebastián de la Gomera	Alto de Garajonay (1,487m)	21,503	6
EL HIERRO	Villa de Valverde	Pico de Malpaso (1,501m)	10,968	7

Canary Islands
↳ Good To Know

GUANCHES

The Guanches were the original inhabitants of the Canaries and are believed to have arrived on the islands from Africa in the 2nd–1st centuries BCE. They lived in caves, had knowledge of geometry and mummified their dead. How they arrived in the Canaries is still unknown: some believe they were exiles from Africa, others that they escaped from pirates, and a few even that they were refugees from the mythical drowned island of Atlantis. In the 15th century, they were conquered by the Spanish.

ISLAND OF THE DOGS

The name of the Canary Islands is likely derived from their Latin name, *Canariae Insulae*. According to the Roman historian Pliny the Elder, the island Canaria contained 'vast multitudes of dogs of very large size'. The connection to dogs is retained in their depiction on the islands' coat-of-arms. The name of the islands is not derived from the canary bird; rather, the birds are named after the islands.

LAS PALMAS, BIGGEST CITY

Las Palmas de Gran Canaria is the biggest city on the islands and, together with Santa Cruz de Tenerife, the capital. Don't confuse the city Las Palmas with the island La Palma. Las Palmas is home to the biggest freight port, while its sister, Santa Cruz, has the biggest fishing port. Both ports have ferries connecting to the majority of all the other islands.

ONE REGION, TWO PROVINCES

The Autonomous Community of the Canary Islands consists of two provinces, Las Palmas and Santa Cruz de Tenerife. The province of Las Palmas consists of Gran Canaria, Fuerteventura and Lanzarote. The province of Santa Cruz de Tenerife governs Tenerife, La Palma, La Gomera and El Hierro.

1402, JEAN DE BÉTHENCOURT

The conquest of the islands by Castilian forces began in 1402 under the command of Jean de Béthencourt. First Lanzarote, Fuerteventura and El Hierro were conquered after which Jean de Béthencourt was crowned 'King of the Canary Islands'. The natives of La Gomera, Gran Canaria, Tenerife and La Palma resisted the Castilian invaders for almost a century.

12 MILLION TOURISTS PER YEAR

Some 6 million go to Tenerife, 4 million to Gran Canaria, 3 million to Lanzarote, and 2 million to Fuerteventura, with considerably fewer going to the other islands. As a reference, Paris attracts 30 million visitors per year. The majority come from the UK, Germany and Spain. Tourism is the highest contributor to the economy accounting for 23 per cent of the GDP, followed by construction and agriculture. Inflow is very stable throughout the year with the peak from December to April.

STARGAZING

Thanks to the absence of light pollution, the elevation and the stable position of the clouds around 2,000m, the highest peaks on some of the Canary Islands are known to be among the best places on the planet for observing the heavens. The Roque de los Muchachos observatory and Teide Observatory, both at approximately 2,300m, host dozens of telescopes and attract international scientists.

MACARONESIA

The Canaries are part of Macaronesia, four volcanic archipelagos in the north Atlantic, off the coasts of Africa and Europe, formed by seamounts on the ocean floor whose peaks have risen above the ocean's surface. The Azores and Madeira are part of Portugal, the Canary Islands are part of Spain, and the rest are part of the island country of Cabo Verde.

2.2 MILLION INHABITANTS

The majority of Canarians live on the two capital islands of Tenerife (43%) and Gran Canaria (40%). The population is steadily growing by 1 per cent per year. Some 75 per cent are Spanish; the rest are foreign migrants from both western Europe and Africa.

CÉSAR MANRIQUE

César Manrique was a Spanish artist, sculptor and environmental activist from Lanzarote, known for his architectural projects that integrated touristic facilities into nature. His works are to be found mostly in Lanzarote – including Jameos del Agua, Mirador del Rio, Jardín del Cactus and the El Diablo restaurant – and the Juguetes del Viento (windmill sculptures) found all across the islands. On other islands he built famous viewpoints such as La Peña in El Hierro and Palmarejo in La Gomera.

GOFIO

Gofio is a traditional food eaten since the Guanche people, made by grinding roasted grains, primarily barley and wheat. It still dominates the local cuisines and is known for its long shelf life as well as its nutritional value, as it is rich in fibre, vitamins, and minerals. It's an excellent source of energy and was important for the sustenance of the island's inhabitants in times of scarcity. It is commonly eaten at breakfast, mixed with milk or yogurt, yet it can also be added to soups and stews as a thickener, or used to make dough for bread.

GOLF

There are 23 golf courses on the Canary Islands. Most of them, nine in total, are located on Tenerife, with six on Gran Canaria, five on Fuerteventura, two on Lanzarote and one on La Gomera. Abama and Buenavista golf clubs in Tenerife, located in the west of the island, and Anfi Tauro in Gran Canaria are the best-rated ones. Most courses are found in south-western Tenerife or in southern Gran Canaria.

PARADORES DE TURISMO DE ESPANA

The Paradores de Turismo de España is a Spanish state-owned chain of luxury hotels, usually located in historic buildings or in scenic areas, created with the double objective of promoting tourism and putting unused historic buildings to use. The first parador was created on the Spanish mainland on 9 October 1928 in Avilla. Today, there are 97 in Spain and five paradores on the Canaries, one on every island except Lanzarote and Fuerteventura. The most legendary ones are in Tenerife, El Hierro and Gran Canaria. The one in Tenerife is located at 2,000m and is very popular among top athletes who benefit from the high altitude. During our stay we ran into a few Olympic champions and the Slovene cyclist Primož Roglič, a Grand Tour winner. The one on Gran Canaria is located in Cruz de Tejeda, close to Roque Nublo. The one in El Hierro has an end-of-the-world vibe, located right next to the beach in the desolate Las Playas valley with a view over the ocean.

CHRISTOPHER COLUMBUS

Columbus voyaged four times to the Americas, always passing the Canary Islands first to make use of the advantageous trade winds. In 1492, he fixed the rudder of one of his ships on Gran Canaria and then went to meet his two other ships in La Gomera, from where they started a five-week journey on 6 September 1492. In the subsequent voyages, the Canary Islands remained a welcome port of call for taking on water and other supplies. Both Gran Canaria and La Gomera have museums dedicated to this historic stopover.

WINE

Wine is made on all main islands, with ten Denominaciones de Origen Protegida (DOPs), of which five are in Tenerife. Wine has been made here since the 15th century, when the Spanish colonized the islands, exporting Malvasia sweet wine, so popular in that time that it was even known to Shakespeare. Lanzarote's El Grifo, founded in 1775, is the oldest bodega in the Canary Islands, in the iconic La Geria region.

Canary Islands
↳ How to use this book

THIS BOOK

The book is conceived as a visual travel guide with the goal of inspiring and guiding the user. After this introductory section, the book is split into two parts, 'The Islands' and 'The Journey'.

The first part takes up the lion's share of the book. This part consists of breathtaking photographs of the scenery and 'highlights' of each island, together with expansive practical information. It contains everything anyone needs when looking for information to plan and book their own journey and holiday.

'The Journey' is a short section that can be considered as an epilogue. It describes our adventure and the emotions and learnings we took away. While 'The Islands' part is written in an informative, neutral way and is written to guide readers, 'The Journey' is written as a story.

THE ISLANDS

Every chapter starts with an informative section designed to introduce someone who is not directly familiar with one of the islands to gradually build up detailed information. You will find a general introduction to the island, followed by a statistical table with some insights. Every island chapter has a map showing the general outlines of the island together with the numbered 'Highlights', so you can orient yourself. Next to this map, you will find a practical page with helpful section on 'where to stay', 'how to move about' and 'best beaches' and a suggested schedule for a two- or three-day stay on the island. The bigger islands get three days' worth of suggestions, the smaller ones two days'.

THE HIGHLIGHTS PER ISLAND

The introductory pages are followed by the 'Highlights', the numbering corresponding to the numbers on the map. There are two types of highlight, 'Stroll' highlights, covering the cities and villages on the island, and 'Explore' highlights, gathering together the best natural and cultural sites. You can scan and read through these highlights and pick and choose which look best, based on your preference.

To further help you, we have scored them 1–5 on a number of aspects: 'Stroll' highlights are scored on recommendation (☆), access (⇎) and hospitality (♀). 'Explore' are scored on recommendation (☆), size (↕) and hospitality (♀). You can find the scoring methodology in the table opposite. This will help guide your choice of destination, based on its characteristics and maybe risks.

THE HIKES

We have followed the GR131, running from Lanzarote in the east to El Hierro in the west. We highlight and share 36 stages spread over eight islands. An introductory section shares basic tips and tricks, followed by a big overview map and table. The table features handy statistics such as length, total ascent and descent, technicality of the trail and, finally, our recommendations based on our experience. Furthermore, every island has its own hike section with more expansive descriptions of the different options. For each island there is also a zoomed-in map so you can identify hikes nearby.

THE JOURNEY

The last part tells the story of the runners, the two support crew, and the dedicated photographer supported by his mother and one-year-old child, Léo. We follow the run, day in, day out, along the GR131 and read how the whole adventure came to life. This part is more personal, sometimes emotional and at times philosophical. It reads like a short story and hopes to deliver a raw, honest insight into what happened in April 2023 when friendship, creativity and resilience were some of the key themes.

Canary Islands
↳ How to choose your highlights

RECOMMENDATION	☆	
Do we recommend this place?	1	no, tourist trap
	2	not sure
	3	recommend
	4	highly recommend
	5	must

HOSPITALITY		AVAILABLE AT LOCATION?	NEARBY?	RECOMMENDATION
Are food & drinks available?	0	no	no, day trip	bring your own drinks
	1	no	long walk, 20'-1h	bring your own drinks
	2	no	medium walk, 5-20'	bring your own drink
	3	no	short walk, 5'	drinks available
	4	yes, few	on the spot	drinks available
	5	yes, plenty	on the spot	drinks available

SIZE	↕	STATUS	INHABITANTS	EXAMPLES
How big is the town?	1	village with no or few facilities	<100	Puertito de los Molinos
	2	village with facilities	>100	Caleta de Famara
	3	town	>1.000	Teguise
	4	city	15.000-50.000	Corralejo, Puerto del Carmen
	5	big city	>50.000	Las Palmas

ACCESS		CAR	ROAD	WALK	WHEELCHAIR	CHILDREN (5+)
Is this place easily reachable	1	no	trail - hard	long	not accessible	not accessible
	2	no	trail - fair	long	not accessible	not accessible
	3	yes	dirt	short	hard	yes
	4	yes	asphalt	short	yes	yes
	5	yes	highway	short	yes	yes

Canary Islands
↳ Hiking on the GR131

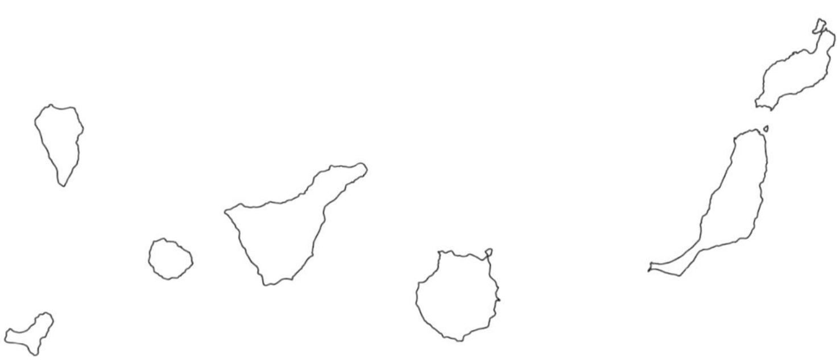

HIKING IN THE CANARIES

The Canary Islands are a paradise for hikers. Year-round spring-like temperatures and ample sunshine and very few rainy days are some of the perks. Couple that with a variety of landscapes, from desert to jungle, and some serious elevation, up to 3,718m on Tenerife, and you get a recipe for success. Lanzarote and Fuerteventura offer arid, desert-like landscapes, Gran Canaria provides ravines, La Gomera plenty of subtropical forests (and ravines), La Palma volcanoes and abundant pine forests, and Tenerife a bit of all the above.

THE GR131

The GR131 is a 560km route that traverses the seven Canary Islands, from east to west. It begins in Lanzarote and finishes on El Hierro and is presented in 32 daily stages. The route is well waymarked, but some navigational skills are required. Most of the terrain is moderately technical, but there are some remote and rocky sections that need to be treated with care. It general, it passes by the highest peaks of each island and it runs from coast to coast, except in Tenerife. On Gran Canaria, the GR is not yet signposted. Lobos, a small island to the north-east of Fuerteventura is also included, but La Graciosa, often referred to as the eighth Canary Island, is not included. Also included is an optional ascent of Mount Teide. The total itinerary encompasses more than 20,000m of elevation gain and would take an average hiker about one month to complete.

The best guide on the GR131 is *Trekking in the Canary Islands* published by Cicerone. It describes every stage of the trail and comes with downloadable GPX files.

HIKES IN THIS BOOK

In this book you will find 'Hike' pages for each island, sharing more information on hike opportunities for the Canaries. We present 36 hikes, of which 32 are GR131 stages. We have added four more stages to enable you to walk from coast to coast in Tenerife (as we did on our own trip). On the eastern side of the island, we have connected Chamorga with La Esperanza, where the GR131 starts, passing through the Anaga forest, leading to three additional stages. In the west, we connected Arona with Los Cristianos.

The average distance of a stage is 15km, which will take an average hiker 4–6 hours. All stages have some elevation gain, with 10 out of 36 having more than 1,000m in elevation gain. These are to be undertaken only with careful planning and preparation. All stages are A-to-B, so it's important to consider practicalities carefully before starting a hike.

	# hikes	hikes	distance (km)	ascent (m)
LANZAROTE	5	1-5	73	1570
LOBOS	1	6	8	150
FUERTEVENTURA	8	7-14	156	3460
GRAN CANARIA	5	15-19	74	3252
TENERIFE	10	A1-3, 20-24	162	8004
LA PALMA	4	27-30	69	4144
LA GOMERA	2	25-26	45	2384
EL HIERRO	2	31-32	40	1683

HIKING TIPS

Much of the routes consists of remote treks through wild landscapes, far away from facilities. Often, you will be exposed to the elements for a significant time so make sure you bring sun protective gear like sun cream, hats and long sleeves and always make sure you are hydrated sufficiently. Hiking is a demanding physical activity so make sure you are bring along a good supply of high-carb foods such as energy bars or bananas.

When climbing, you should take into account the lower speeds per kilometre. In steep climbs, 300m/h is a solid pace, 500m/h is a great pace, 700m/h-plus is for experts. Plan your timing carefully so you don't miss the bus you are counting on catching.

WHICH HIKES TO PICK

On the 'Hike' pages for each island, and in the overview table on page 21, we share the different stages along with a short summary of what to expect and some quantitative information to help you make your decision. For each hike, the following data will be shown: distance, total vertical ascent and descent, and asphalt percentage. In addition to this factual data, we have added scores in terms of technicality, the availability of facilities and, finally, our level of recommendation. These ratings are scored out of a maximum of 4. A low number for technicality means 'easy terrain, suitable for most abilities'. A low number for facilities means 'few facilities present, so take precautions'. For recommendations, we have the following definitions: 1 means 'not recommended'; 2, 'recommended, but there are better alternatives on the island'; 3, 'highly recommended', and 4, 'unique experience'.

Faced with this combination of distance, elevation, asphalt percentage and technicality, you should be able to determine whether a hike is suitable for you, how to prepare and estimate injury risk. Distances over 20km, ascents over 700m, or technicality levels of 3 or upwards carry some challenge or risk.

OUR TOP SEVEN HIKES

Most of the hikes come recommended. There are a few we consider 'mind-blowing'. You can find these below:

1. Tenerife, El Portillo to Teide Summit, GR131, Stage 22A
2. Tenerife, Teide Summit to Parador, GR131, Stage 22B
3. Tenerife, Charmorga to Taborno, non-GR, Stage A1
4. La Palma, Ruta de los Volcanes, GR131, Stage 28
5. La Palma, Caldera de la Taburiente, GR131, Stage 29
6. Gran Canaria, Tunte to Cruz de Tejeda, GR131, Stage 17
7. Fuerteventura, La Pared to Barranco, GR131, Stage 12

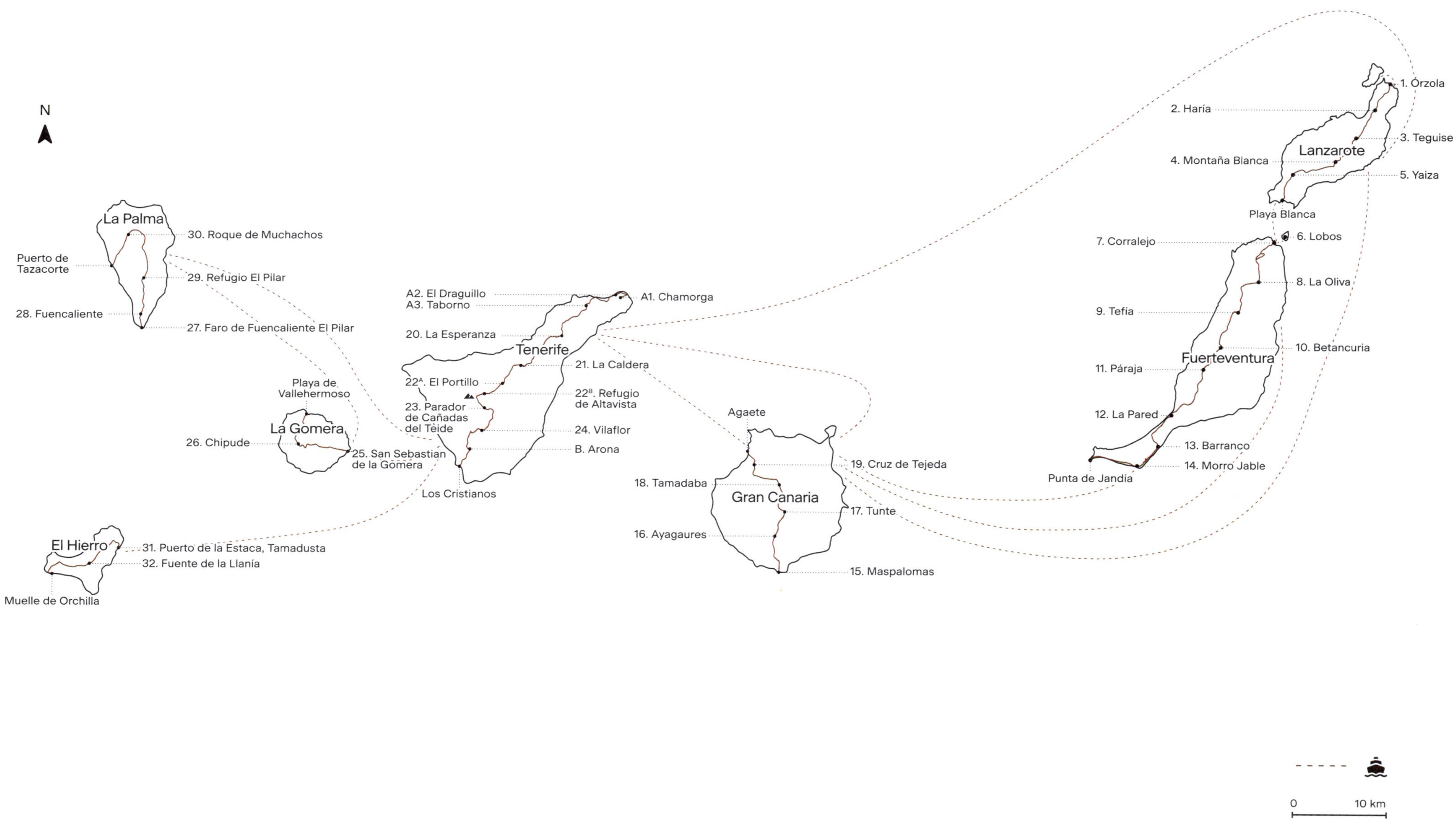
N
La Palma
30. Roque de Muchachos
Puerto de Tazacorte
29. Refugio El Pilar
28. Fuencaliente
27. Faro de Fuencaliente El Pilar
Playa de Vallehermoso
La Gomera
26. Chipude
25. San Sebastian de la Gomera
El Hierro
31. Puerto de la Estaca, Tamadusta
32. Fuente de la Llanía
Muelle de Orchilla
A2. El Draguillo
A3. Taborno
A1. Chamorga
20. La Esperanza
Tenerife
21. La Caldera
22ᴬ. El Portillo
22ᴮ. Refugio de Altavista
23. Parador de Cañadas del Teide
24. Vilaflor
B. Arona
Los Cristianos
Agaete
19. Cruz de Tejeda
18. Tamadaba
Gran Canaria
17. Tunte
16. Ayagaures
15. Maspalomas
1. Órzola
2. Haría
3. Teguise
Lanzarote
4. Montaña Blanca
5. Yaiza
Playa Blanca
6. Lobos
7. Corralejo
8. La Oliva
9. Tefía
10. Betancuria
Fuerteventura
11. Páraja
12. La Pared
13. Barranco
14. Morro Jable
Punta de Jandía
0
10 km

island	stage	type	from	to	distance (km)	ascent (m)	descent (m)	asphalt	facilities	technicality	recommendation
LANZAROTE	1	GR131	Órzola	Haría	12	470	190	43%	🍷🍷	⛰⛰	☆☆
	2	GR131	Haría	Teguise	13	360	340	19%	🍷🍷	⛰⛰	☆☆☆
	3	GR131	Teguise	Montaña Blanca	15.5	270	300	26%	🍷🍷	⛰	☆☆
	4	GR131	Montaña Blanca	Yaiza	17	390	480	39%	🍷🍷	⛰⛰	☆☆☆
	5	GR131	Yaiza	Playa Blanca	15.5	80	260	30%	🍷🍷	⛰⛰	☆☆
FUERTEVENTURA	6	GR131	Lobos	Lobos	8	150	150	0%	🍷🍷	⛰	☆☆
	7	GR131	Corralejo	La Oliva	25	480	260	40%	🍷🍷	⛰⛰	☆☆☆
	8	GR131	La Oliva	Tefía	17.5	210	230	22%	🍷🍷	⛰	☆☆
	9	GR131	Tefía	Betancuria	17.5	530	340	32%	🍷🍷	⛰⛰	☆☆☆
	10	GR131	Betancuria	Pajara	17	520	710	24%	🍷🍷🍷	⛰⛰⛰	☆☆
	11	GR131	Pájara	La Pared	26	750	910	19%	🍷	⛰⛰⛰	☆☆☆
	12	GR131	La Pared	Barranco	16	290	280	1%	🍷	⛰⛰	☆☆☆☆
	13	GR131	Barranco	Morro Jable	16.5	400	450	8%	🍷🍷	⛰⛰	☆☆☆
	14	GR131	Morro Jable	Punta de Jandia	20.5	280	280	16%	🍷🍷	⛰⛰	☆☆☆
GRAN CANARIA	15	GR131	Maspalomas	Ayagaures	18	530	220	72%	🍷🍷🍷🍷	⛰	☆
	16	GR131	Ayagaures	Tunte	12.5	900	320	24%	🍷	⛰⛰⛰	☆☆☆
	17	GR131	Tunte	Cruz de Tejeda	15.5	1020	400	6%	🍷🍷	⛰⛰⛰	☆☆☆☆
	18	GR131	Cruz de Tejeda	Tamadaba	17.5	750	1060	11%	🍷🍷	⛰	☆☆
	19	GR131	Tamadaba	Puerto de las Nieves	10.5	50	1250	10%	🍷🍷🍷	⛰⛰⛰	☆☆☆
TENERIFE	A1	Selfmade	Chamorga	El Draguillo	10.4	670	940	0%	🍷	⛰⛰⛰⛰	☆☆☆☆
	A2	Selfmade	El Draguillo	Taborno	18	1360	950	22%	🍷🍷	⛰⛰⛰⛰	☆☆☆
	A3	Selfmade	Taborno	La Esperanza	24	1040	730	42%	🍷🍷🍷	⛰⛰⛰	☆☆
	20	GR131	La Esperanza	La Caldera	29.5	1650	1360	5%	🍷	⛰⛰	☆☆☆
	21	GR131	La Caldera	El Portillo	13.5	1090	240	2%	🍷🍷	⛰⛰⛰	☆☆☆
	22[A]	GR131	El Portillo	Altavista	11.5	1250	20	0%	🍷	⛰⛰⛰	☆☆☆☆
	22[b]	GR131	Altavista	Parador	13	450	1570	0%	🍷	⛰⛰⛰⛰	☆☆☆☆
	23	GR131	Parador	Vilaflor	15.5	380	1100	0%	🍷🍷	⛰⛰⛰	☆☆☆
	24	GR131	Vilaflor	Arona	18	450	1260	22%	🍷🍷	⛰⛰⛰	☆☆☆
	B	Other	Arona	Los Cristianos	8.5	0	620	82%	🍷🍷🍷	⛰	☆
LA GOMERA	25	GR131	San Sebastián de la Gomera	Chipude	27	1960	880	19%	🍷🍷	⛰⛰⛰	☆☆☆
	26	GR131	Chipude	Playa Vallehermoso	18.5	420	1500	27%	🍷🍷🍷	⛰⛰⛰	☆☆☆
LA PALMA	27	GR131	Fuencaliente	Los Canarios	7	710	0	14%	🍷🍷	⛰⛰	☆☆☆
	28	GR131	Los Canarios	El Pilar	17.5	1450	720	3%	🍷	⛰⛰	☆☆☆☆
	29	GR131	El Pilar	Roque de los Muchachos	27	1880	900	1%	🍷🍷	⛰⛰⛰	☆☆☆☆
	30	GR131	Roque de los Muchachos	Puerto de Tazacorte	18	1440	100	18%	🍷🍷	⛰⛰⛰	☆☆☆
EL HIERRO	31	GR131	Puerto de la Estaca	Fuente de Llanía	18	1440	100	18%	🍷🍷	⛰⛰	☆☆☆
	32	GR131	Fuente de Llanía	Muelle de Orchilla	22	240	1580	27%	🍷	⛰⛰	☆☆☆

↱ Island 1 / 7
Lanzarote

846km²
152,289 residents

1

→ VOLCÁN DE LA CORONA
29.18472° N / 13.48083 °W
HEIGHT 609M

↳ Welcome to Lanzarote, the most easterly of the seven islands. 'Lanza' feels like one big Hollywood movie set for a film set on Mars. With over 300 volcanoes – red, amber or black – it features one of the driest and most alien landscapes of the archipelago. It is a real playground for sport fanatics – with all-year-long spring-like temperatures and an abundance of waves, hills and wind – as well as for culture lovers, who come to see the architecture and sculpture of local hero and visionary César Manrique scattered across the island. Despite its barren and often-menacing look, the island has abundant vegetation and is home to hundreds of vineyards, or bodegas, the colours of the vineyards offering a vivid contrast to the black volcanic backdrop.

Lanzarote
Fire Island

Coastline: 212km
Highest point: 670m

Fire Island, famous for its moon-like black-and-red landscapes and volcanoes

↳ Lanzarote can be divided into three main areas. Mountains in the north-east, volcanoes in the west and beaches in the south. The beach resorts of Puerto del Carmen and Playa Blanca play host to most of the restaurants, hotels and tourists on the island. Peace and quiet away from the hordes, can be found in the mountains in the north among the white villages tucked away in the palm-tree-filled valleys. The few souls you'll see there – perhaps at Mirador del Río or Famara – are likely to be of the cultural or adventurous kind. Don't forget to go in search of hidden beauty in the Jameos del Agua complex formed by a massive volcanic tunnel. The famous postcard views of black lava of ancient volcanoes are found in the Timanfaya and Los Volcanes National Parks, home to many craters, some of them accessible on foot. Where the lava meets the ocean in the west, Los Hervideros and Lago Verde offer a wealth of natural beauty that appeals to every sense. The El Jable plain, a strip of dusty desert south of Famara, separates the eastern mountains from the western volcanoes.

CASTILLO DE SANTA BÁRBARA

Lanzarote
↳ Introduction

HOW TO GET AROUND

Planes touch down from anywhere in Europe in Lanzarote Airport (ACE), named after César Manrique. The airport is conveniently close to the main tourist area of Puerto del Carmen.

Arrecife is connected by boat to Cadiz, La Palma, Gran Canaria, Tenerife and Fuerteventura at Puerto del Rosario.

A shorter connection between Lanzarote and Fuerteventura can be found at Playa Blanca, with a 20-minute journey time to Corralejo.

The ferry to the northern island of La Graciosa departs from the small docks in Órzola, which is also the starting place of the GR131.

The best roads, LZ1 and LZ2, run along the eastern coast from Playa Blanca in the south to Órzola in the north. All the towns are easily accessible by car, and, unlike in Lanzarote's southern neighbour, Fuerteventura, the asphalt is mostly in a good condition, much to the appreciation of the many cyclists.

WHERE TO STAY

If you are a surfer or triathlete, you will likely base yourself close to La Santa or Caleta de Famara where you'll find your natural habitat in the shape of pools or waves. If you like a drink or two and convenience, you'll lay your head anywhere on the coastline between Puerto del Carmen, Arrecife and Teguise, though you'll find many of your fellow tourists there as well.

Puerto del Carmen is the place that offers the most possibilities, from beach to shops to restaurants to hotels. Arrecife, the capital, is not the most common place to stay. We would probably recommend staying close to Teguise – the old city in the centre, not the part on the seafront – where you have the convenience of being close to the cities, the charm of the whitewashed old buildings and the natural beauty of the El Jable plain and Famara Cliffs.

Anywhere close to Haría is a bit remote from everywhere else, and don't bother trying in Timanfaya, as this is a restricted nature reserve.

BEACHES

There are good beaches to be found across the island but they are relatively rare owing to the generally rocky coastline. There is the picturesque Playa Papagayo in the west, the Playa Flamingo in Playa Blanca, the more touristy beaches in Puerto de Carmen of which Playa Chica is the prettiest, the surf beach of Famara in the north, and the remote Playa de las Concas at La Graciosa.

THREE-DAY STAY

Day 1 – The north
Early hike to Mirador del Río. Visit Jameos del Agua. Coffee in Haría. Lunch in Caleta de Famara. Surf session on Famara beach. Aperitif and dinner in Teguise or Jameos.

Day 2 – Volcanoes
Sunrise hike on Caldera Blanca. Breakfast in Mancha Blanca or on the crater. Lunch in El Diablo restaurant in Timanfaya, with tour before. Afternoon at El Golfo, Los Hervideros and Lago Verde. Dinner at a fish restaurant in El Golfo.

Day 3 – Culture and beach
Culture in the morning at the César Manrique Foundation in Tahíche. Lunch in a bodega. Beach in Playa Blanca or Puerto del Carmen. Vineyards in La Geria in late afternoon. Dine in a bodega.

LANZAROTE

EXPLORE / HIGHLIGHTS

1 La Graciosa
2 Mirador del Río
3 Monte Corona
4 Cueva de Los Verdes
5 Jameos del Agua
6 Famara Cliffs
7 Jardín de Cactus
8 Castillo de Santa Bárbara
9 César Manrique Foundation
10 Club La Santa
11 Los Grietas
12 Montaña Colorada
13 Volcan El Cuervo
14 Caldera Blanca
15 Timanfaya National Park
16 La Geria
17 Lago Verde
18 Los Hervideros
19 Salinas de Janubio
20 Playa de Papagayo
21 Montaña Roja

STROLL / HIGHLIGHTS

A Haría
B Caleta de Famara
C Teguise
D Puerto del Carmen
E Mancha Blanca
F El Golfo
G Playa Blanca

Lanzarote
↳ Key Facts

WHEREABOUTS	Name	Lanzarote
	Origin of name	Derived from Insula de Lanzarotus Marocelus, the name given by Italian-Majorcan cartographer Angelino Dulcert in honour of Genoese navigator Lancelotto Malocello
	Nickname	'Fire Island' – due to the red-black volcanic landscape, black sand beaches and desert-like terrain
	Key towns and villages	Teguise, Haría, Caleta de Famara
DEMOGRAPHICS	Population	152,289 people, 7% of the Canary Islands, 3rd in rank
	Capital	Arrecife (pop. approx. 63,750)
	Biggest cities	Puerto del Carmen, Teguise, Playa Blanca
INFRASTRUCTURE	Commercial Airport	César Manrique-Lanzarote Airport (ACE), close to Arrecife
	Commercial Ports	Port of Arrecife – ferries to Las Palmas de Gran Canaria, Santa Cruz de Tenerife and Cadiz Port of Playa Blanca, the island's southernmost town – ferry to Fuerteventura Port of Órzola – ferry to the island of La Graciosa
	Agriculture	White wine, Malvasia wine, sweet potatoes, tomatoes, cacti, aloe vera, salt
GEOGRAPHY	Size	846km2, 4th in rank
	Highest point	Peñas del Chache (672m)
	Dimensions	60km from north to south and 25km from west to east
	Coastline	213km – 10km sand, 16.5km beach, remainder is rocky
	Geologic origins	The island emerged about 15 million years ago as a product of the Canary hotspot, making it the oldest of the Canary Islands
HISTORY	1402	French explorer Jean de Béthencourt arrives and conquers the island.
	1730-1736	A series of violent eruptions takes place, creating 32 volcanoes and causing large-scale immigration
	1775	The Bodega El Grifo is opened, still in existence as Lanzarote's oldest working winery

Lanzarote
↳ Where to Hike

OVERVIEW

The five stages through Lanzarote give a good impression on the make-up and the look and feel of the island.

Stage 1 and 2 offer more mountainous terrain, far away from civilization. Stage 3 crosses the El Jable desert plain. Stage 4 connects the midland to volcanic country and the La Geria vineyards and Stage 5 descends through lava fields back to the ocean.

TERRAIN

Lanzarote offers mostly easy rolling dirt roads, often through wide open landscapes. Although the surrounding terrain looks wild and barren, the technicality or ascents of the trails are the most gentle of all the islands. Facilities are relatively scarce on the track itself but the island is not so big so the nearest town is often not very far away.

WHICH STAGE TO PICK

If we had to select wo stages out of the five available on Lanzarote, we would go for Stage 2 and Stage 4. Stage 2 offers the vertical drop of the Famara Cliffs with a view on Famara beach and the stunning descent to Teguise and El Jable plain. Mornings can be misty in this area, so if you want to enjoy the views it is better in the afternoon. This stage gives you a flavour of mountains, cliffs, desert and finally the charm of Teguise. Stage 4 connects the midland with a view on the ocean with the extra terrestrial region of the La Geria Vineyards. If you want to witness something truly unique which you will not find anywhere else in the world, pick Stage 5.

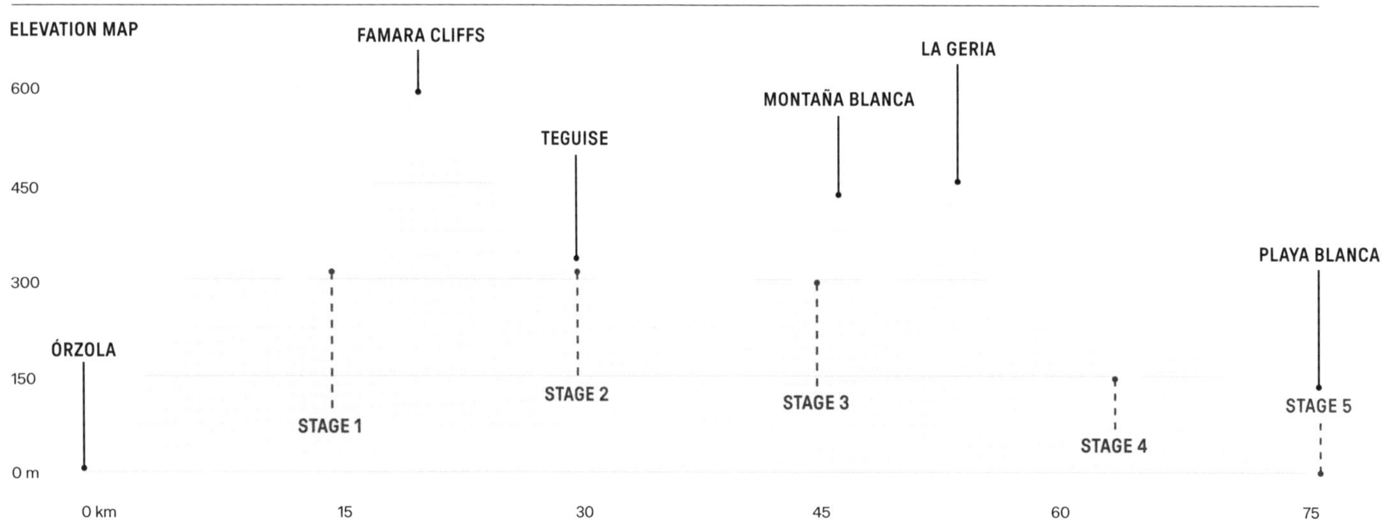

Lanzarote
↳ Hikes Overview

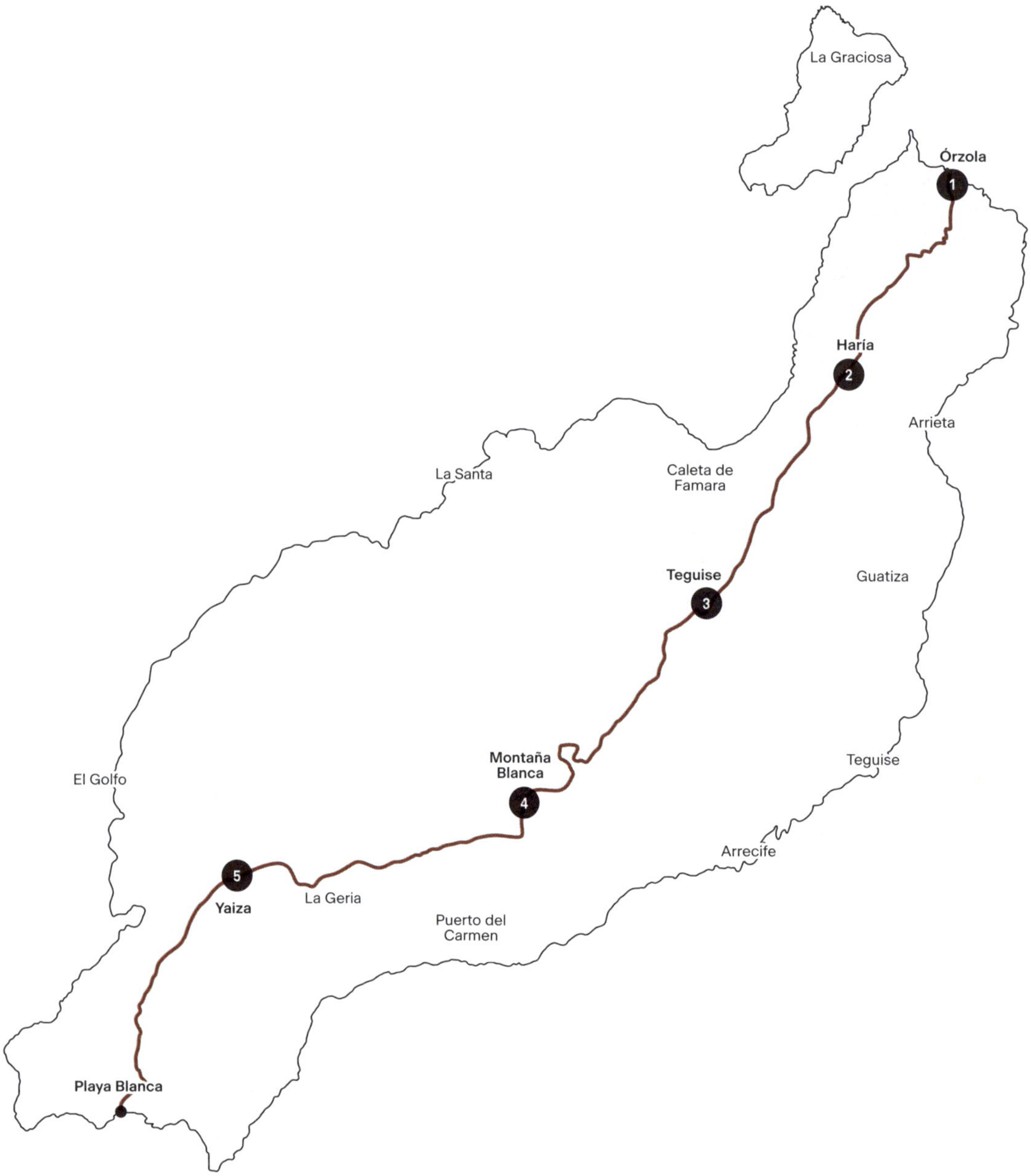

STAGE 1	ORZOLA TO HARIA	**Distance** 12km **Ascent** 470m **Decent** 190m **Asphalt** 43%
	Dirt roads and single tracks through the black-sand lava plains on Malpaís de La Corona, passing the Volcán de La Corona. Recommendation: 2 / 4 Technicality: 2 / 4 Facilities: 2 / 4 Type: GR131	The GR131 starts in the remote town of Órzola, first following an asphalt road. After taking a right turn, the path gently rises on a wide dirt trail, entering the wild Malpaís de La Corona, an area characterized by its volcanic cone and dotted with small vineyards. The trail winds through fertile fields of black volcanic ash near the village of Máguez, to cross over a hill to arrive at the neighbouring village of Haría. Haría is renowned for its picturesque white houses and serves as an ideal spot for a coffee break or a lunch at one of the local bars.

STAGE 2	HARIA TO TEGUISE	**Distance** 13km **Ascent** 360m **Decent** 340m **Asphalt** 19%
	Dirt road to the highest peak of the island, single track along 600m-high cliffs, then a gentle dirt-road descent with fantastic views over the Teguise valley. Recommendation: 3 / 4 Technicality: 2 / 4 Facilities: 2 / 4 Type: GR131	This stage climbs almost to the highest point on Lanzarote, though the summit of Peñas del Chache is occupied by a military installation. Most of the ascent is broad dirt road. Once the summit is reached, you can hike along a mountain ridge that has wonderful views over Famara beach and cliffs. Once you reach the Ermita de las Nieves, there's a gentle descent along dirt roads with views over the El Jable plains, leading to the lovely ancient town of Teguise, whose narrow, cobbled streets are made for wandering and exploring.

STAGE 3	TEGUISE TO MONTANA BLANCA	**Distance** 15.5km **Ascent** 270m **Decent** 300m **Asphalt** 26%
	Desert-crossing dirt roads from the mountains to the volcanoes. Recommendation: 2 / 4 Technicality: 1 / 4 Facilities: 2 / 4 Type: GR131	From Teguise on, an easy walk along dirt roads leads to the desert plains of El Jable in the middle of the island, where there is an immense feeling of space and views to the surrounding hills. From here the stage takes you from the northern mountains, through the deserts, towards volcano country. After the village of San Bartolomé, the road does an absurd loop around a volcano to arrive almost at the same point, leading you close to the first small vineyard and one of the typical local walls built to protect the grapes.

STAGE 4	MONTAÑA BLANCA TO YAIZA	**Distance** 17km **Ascent** 390m **Decent** 480m **Asphalt** 39%
	A stage of dirt roads with stunning views from Montaña Blanca over Puerto del Carmen and a finale through the black La Geria vineyards. Recommendation: 3 / 4 Technicality: 2 / 4 Facilities: 2 / 4 Type: GR131	The first part of the trail passes Montaña Blanca over dirt roads with a descent offering great views over whitewashed Puerto del Carmen, Arrecife and the Atlantic Ocean. Next is a longer stretch of asphalt road with a number of villages, though all with sparse facilities. Towards the second part of the stage is La Geria, approached along a black dirt road with first a climb followed by a long descent with a view over the spectacular wine valley. In the last section of the day's hike, there is a single trail through rock-hard lava prior to reaching Yaiza.

STAGE 5	YAIZA TO PLAYA BLANCA	**Distance** 15.5km **Ascent** 80m **Decent** 260m **Asphalt** 30%
	Descent along a single trail amid ochre-coloured lava fields. Recommendation: 2 / 4 Technicality: 2 / 4 Facilities: 2 / 4 Type: GR131	A gentle descent towards Playa Blanca, in large part on a single trail with ochre-coloured lava fields as far the eye can see and the mountains of La Geria in the background. It's easy to twist an ankle on a single track like this, especially if you're in a hurry to catch a ferry.

VOLCÁN DE LA CORONA

Lanzarote
↳ To Explore

1 **LA GRACIOSA** ☆^{4} ⇨^{2} 🍷^{2}

La Graciosa is a paradise for people looking to enjoy remote white beaches or avian or maritime wildlife (it's a magnet for divers). Biking or hiking is the sole mode of transport as the island has no asphalted roads. Climbing the island's summit of Las Agujas (266m) should be on your bucket list.

La Graciosa is the biggest island of the Chinijo Archipelago, a small group of islands just north of Lanzarote that includes, at 700km^2, the largest marine reserve in Europe. La Graciosa is the only inhabited island, with a population of around 700, mostly living in the port town of Caleta del Sebo.

Each year, in early November, people swim 2,650m across the channel between Lanzarote and La Graciosa, in a swimming event named after the Strait of El Río.

2 **MIRADOR DEL RÍO** ☆^{5} ⇨^{5} 🍷^{4}

A must-see when visiting the north of Lanzarote, Mirador del Río is an impressive viewpoint carved out of the 475m-high Famara Cliffs overlooking the island of La Graciosa and the Strait of El Río. Local artist and visionary César Manrique created this magical place between 1971 and 1973 in his typical style, including a balustrade café, shop and viewing platform, with views over Salinas del Río and the salt marshes below, the oldest marshes on the Canaries.

The large windows look like a pair of eyes, their gaze wandering over Salinas del Río. Before César laid his hands on the place, the spot was used to spot smugglers or pirates.

3 **MONTE CORONA** ☆^{4} ⇨^{2} 🍷^{2}

Volcán de la Corona (Monte Corona), at 609m the highest volcano on the island, is currently extinct but some four thousand years ago its violent eruption created massive lava streams covering the north-east of the island with a hot paste. This rough, now-petrified field is called Malpaís de La Corona and gave birth to the island's most visited geological attractions, the Cueva de los Verdes and Jameos del Agua. You can hike up the volcano using a track that starts in the village of Yé, leading you through vineyards to the top.

4 **CUEVA DE LOS VERDES** ☆^{4} ⇨^{3} 🍷^{2}

Cueva de los Verdes is a cave that forms part of a lava tube (pyroduct) situated in the north of Lanzarote. It is open to visitors and is even used for concerts. The cave was created when the top of the lava stream (from Monte Corona, remember?) cooled and developed a solid crust. The lava stream beneath later drained away, forming a large tunnel with the crust as its roof.

The pyroduct extends for 6km above sea level and for another 1.5km below. The latter part is called the Tunnel of Atlantis and is the largest underwater lava tunnel in the world. In about 20 spots, the roof of the pyroduct has collapsed, forming caverns known locally as jameos. One jameo forms the entrance to the Cueva de los Verdes; other jameos can be found a bit further north in Jameos del Agua.

Around 2km of of the cave system were developed for tourists in the 1960s, with the cave walls illuminated by coloured lights. The cave is also famous for its concert hall which is located near the entrance and can seat up to 500 people. In earlier centuries, inhabitants throughout Lanzarote hid in this cave to protect themselves from European pirates and Muslim slave raiders.

5 JAMEOS DEL AGUA ☆ 5 ⇨ 4 🍷 5

Jameos del Agua is a surreal art centre built inside one of the largest volcanic tunnels in the world and features turquoise or emerald-green pools, underground lakes, an auditorium and a restaurant. The spaces were built by César Manrique in three different caves – Jameo Chico, Jameo Grande and Jameo la Cazuela – all features created by the Monte Corona eruption.

You'll find not only hordes of tourists here but a unique species of squat lobster, endemic to the island, known as the blind albino cave crab or *jameíto (Munidopsis polymorpha)*. This blind, yellowish-white crustacean is hardly 1cm long and is one of the animal symbol of the place. At the entrance of the art centre is a sculpture erected by Manrique in its honour.

The smooth-bordered pools with crystal-clear blue water look inviting for a bath but unfortunately swimming is forbidden. An urban legend has it that only the Spanish monarch can dip their royal toes into the waters.

The auditorium is used for classical concerts as it has excellent acoustics and also for film screenings. Pedro Almodóvar's film *Broken Embraces*, which was partially shot in Lanzarote, had its premiere here in 2010. The restaurant offers à la carte meals and traditional folk dancing and music on Tuesdays and Saturdays.

6 FAMARA CLIFFS ☆ 3 ⇨ 3 🍷 3

The Famara Cliffs – Risco de Famara – tower above the renowned surfing beach and are the remains of a 10km-diameter caldera that once lay to the south of La Graciosa. The cliffs peak at 671m at the Peñas del Chache, the highest point of the island.

On the cliffs, surrounded by palm trees, and often bathed in fog, is the white-painted chapel of Ermita de las Nieves, dedicated to the Virgen de las Nieves (Our Lady of the Snows), patron saint of Lanzarote, who is said to bring rain to water the crops of local farmers. Legend has it that in 1427 the Virgin appeared to a shepherd, after which a small chapel was built.

7 JARDÍN DE CACTUS ☆ 3 ⇨ 4 🍷 4

This famous cactus garden, created by César Manrique, brings together more than 4,500 cacti of 450 species from North and South America, southern Madagascar, and other desert and arid areas. It was created in 1991, next to the village of Guatiza, in the north of the island. It was the last project of César Manrique, aided by the botanist Estanislao González Ferrer who was responsible for the selection and planting of the specimens. The site chosen was an old quarry, which protects the cacti from the wind. They grow on balconies and terraces in the shape of a large amphitheatre. Their roots enjoy the picón, the black volcanic sand, which create a striking backdrop for the plants' bright green, yellow and red colours.

The highest point of the site is marked with a restored windmill, once used in the production of gofio. The park is open every day, and most of the paths are wheelchair accessible.

8 CASTILLO DE SANTA BÁRBARA ☆ 3 ⇨ 4 🍷 4

Castillo de Santa Barbara, the oldest castle in the Canaries, clings to the slope of the Volcán de Guanapay, overlooking Teguise and the El Jable valley, making use of its panoramic views to protect the city from pirates, who used the archipelago as a key stopover on their routes to the Americas. Built 1km from Teguise on the rim of the volcano, the Castillo de Santa Bárbara (or Castillo de Guanapay as it is also known) dates to the 14th century and now houses the Museo de la Piratería (Museum of Piracy), taking us back to the most infamous pirates of the past. Among the objects on display are the various weapons used in their attacks: pistols, swords, cannons.

9 **CÉSAR MANRIQUE FOUNDATION** ☆4 ⇨5 ♀4

A museum dedicated to the work and life of César Manrique, Lanzarote's most influential architect and artist. César Manrique (24 April 1919 – 25 September 1992) was a painter, architect and sculptor who was born in Lanzarote and returned from New York in 1968 with a mission to preserve Lanzarote's natural beauty in the wake of rising tourism. It's hard to overestimate the impact Manrique had on the island, making his mark on many art projects including Jameos del Agua (1963–87); his Volcano House, Taro de Tahíche (1968), subsequently converted into the César Manrique Foundation; the restaurant at the restored Castillo de San José at Arrecife (1976); the visitor centre at the Timanfaya National Park (1971); the Palm Grove House at Haría (1986); the Mirador del Río (1973), the Jardín de Cactus at Guatiza and the series of 'windmill sculptures' known as the Juguetes del Viento on a handful of roundabouts on the island. His importance is such that the island's airport is named after him!

The César Manrique Foundation, constructed on five volcanic bubbles, is an example of the artist's own style of architecture, mixing art with nature to respect the landscape and the traditions of the island. The museum contains both art created and collected by the artist, the latter including works by Miró and Picasso. Manrique supervised the conversion of the Volcano House before his death. It can be visited daily from 10am until 6pm.

10 **CLUB LA SANTA** ☆4 ⇨5 ♀5

Club La Santa is one of the best-known and specialized sport hotels in the world, built in 1983 and offering activities across more than 40 sports to over 1,600 guests. It includes an athletic track, a sailing bay and three Olympic-size swimming pools.

11 **LAS GRIETAS** ☆2 ⇨3 ♀2

Las Grietas – Spanish for 'The Cracks' – is a canyon-shaped rock formation formed on the slope of the 600m-high Montaña Blanca. The three parallel cracks – one main one and two secondary ones – are separated by only a few metres and extend for some 20m through narrow corridors of solidified lava before reaching a final wall. These small canyons have been drilled into Montaña Blanca by the action of the water over thousands of years.

You can reach Las Grietas by parking on the right-hand side of the LZ35 road from Tias to San Bartolomé; the rock formation is on the other side of the road. As with many other sights in Lanzarote, the parking is slightly off-road and on the other side of the road to the sight itself.We recommend to visit mid-morning or mid-afternoon to get the most out of the contrasts of colour. Parking is at 28.973151, -13.635757.

12 **MONTAÑA COLORADA** ☆3 ⇨2 ♀2

This red-coloured 429m volcano lies close to the village of Masdache and the neighbouring Volcán El Cuervo.

There is an easy 3km hike with limited elevation around the volcano, popular among hikers on the island. You can start the hike at a car park at 29.004721, -13.6839523.

13 **VOLCAN EL CUERVO** ☆4 ⇨2 ♀2

Volcán El Cuervo is located between the Timanfaya National Park and the protected area of La Geria. It was the first volcano formed during the 1730 eruption.

Unlike the friendly-looking Caldera Blanca, El Cuervo has a darker, grimmer and pointier look. There is a 5km trail leading you to the crater with the highest point at 391m. The trail is family-friendly and one of the easiest and most popular routes in Lanzarote.

Just a 5-minute ride by car from the Cuervo Volcano, you can find the best of Lanzarote's volcanic wines.

14 **CALDERA BLANCA** ☆ 5 ⇦ 2 ♀ 2

Caldera Blanca is a large white-stoned volcano near the village of Mancha Blanca and part of 'Los Islotes' (The Islets) – three volcanoes formed between 1730 and 1736. They look as though they have been sculpted out of the landscape with a huge ice-cream scoop.

The volcano's crater is 1,200m wide, with its highest point 458m, from where you can see the town of Tinajo and the Timanfaya National Park. Caldera Blanca is part of the Los Volcanes Natural Park, located in the vicinity of Timanfaya, but unlike that park can be visited without restrictions. You can walk to the crater along the famous Camino al Crater – Path to the Crater – passing the smaller Montaña Caldereta with its 300m-diameter crater and highest point at 328m.

Risco Quebrado – the third of the volcanoes – is not on the track and is the furthest from the village of Mancha Blanca. It can be seen from the crater of Caldera Blanca.

15 **TIMANFAYA NATURAL PARK** ☆ 5 ⇦ 3 ♀ 5

You cannot leave Lanzarote without visiting Timanfaya National Park, encompassing the Montañas del Fuego (Mountains of Fire). Looking down from a plane, you see a huge black area to the west of the island, the result of the famous eruptions of 1730–36, when 50km^2 of Lanzarote – more than a quarter of the island – was covered with black lava basalt, with 25 craters and more than a hundred volcano cones. Timanfaya is one of the four national parks in the Canaries and a protected area so you can't wander around it freely. That doesn't mean you can't explore it, however. You need to buy a ticket to be granted access to the park and its visitor centre, and a 40-minute guided bus tour is included in the price. There are several guided walking tours, too – the most famous one being the 14km-long Ruta de los Volcanes. Places on these are limited to protect nature, so you might want to reserve your place several months in advance.

César Manrique had a hand in promoting Timanfaya, too, having designed the park's logo – a devil – as well as the famous El Diablo restaurant, on Islet Hilario. There meat is grilled using the lava streams which are still active below the soil, with temperatures rising up to 600 °C just a few metres beneath your feet. The view over the surrounding black sea of cones and stones is incredible. In the Montañas del Fuego visitor centre you can learn more about the region and watch guides dropping straws down holes where they burst into flames or book a camel ride, only a few hundred metres away from the centre.

16 **LA GERIA** ☆ 5 ⇦ 4 ♀ 5

The valley of La Geria is Lanzarote's main winegrowing region and a place like nowhere else on Earth. It's home to more than ten thousand gerias – funnel-shaped hollows and walls, dug and built into the thick layers of picón, the dark volcanic ash scattered across the valley. Without this human effort and creativity, the merciless winds and aridity would make viniculture impossible. You will see gerias as far as the eye can see over 52km^2 alongside the road from Masdache to Uga, a region declared a Protected Area. Fans of sweet white wine will enjoy the Malvasia grape, one of the oldest known grape varieties, its yellow colour and sweet and rich flavour pleasing many wine lovers, including Shakespeare who mentioned it in three plays, *Love's Labour's Lost*, *Henry IV Part 2* and *King Richard III*.

You can follow a 'wine trail', which passes by 30 wineries or bodegas, ideally starting from Uga, where you will find the local farmers market on Saturday mornings. Some of our favourite bodegas include the most visited, La Geria, located in the main wine valley where all the coaches stop; Rubicon, just across the road from La Geria, built by the Rijo family towards the end of the 19th century and one of Lanzarote's oldest; the modern winery Bodega Stratvs, just to the north; and El Grifo, the oldest in the Canary Islands, opened in 1775. Other great but lesser-known bodegas include: La Querencia, La Florida and Vega de Yuco.

through the caves. The collision creates geyser-like phenomena, with sprays of white water suspended in mid-air, as if the water is boiling; *hervir* is the Spanish for 'to boil'.

Little paths, balconies and sitting places have been dug into and carved out of the lava rock, which makes access more enjoyable but still hard for those using wheelchairs or prams. Access is free but the place can be crowded, so it's best to go early in the morning for your cold shower.

17 **LAGO VERDE** ☆4 🪧3 🍷3

Lago Verde is a green-coloured lake in an old volcano crater at the side of the ocean, a few hundred metres from the village of El Golfo. Water passes along underground channels and its green colour is a result of algae living in the salty water, not of sulphur or any other volcanic substance, despite popular belief. The steep slope next to the lake is what remains of the original crater of the volcano, today half eroded by the elements. You can reach Lago Verde by driving to El Golfo, where you find free parking on the left of the road, and then following a path to a viewing point. If you want to get closer, there is a descending track at the left, which allows you to get to within a few metres of the lake, which is separated from visitors by a rope. The best time to visit is between 2pm and 4pm when the sun throws hardly any shadows on the spectacle.

18 **LOS HERVIDEROS** ☆4 🪧3 🍷2

Los Hervideros is a series of lava rocks where the land meets the sea, unique because of the tunnels and coves cut out by the forces of pyroclastic flow and water erosion. People go here to enjoy the spectacle of roaring waves crashing against the rocks and making its way

19 **SALINAS DE JANUBIO** ☆4 🪧4 🍷3

These are the largest salt pans still in operation in the Canary Islands, on the Costa de Yaiza. These bluish-white fields, created 120 years ago and stretching across 168ha, form a striking contrast with the dark soils of the adjoining Timanfaya National Park. They are a perfect illustration of the ingenuity of the people of Lanzarote in dealing with the harsh climate and conditions of the island. Only two salt pans remain active on Lanzarote, the Salinas de Janubio and the Salinas Los Agujeros, the only survivors of a centuries-old tradition of salt production which has seen the disappearance of nearly 30 such enterprises in recent years. The Padrón Lleó family remains at the helm of the undertaking. The top-flight product, flor de sal, is obtained by scraping off the top layer from the salt floating in the salt pans, which have the appearance of giant stamps. This sought-after product, said to contain high amounts of iodine, is sold at the onsite bodega.

20 **PLAYA DE PAPAGAYO** ☆4 🪧4 🍷3

One of the most beautiful beaches on the island, 4km east of Playa Blanca, offers white sand and blue water protected from the wind in a moon-shaped bay. Due to its shape, it's often referred to as 'The Shell' by locals. Its clear, shallow water makes it a great place for families. It is reached by a short, descending track. As it is located in the Monumento Natural de los Ajaches, you can combine your visit to the beach with walks in the nature park. There is a small beach bar on the hillside where you can buy drinks or something to eat. The best time to enjoy it is evening time. Note that the nearby car park is a busy one and is not free of charge.

21 **MONTAÑA ROJA** ☆3 🪧2 🍷2

This 159m red volcano lies close to Playa Blanca, with an easy, short 3km hike to and around the crater. The hike starts here: 28.871725, -13.848604

Lanzarote
↳ To Stroll

A **HARÍA** ☆ 4 ↕ 2 🍷 3

This hidden gem in the Valley of a Thousand Palms, with its white houses and narrow streets, is protected from mass tourism. The village is set in the most fertile region of the island thanks to the slightly higher rainfall and volcanic soil resulting from ancient eruptions of the three surrounding volcanoes. There is not much to do apart from wandering beneath the shady trees on Plaza Leon y Castillo, enjoying some tapas, browsing the Saturday market, or visiting the old house of local hero César Manrique.

B **CALETA DE FAMARA** ☆ 3 ↕ 2 🍷 3

Caleta de Famara is a good blend between a cowboy town with dusty roads and a surfer resort where your wild soul is awakened by the bare-chested surfers carrying their boards home after 'a sesh' at the nearby Famara beach. The beach is the place to surf on the island, both for beginners and experts. It's also the biggest sand beach so is a great place whether you want to be active or chill.

Recently, this sleepy Spanish town has seen a wave of surf-related commerce and you'll find rentals, coffee bars and B&Bs. The walk to the beach is a short one, and the Famara Cliffs tower over the bay. A great camp for a day out – to surf or hike – and a relaxing drink afterwards.

C **TEGUISE** ☆ 5 ↕ 3 🍷 5

Teguise is the most charming town on Lanzarote with characteristic white houses and little squares. Founded in 1402, Teguise is the oldest settlement in the Canary Islands and was Lanzarote's capital for 450 years, thanks to its elevated position, making it hard to conquer. It's full of attractive white buildings, squares and palm trees, with a great Sunday market on Plaza de la Constitución where buying local cheese and a leather bag is obligatory!

Nuestra Señora de Guadalupe is the main church and dates to the 16th century. There are nice cobbled streets to wander along like Calle Los Árboles with its very strange-shaped trees. In the nearby village of Nazaret, you'll find the LagOmar museum and art gallery, another Manrique creation, and formerly the home of Omar Sharif, incorporating natural lava caves and furnished with flotsam and jetsam. Once you're done with exploring, pop into the stylish museum restaurant.

D **PUERTO DEL CARMEN** ☆ 5 ↕ 5 🍷 5

With its 6km-long promenade and numerous beaches, Puerto del Carmen is the most popular beach resort in Lanzarote and the place where you'll find the most shops, bars and restaurants as well as the inevitable tourists. One could compare it to Playa Inglés in Gran Canaria and Las Americas in Tenerife but because of the maximum four storeys vertical threshold rule on buildings and the unified colour palette, the resort doesn't give the same impression of mass tourism as its peers on the other island.

It's a great place if you like nightlife and if you want to be close to the beach. Playa Grande or Playa Blanca is the biggest and most popular beach. A bigger, less busy beach is Playa de los Pocillos. Closer to the airport you can find Playa de Matagorda. It's well located, less than 10 minutes from the airport – which you can actually see from the cycling and walking path that runs around the town – and close to Rancho Texas, a famous animal and water park.

E **MANCHA BLANCA** ☆ 2 ↕ 2 🍷 5

Mancha Blanca is a little village situated in Tinajo municipality, on the western side of the island, and is squeezed between two national parks, Timanfaya in the west and Los Volcanos in the east, making it a great stopover or stayover for hikers and nature lovers. The most famous volcano on the island – Caldera Blanca

– is only 4km away, making a walk around its crater irresistible. The name of the village – meaning 'white spot' – originates from the chalk areas on the Caldera Blanca. Its charming white church is dedicated to the Virgen de los Dolores whom locals prayed to during the 18th-century eruptions asking her to spare their fields and homes. In honour of their protector, they have built the church exactly on the spot where the lava stopped in 1736. Every Sunday there is a local market held in front of the church and housed in stables built of lava stone.

F **EL GOLFO** ☆ 4 ↕ 1 🍷 2

El Golfo is a small fishing town in the west of the island, named after the ancient El Golfo volcano, nowadays half covered by the sea. It's famous for the nearby spots of Lago Verde and Los Hervideros. Despite its remote location and small population of a few dozen inhabitants, there are a dozen fish restaurants and a few hotels. Nearby beaches are small and rocky, and less frequented, and unique because of the contrast between the black beach, ochre rocks and blue water.

G **PLAYA BLANCA** ☆ 3 ↕ 3 🍷 4

Situated in the very south of Lanzarote, with a view to the neighbouring island of Fuerteventura, is the beach resort of Playa Blanca. Playa Blanca can be seen as Puerto del Carmen's little brother, with the same offering but on a smaller scale and with a slightly less mass-touristy vibe. You can stroll along Avenida Marítima with its sea views, shop in the car-free Zona Peatonal Los Limones. or enjoy the sun on Playa Dorada. Tourism is pushing the little town to grow ever larger, and it now stretches from Faro de Pechiguera almost to the picturesque beach of Playa del Papagayo.

MIRADOR DEL RÍO & THE STRAIT OF EL RÍO

GR131, VOLCÁN DE LA CORONA

↰ HARÍA

MÁGUEZ ↴

CALDERA BLANCA, PARQUE DE LOS VOLCANES

GR131, CASTILLO DE SANTA BÁRBARA
ROAD TO TEGUISE

↙ GR131, PUERTO DEL CARMEN

FAMARA BEACH, WITH LA GRACIOSA (L) AND FAMARA CLIFFS (R) ON THE HORIZON ↗

LA GERIA

GR131, LA GERIA VINEYARDS

LA GERIA

LAS GRIETAS

↰ LAGO VERDE

LAS SALINAS DE JANUBIO ↴

LOS HERVIDEROS

↑ VOLCÁN EL CUERVO

EL GOLFO ↓

28.8398° N

13.8417°
W

↱ Island 2 / 7
Fuerteventura

1,660km²
116,886 residents

2

→ LEAVING CARDÓN
28.2406 W° / 14.15263 N°

↳ Welcome to Fuerteventura, known as a water sport paradise for its sandy beaches and constant winds, propelling kiters and surfers across its emerald-blue waters. Twin island to Lanzarote, Fuerte has a similar arid look with little vegetation, though it is lighter and more varied in tone, offering fifty shades of brown along its L-shaped form. What it lacks in variety of colour, it compensates for in the variety of its attractions. Sea lovers can choose between gorgeous turquoise lagoons or wild waves. Dirt eaters find yellow-sand deserts and dunes and can wander over ochre rolling hills and plains that stretch as far as the eye can see. Hill seekers can climb volcanoes or travel along remote and windy ridges where no living soul is to be found. Last but not least, beach boys and girls have an astonishing smorgasbord to choose from – whether sheltered shell-shaped coves only accessible by 4x4 or long sandy beaches where an ice cream is only ever just a stroll away.

Fuerteventura
Windy Island

Coastline: 304km
Highest point: 807m

CORRALEJO
LOBOS ISLAND

The Windy Island, with an abundance of sandy beaches, dunes and far-stretching plains

↳ Fuerteventura can be divided into three parts: the diverse north around Corralejo, the desolate and mountainy middle around Betancuria, and the sandy Jandía Peninsula in the south.

The north is hard to pin down in one compelling description, and it's that diversity that makes it so attractive. A diverse crowd is drawn to the lagoons and sunsets around El Cotillo, the bars in Corralejo, the dunes in the north-east and the volcanoes around Lajares. All this is punctuated by plenty of beaches, perfect for both kites and boards, creating the area's exotic surfer vibe. Once you pass La Oliva, the tourists fade away into the brown of boulders, plains and hills. Tucked between the peaks you'll find Betancuria, a charming white village surrounded by splendid viewpoints, such as the Morro Velosa Viewpoint created by César Manrique. On the coasts you will find tiny villages and remote beaches such as de Los Molinos, Garcey, Jarubio and Ajuy, where hikes or hidden caves reward those who have made the journey. At La Pared, the mountains give way to a vast desert, marking the start of the Jandía Peninsula with its spectacular landscapes – from the dunes of the isthmus of La Pared to the endless sandy beaches of La Cofete and the famous blue lagoons of Sotavento.

ISTMO DE LA PARED

Fuerteventura
↳ Introduction

HOW TO GET AROUND

Puerto del Rosario on the eastern side of the island is your first port of call whether you arrive by plane or boat, but it's an unattractive no-man's-land, the arriving tourists flocking either to the north around Corralejo or to the south around Sotavento or Morro Jable. The FV1 and FV2 highways along the eastern shore provide a good connection from north to south, but many of the roads that lead further afield and to the island's loveliest beaches are little more than dirt tracks. So if you like to get around, you should get a sturdy car or good car insurance. A quick 20-minute ferry ride gets you from Corralejo to Lanzarote, while the ride to the city of Las Palmas on neighbouring Gran Canaria takes more than two hours. Both Morro Jable and Puerto del Rosaria offer ferry routes running out of them, though Morro Jable is your best option, with shorter ferry times, higher frequency and also connections to Tenerife.

WHERE TO STAY

The choice here can feel rather binary, with most people staying either in the south or in the north, with nothing in between. In the north, Corralejo will offer the widest range of options and good access, but El Cotillo, with its beaches, lagoons and gorgeous sunsets, is also a good pick as is the inland village of Lajares with many scattered villas in the stony countryside, is a great choice. In the south, the Sotavento resorts or the city of Morro Jable offer roofs and ocean views to tourists. Both sides of the island welcome both the sunbathing and sporty tourists.

BEACHES

Fuerte has 300km of beaches. While most of the coastline is inaccessible rock, more than 70km offer incredible places to relax. Beaches come in all shapes and sizes. In the north-east are the urban beaches of Corralejo, the remote ones of Lobos or the 10km stretch of sand along the Corralejo Dunes Natural Park. The north-west offers surfers the beaches of Punta Blanca and families the Playa de los Charcos lagoons around Tostón Lighthouse or the famous C-shaped Playa de la Concha in El Cotillo. In the centre, are the remote, less accessible beaches of Jarubio, Garcey and Los Molinos. The south-west offers the spectacular Playa Cofete or the waves of Playa del Viejo Reyes near La Pared. In the south-east, the Sotavento Lagoon marks the beginning of a long stretch of sand heading towards the popular Morro Jable beaches.

THREE-DAY STAY

Day 1 – The versatile north
Start the day with an early hike on Volcán Calderón Hondo or a surf session in Punta Blanca. Have breakfast in Corralejo and take a picnic to Lobos Island or the Parque Natural de las Dunas de Corralejo to enjoy some beach time and peace and quiet. The wind usually picks up in the afternoon so, if you want a kite session, this is the place to be. Enjoy the sunset in El Cotillo with a *barraquito* (a kind of coffee liqueur) and have dinner here or in Corralejo.

Day 2 – The inland mountains
The GR131 offers great views just north of the viewpoint of Guise y Ajose or on the Morro del Cortijo, just after Betancuria. After breakfast or a coffee in Betancuria, drive south along the scenic FV30 and take the time to spot the Ermita de las Peñitas chapel after a short hike to the Mirador del Risco de las Peñas. Spend the afternoon on a remote beach such as Ayuy or Garcey.

Day 3 – The vast beaches of La Pared
Start the day with a long hike on La Pared. In the afternoon, choose between the remote Cofete or the buzzing Sotavento Lagoon. Before heading home or for the next island, Morro Jable offers a wide array of places to dine.

FUERTEVENTURA

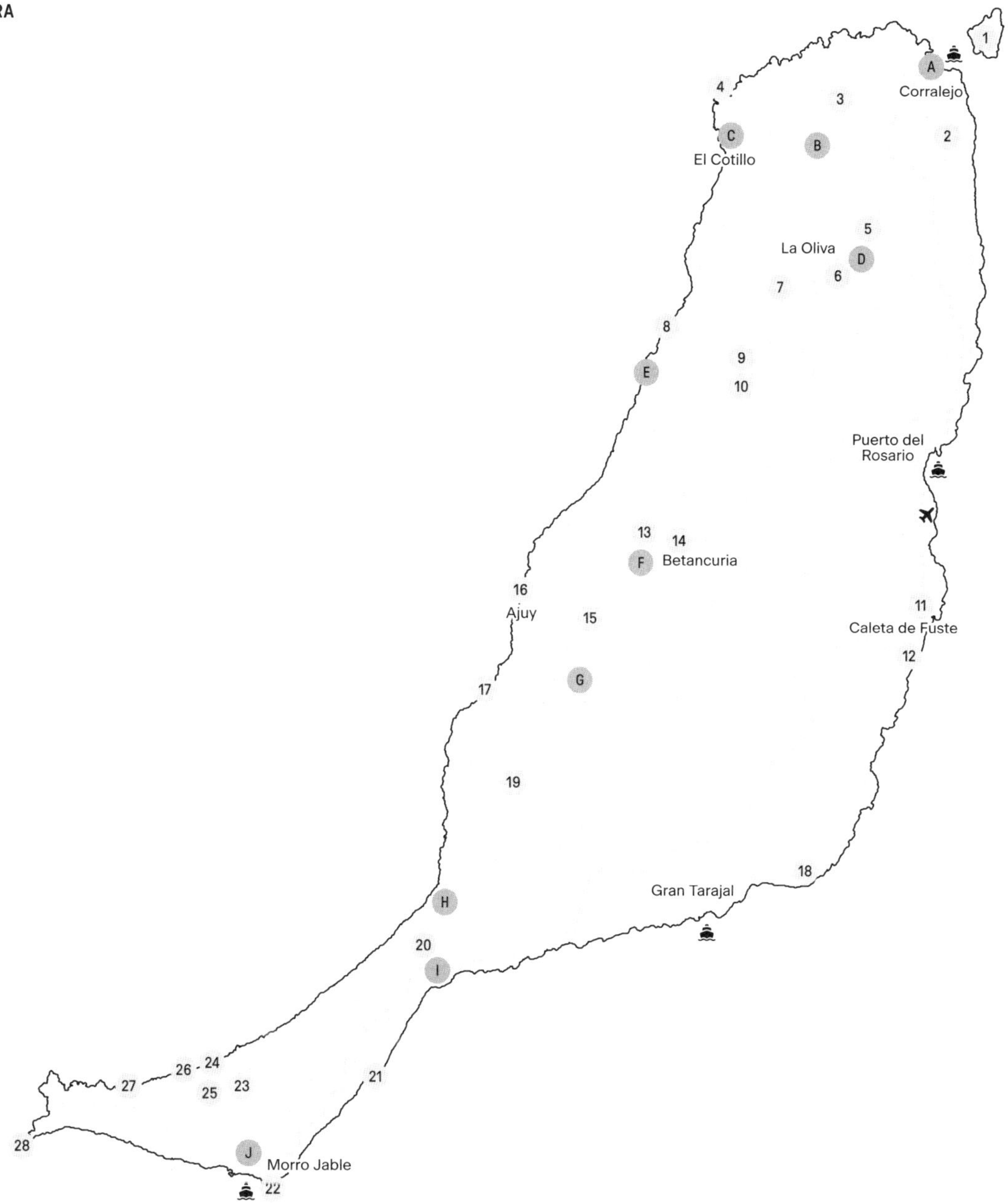

EXPLORE / HIGHLIGHTS

1 Lobos Island
2 Parque Natural de Corralejo
3 Volcán Calderón Hondo
4 Tostón Lighthouse
5 Molinos de Villaverde
6 Casa de los Coroneles
7 Tindaya Mountain
8 Playa de Jarubio
9 Molino de Tefía
10 Ecomuseo de la Alcogida
11 Castillo de Caleta de Fuste
12 Salinas del Carmen
13 Mirador de Guise y Ayose
14 Mirador de Morro Velosa
15 Ermita de las Peñitas
16 Ajuy Caves
17 Playa de Garcey
18 Faro de la Entallada
19 Sicasumbre Astronomical Viewpoint
20 Istmo de la Pared
21 Sotavento Lagoon
22 Morro Jable Lighthouse
23 Pico de la Zarza
24 Playa de Cofete
25 Casa Winter
26 Cofete Cemetery
27 Roque del Moro
28 Punta Jandía Lighthouse

STROLL / HIGHLIGHTS

A Corralejo
B Lajares
C El Cotillo
D La Oliva
E Puertito de los Molinos
F Betancuria
G Pájara
H La Pared
I Costa Calma at Sotavento
J Morro Jable

Fuerteventura
↳ Key Facts

WHEREABOUTS	Name	Fuerteventura
	Origin of name	The Romans referred to the Canaries as the *Fortunatae Insulae* (Fortunate Isles). While many link the name to the strong winds, it's probably linked to luck or destiny.
	Nickname	Windy Island, because of its consistent winds, making it a paradise for kite and wind surfers.
	Key towns and villages	Betancuria, Lajares , El Cotillo, Puertito de los Molinos
DEMOGRAPHICS	Population	122,629 people, 5% of the total population of the Canary Islands, 4th in rank
	Capital	Puerto del Rosario (pop. approx. 38,000)
	Biggest cities	Corralejo, Morro Jable, Puerto del Rosario
INFRASTRUCTURE	Commercial Airport	Fuerteventura Airport (FUE), El Matorral, Puerto del Rosario
	Commercial Ports	Port of Corralejo - ferry to Lanzarote & Lobos Port of Gran Tarajal - ferry to Gran Canaria Port of Morro Jable - ferries to Gran Canaria and Tenerife
	Agriculture	Wheat, cereals, Majorero goat cheese
GEOGRAPHY	Size	1660km², 2nd in rank
	Highest point	Pico de la Zarza (807m)
	Dimensions	100km from north to south, max. 30km from west to east and min. 6km at La Pared
	Coastline	304km, including 50km of white sand and 25km of black volcanic shingle
	Geologic origins	The island emerged 5 million years ago, one of the oldest of the Canaries. The last volcanic activity occurred between 4,000 and 5,000 years ago.
HISTORY	1340	The island is divided by a wall into two Guanches kingdoms, with the northern Maxorata ruled by King Guize and the southern Jandía ruled by King Ayoze
	1402 - 1405	Conquest of the island by Jean de Béthencourt who founded Betancuria, the first settlement and later capital of the island, in 1404
	1960	Arrival of mass tourism

Fuerteventura
↳ Where to Hike

OVERVIEW

Together with Tenerife, Fuerteventura offers the longest stretch of GR131. The barren landscapes with wide views are impressive and offer a feeling of both desolation and peace. Fuerteventura has the most arid feel of all the islands, and this vibe is apparent in all the hikes presented here. The nine stages comprise eight on the island of Fuerteventura itself plus one on the little island of Lobos off the north-east coast. The hilliest stages can be found in the middle of the island around Betancuria.

TERRAIN

Like Lanzarote, Fuerte offers a lot of easily walkable dirt roads, but in the area between Betancuria and La Pared, more technical single trails can be found. Due to the lack of vegetation and the wide-open landscapes, you are often exposed to the elements of wind and sun, so come protected for both.

Facilities are scarce on this, the most desolate island of the seven, though the terrain is not as unforgiving as you find in Tenerife or Gran Canaria.

WHICH STAGE TO PICK

The eight stages on Fuerte offer plenty of opportunity for great hikes. Stage 7 is both convenient and amazing. It's close to Corralejo and Lajares, where many people choose to stay, and it offers a hike to the crater of one of the most spectacular volcanoes on the island.

Stages 9 and 10 have some hefty climbs, which can be combined with a visit to Betancuria. A must is Stage 11 where you cross desolate desert dunes with the blue ocean on the right. Stage 12 and 13 offer ocean views, not too far from the tourist hotspot of Morro Jable.

ELEVATION MAP

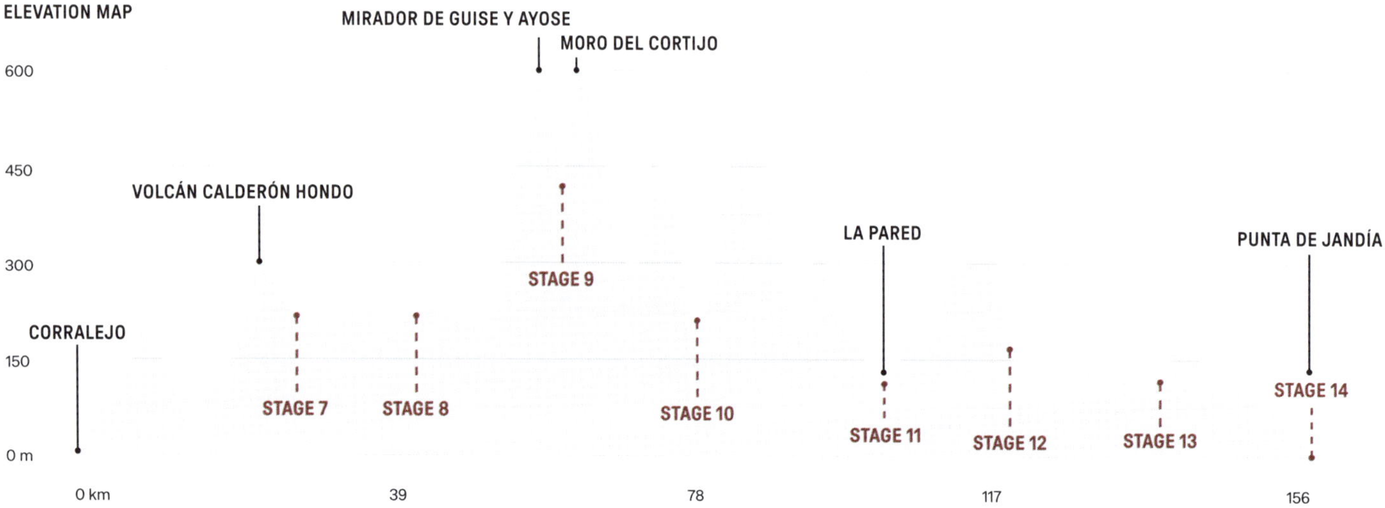

Fuerteventura
↳ Hikes Overview

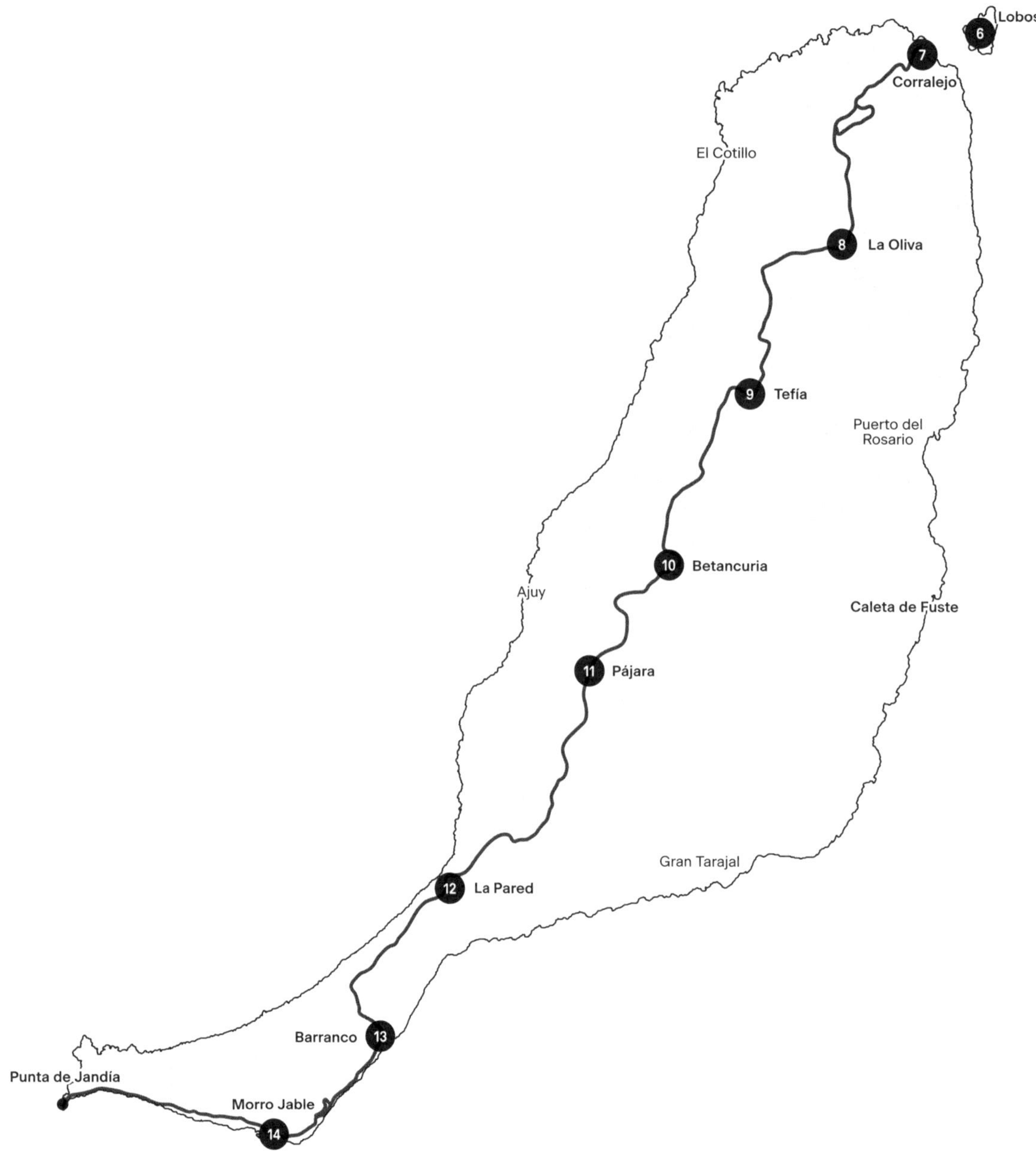

STAGE 6

LOBOS

Distance 8km **Ascent** 150m **Decent** 150m **Asphalt** 0%

Circular path on the island of Lobos, with views on its little village and lighthouse, pristine beaches and Corralejo and Lanzarote a few miles away.

Recommendation: 2 / 4
Technicality: 1 / 4
Facilities: 2 / 4
Type: GR131

The route through Lobos is short and easy, and goes from the little port to the lighthouse and back. Walking the dirt roads, taking in the hamlet of El Puertito, views of Las Lagunitas marshes and the small Punta Martiño lighthouse, before returning along the GR131. A ferry brings you back and forth from Corralejo, tickets can be bought in the harbour of Corralejo.

STAGE 7

CORRALEJO TO LA OLIVA

Distance 25km **Ascent** 480m **Decent** 260m **Asphalt** 40%

Spectacular volcano and panoramic views over lava landscapes. The start of the stage is urban and not great, but most of the hike is stunning.

Recommendation: 3 / 4
Technicality: 2 / 4
Facilities: 2 / 4
Type: GR131

Once you leave the beach resort of Corralejo, you follow winding dirt roads over rugged *malpais* ('bad land') slopes around a range of volcanic hills. There is an option to climb the crater of Calderón Hondo, or stay on the GR131 to reach the village of Lajares. The view over the Lajares valley during the descent from the Calderon hills is stunning. Another rugged malpais area is crossed on the slopes of Montaña de la Arena, with again offers great views over the valley, before a gentle descent to La Oliva.

STAGE 8

LA OLIVA TO TEFÍA

Distance 17.5km **Ascent** 210m **Decent** 230m **Asphalt** 22%

Dirt roads through stony deserts around the sacred mountain of Tindaya.

Recommendation: 2 / 4
Technicality: 1 / 4
Facilities: 2 / 4
Type: GR131

The whole of this stage is spent following broad dirt roads across extensive, stony semi-desert. The splendid little 'sacred' mountain of Montaña Tindaya commands the view most of the day, and it can be climbed from the GR131. The route provides a hike through a typical Fuerte desert landscape, but is not the most engaging on the island.

STAGE 9

TEFÍA TO BETANCURIA

Distance 17.5km **Ascent** 530m **Decent** 340m **Asphalt** 32%

Dirt roads through large desert plains, followed by single trail towards a viewpoint, with dazzling views over both the plains and Betancuria.

Recommendation: 3 / 4
Technicality: 2 / 4
Facilities: 2 / 4
Type: GR131

The first section comprises easy dirt roads and tracks across stony plains, passing through a succession of villages and the Ecomuseum and Mill of Tefía. In the second section, a more rugged single trail path climbs steeply along an open mountain flank – the biggest climb so far on the GR131 – to a mountain gap where we find the viewpoint and the statues of the Guanche kings Guise and Ayose, followed by a descent with a great view over Betancuria.

STAGE 10

BETANCURIA TO PÁJARA

Distance 17km **Ascent** 520m **Decent** 710m **Asphalt** 24%

Mountain stage with medium technical climbs, passing highest point of the GR131 in Fuerteventura, moving from panoramic views to valleys.

Recommendation: 3 / 4
Technicality: 3 / 4
Facilities: 2 / 4
Type: GR131

On this stage the GR131 finally gives you a real taste of the mountains, as we leave the stony deserts plains behind. Leaving Betancuria, the route climbs directly to the summit of Morro del Cortijo, which is the highest point on the Fuerteventura part of the trail. Descending to the village of Vega de Río Palmas, the landscape changes definitively to a more densely hilly terrain with no surrounding plains. The second climb of the day is a rugged and technical path crossing the mountain gap of Degollada de los Granadillos.After a single-trail technical descent, this stage ends with an easy walk between the villages of Toto and Pájara.

STAGE 11

PÁJARA TO LA PARED

Mountain stage with medium technical climbs through barren, exposed, open rolling hills as far as the eye can see.

Recommendation: 3 / 4
Technicality: 3 / 4
Facilities: 1 / 4
Type: GR131

Distance 26km **Ascent** 750m **Decent** 910m **Asphalt** 19%

A long and difficult stage through a barren landscape, which you could break by overnighting at the halfway village of Cardón, if you organize a pick-up or taxi. It starts with a walk along a high, often windy mountain crest, followed by a traverse of mountain slopes, on often more technical terrain. The technicality, combined with the gradient and potential strong winds, can make this stage hard to navigate. After Cardón, a more gradual ascent leads to more protected descent towards La Pared, which is a resort built between the mountains and the sandy desert of El Jable.

STAGE 12

LA PARED TO BARRANCO

Must-do desert and dune stage on the isthmus of La Pared with the ocean on both sides.

Recommendation: 4 / 4
Technicality: 2 / 4
Facilities: 1 / 4
Type: GR131

Distance 16km **Ascent** 290m **Decent** 280m **Asphalt** 1%

The main part of this stage follows the coast and hops from rocky cliff to beach with the blue Atlantic on your left. To get there, you first have to navigate out of the Istmo La Pared desert along a 2km-long dry river bed through dune desert terrain. Towards the end of the stage, you'll come across more and more tourist facilities before finally reaching the resort of Morro Jable.

STAGE 13

BARRANCO TO MORRO JABLE

Up-and-down single trail along the coastline with the ocean at your feet.

Recommendation: 3 / 4
Technicality: 2 / 4
Facilities: 2 / 4
Type: GR131

Distance 16.5km **Ascent** 400m **Decent** 450m **Asphalt** 8%

The main part of the stage follows the coast and hops from rocky cliff to beach with the blue Atlantic on the left. To get there, you first have to navigate out of the Istmo La Pared desert through a 2km long dried river bank through duny desert terrain. Towards the end of the stage, we see more and more tourist facilities to end in theresort of Morro Jable.

STAGE 14

MORRO JABLE TO PUNTA DE JANDÍA

Rolling single trail through the stony desert plains of the Jandia Peninsula and on towards the lighthouse.

Recommendation: 3 / 4
Technicality: 2 / 4
Facilities: 2 / 4
Type: GR131

Distance 20.5km **Ascent** 280m **Decent** 280m **Asphalt** 16%

The final stage of the GR131 through Fuerteventura continues the theme of stony semi-desert. The trail makes every effort to avoid the dirt road from Morro Jable to the lighthouse, picking is way across stony slopes then following the coast. We again hop from beach to cliff on a single trail, with the lighthouse of Faro de Jandía often in view on the open plains of the peninsula with the mountains in the back. Be sure to have a good plan at hand if you want to transfer to Gran Canaria to continue along the next stage of the route.

PARQUE NATURAL DE CORRALEJO

LANZAROTE
LOBOS

Fuerteventura
↳ To Explore

1 **LOBOS** ☆ 4 ⇨ 3 🍷 4

Lobos is a small island 3km north-east of Fuerteventura, almost like an escapee from neighbouring Lanzarote. No one has lived on the island since 1968 when the lighthouse keeper left the place, but the remaining houses, now mostly in a state of decay, are a reminder of the past. It's a popular destination to spend an afternoon, with a walk to the lighthouse in the north, a hike on the Montaña La Caldera – at 127m the highest point on the island – or to take in the unique view of Corralejo from the white-sand beach of Playa de la Concha de Lobos. There are a couple of restaurants and a handful of boat trips back and forth to Fuerteventura each day. You'll find only dirt roads and no cars on the island, so access for those with a physical disability might be tricky.

2 **PARQUE NATURAL DE CORRALEJO** ☆ 5 ⇨ 2 🍷 2

The Parque Natural de Corralejo offers remote natural beauty of striking contrasts, in an almost perfect rectangular-shaped area of 2.5 by 10.5km on the north-east of the island. In the north, you'll find the largest dune formations in the Canaries, made up of white sands that stand out against the turquoise waters of the Atlantic, which nowadays play host to hundreds of kiters who camp on the island for its favourable wind conditions. In the southern part of the park, the earth turns darker and the texture harder into irregular ochre-red volcanic shapes. The park offers almost perfectly pristine access to the ocean, apart from the occasional kite rental shop and the two monster hotel complexes approximately halfway along the coast, which serve as a landmark for kiters who've lost their way.

3 **VOLCÁN CALDERÓN HONDO** ☆ 5 ⇨ 3 🍷 2

A hike up this impressive volcano and crater offers great views over the valleys of Corralejo and Lajares. A cobbled path – part of a detour of the GR131 – leads up to a viewpoint shielded by a metal fence protecting you from the 70m-deep crater. Make sure to bring some nuts because you'll most likely be joined by a handful of eager, hungry chipmunks.

4 **EL TOSTÓN LIGHTHOUSE & LAGOONS** ☆ 5 ⇨ 4 🍷 2

The lighthouse is a must-see location in the north of El Cotillo. It is known for its spectacular for spectacular sunsets and crystalline turquoise water lagoons protected by reefs that offer ideal swimming conditions for all the family. The lighthouse, built in 1987 to protect ships in the Bocaina Strait, is still active today and houses the Traditional Fishing Museum.

5 **MOLINOS DE VILLAVERDE** ☆ 2 ⇨ 4 🍷 2

These 18th-century windmills were built to ground grains, oats, rye and chickpeas, usually into gofio, a staple of the local cuisine.

6 **CASA DE LOS CORONELES** ☆ 3 ⇨ 4 🍷 4

On the outskirts of La Oliva, you can find one of the most interesting and historic buildings in Fuerteventura. The origins of the Casa de los Coroneles (The Colonels' House) can be traced to the 17th century but the present structure was built in 1740 by the Sánchez-Dumpiérrez family – who served as the island's hereditary military governors until the end of the 18th century. The imposing, symmetrical mansion contrasts sharply with the desolate, irregular plains of Malpaís de La Arena where it is located and today houses a museum devoted to the island's history.

7 **THE SACRED MOUNTAIN OF TINDAYA (400M)** ☆ 3 ⇨ 2 🍷 2

The cone-shaped mountain of Tindaya, dominating the surrounding plains, was considered sacred by the Mahoreros, the native population of Fuerteventura. Close to its summit, which you can reach on foot, you can find *podomorfos*, or carved foot-shaped markings.

8 **PLAYA DE JARUBIO** ☆ 3 ⇨ 2 🍷 1

Playa de Jarubio is one of the most remote beaches of Fuerteventura, located near Tindaya and El Cotillo in the north-west of the island. Don't expect ice creams, bunting or the fried doughnuts known as *boules de Berlin*. This hidden beach only 250m long offers nothing but peace and quiet, and you'll likely be enjoying the feel of sand between your toes alone. We do not recommend swimming because of the strong current and waves and the absence of lifeguards. There is a fairly short and easy hike between this beach and the nearby village of Los Molinos.

9 **MOLINO DE TEFIA** ☆ 3 ⇨ 4 🍷 2

The Molino de Tefía is one of the many windmills you'll find on the island. Together with Lanzarote, Fuerteventura historically supplied grains to the other Canary Islands. This specific molino has overlooked the plains of Tefía since 1930. Noteworthy are the traditional walls made from volcanic rocks and white chalk cement. Location: 28.52556, -14.00705

10 **ECOMUSEO DE LA ALCOGIDA** ☆ 3 ⇨ 4 🍷 4

The Ecomuseo de la Alcogida, in Tefía in the centre of the island, is a reconstructed farming village, where visitors can discover how farming was done in the 1900s.

11 **CASTILLO DE CALETA DE FUSTE** ☆ 3 ⇨ 5 🍷 4

Few people might guess that the town of Caleta de Fuste, currently known as a family resort, was once one of the favourite docking places for pirates trying to conquer the island in the 17th and 18th century. With its remarkable circular defensive towers, the Castillo de Caleta de Fuste – also known as the Castillo de San Buenaventura – was built to protect the people from the feared invaders.

12 **SALINAS DEL CARMEN** ☆ 5 ⇨ 3 🍷 1

Salinas del Carmen, founded in 1910, are the only saltworks in Fuerteventura still in operation, extending over 26,100m^2. In appearance it looks like an array of car-sized postage stamps and consists of a grid of over a hundred salt pans stretching as far as the eye can see.

The salt marshes are located on the Antigua Coast, on the east side of the island, and include a salt warehouse, a salt worker's house, the remains of an old quay and a museum.

13 **MIRADOR DE GUISE Y AYOSE** ☆ 4 ⇨ 5 🍷 4

Right on the GR131, with great views over the Tindaya valley in the north and Betancuria in the south, you will find two bronze statues representing Fuerteventura's ancient kings. At the time of the European conquest, native Guanche kings ruled over the island: Guize ruling the north, and Ayose the Jandía Peninsula in the south.

It's a great place for a stop, but if you want a drink and a bite to eat, go to the nearby Morro Velosa Viewpoint or to Betancuria.

14 **MIRADOR DE MORRO VELOSA** ☆ 5 ⇨ 5 🍷 5

This viewpoint close to the former capital, Betancuria, was built by Lanzarote's Michelangelo, César Manrique, who expanded his mission to integrate architecture and nature to the neighbouring island of Fuerteventura.

The viewer can enjoy a diverse landscape of canyons, small villages and ochre-coloured rolling hills. On clear days you might even see the north of the island and the white sand dunes of Corralejo.

Inside you can enjoy a cup of coffee in the mountain-top restaurant and a gallery which includes a big maquette of the island. If the barrier is closed, so is the restaurant.

15 **ERMITA DE LAS PEÑITAS** ☆ 3 · 2 · 2

In between Betancuria and Pájara, you can find the tiny, whitewashed Ermita de las Peñitas hidden in the depths of the Barranco de las Peñitas. This secluded gem has long been a place of pilgrimage for the inhabitants of Fuerteventura. Its remote, hazardous location wasn't deemed sufficiently inclusive, however, so an alternative church was built in Vega de Río Palmas for the benefit of less surefooted pilgrims. A much-frequented path leads from the car park (at the end of Cam. Pájara, 28.385787, -14.106037), through the valley and to the top of an awe-inspiring rocky gorge: 500m further along the path you'll find the chapel.

16 **AJUY CAVES** ☆ 4 · 2 · 2

These cliff caves, 2km north of Pájara, close to the village of Ajuy, are accessible via an adventurous path with a splendid view over the coastline. The path begins at the northern end of the black sand beach and includes some tricky steps – as a reward for the hike, you get to enter the caves free of charge.

17 **PLAYA DE GARCEY** ☆ 3 · 2 · 2

Playa de Garcey is a remote beach which was famous for the wrecked ship laying in the water just offshore. 'Was' because in 2007 previously visible parts of the SS *American Star* – a US ocean cruise ship built in 1940 and wrecked in 1994 – disappeared beneath the waves for good. Nonetheless, the beach, or rather the 'journey' to it, is still worth the trip. You get to the beach, ideally in a sturdy 4x4, along a dirt road – a right-hand turn-off on the Pájara and La Pared highway – that passes through a series of little canyons. Like Jarubio, the beach itself is remote and quiet, surrounded by high rocks, and with similar conditions conditions: dangerous currents and jellyfish make bathing not advisable.

18 **FARO DE LA ENTALLADA** ☆ 5 · 5 · 2

Faro de la Entellada is not your everyday lighthouse. It's built on a 200m-high cliff towering over the ocean, marking the closest point to Africa, roughly 100km away. The building is a perfect symbol to represent the island, as it's constructed in the typical Moorish style you'll find all over the island – featuring round volcanic stones held together with white cement – and has a pleasing symmetric shape, as if it was built like a temple dedicated to the gods of the sea.

19 **SICASUMBRE ASTRONOMICAL VIEWPOINT (231M)** ☆ 3 · 2 · 1

The Sisacumbre viewing point, in the south of Fuerteventura around Pájara, is a place to lose yourself in stargazing. Don't forget warm clothes because it can get very windy. A trail of 5–10 minutes will get you from the car park to the platform for a cosy, nocturnal look at the heavens.

20 **ISTMO DE LA PARED** ☆ 5 · 2 · 1

La Pared is a quiet, surfer town on the western side of the island, contrasting with the touristy eastern side. Its name means 'wall', commemorating the legendary wall that once separated the northern and southern Guanche kingdoms that made up the island. Today, the wall is gone, yet the town marks the beginning of a unique desert-like stretch of land.

For the next 10km southwards, you'll find a vast emptiness of dune desert, which has featured in many movies, including the *Star Wars* series. It's a must-see on the island and a fitting setting for a serene hike through nothingness. The nearby beaches of del Viejo Rey and Playa La Pared are frequented by surfers.

21 **SOTAVENTO LAGOON & BEACH** ☆ 5 · 3 · 5

This turquoise-blue, mirror-flat, shallow-water lagoon in the south-east of the island attracts most of the sunbathing tourists and kite and wind surfers in the area. Many hotels and facilities can be found along its 4km stretch.

ISTMO DE LA PARED

22 **MORRO JABLE LIGHTHOUSE** ☆ 3 ⇨ 4 🍷 5

This is the tallest lighthouse in the Canaries, its 59m-high tower visible from far afield and from the ferries that serve the port of Morro Jable. The white tower marks the southern tip of Fuerteventura and is surrounded by long sandy beaches where you can enjoy some sunbathing.

23 **PICO DE LA ZARZA (807M)** ☆ 4 ⇨ 1 🍷 1

Pico de la Zarza is the highest point of the island with a stunning view over Cofete Beach. There is a beautiful and technically easy hike to the top.

24 **COFETE BEACH** ☆ 5 ⇨ 2 🍷 2

Cofete Beach, on the south-west of the Island, is one of the remotest and largest beaches in the Canaries.
The 12km stretch of sand is impressive because of its sheer desolateness, and made all the dramatic by the wall of cliffs overlooking its white sands and the blue Atlantic beyond. It's quite a drive to get there, as it's only accessible via the road from Morro Jable in the south, but it's a must-visit on the island. There are a few funky hidden gems scattered around the beach in the shape of an enigmatic villa, one of the most remote cemeteries in the world, and a famous monolith, formed by wind and water erosion. Cofete itself is a small village but don't expect many bars or restaurants here, so come prepared.

25 **CASA WINTER** ☆ 4 ⇨ 2 🍷 2

On the west side of Cofete Beach, set 130m above the sands, you will find one of the most enigmatic villas in the world – Casa Winter. Built by the German engineer Gustav Winter in the 1940s, the villa is the subject of several conspiracy theories, often involving Nazis.

One story claims the villa was used as a secret lighthouse to signal to German U-boats. The Winters always claimed the villa was just built to support local agriculture in the remote area of Cofete. Location: 28.10187, -14.37511

26 **COFETE CEMETERY** ☆ 3 ⇨ 2 🍷 2

Cofete Cemetery is one of the most unique and remote in the world. It was built in the 19th century as an alternative to the rather stinky business of transporting dead bodies on dromedaries, which had to travel 50km of challenging desert tracks to reach the closest cemetery in Pájara. Today dromedaries are no longer used to carry corpses, though you can still take a ride on one on several of the islands. Location: 28.11019, -14.38881

27 **ROQUE EL MORO** ☆ 3 ⇨ 1 🍷 1

Roque del Moro, marking the southern end of Cofete Beach, is a monolith (lone rock formation) rising out of the water withstanding erosion. To reach this wonder of nature, you have to walk 4km along the beach so you can be sure to be one of the only ones on this mission. The rock features veined trachyte, an igneous rock resembling marble.

28 **PUNTA JANDIA LIGHTHOUSE** ☆ 3 ⇨ 1 🍷 1

This small lighthouse built on a rocky promontory marks the western extremity of Fuerteventura. The building itself is not special and cannot be visited, but the trip to it has an end-of-the-world vibe. Close by the GR131 makes its way just a few metres from the ocean. Half a kilometre further on are the ghostly remains of an abandoned village.

Fuerteventura
↳ To Stroll

A **CORRALEJO** ☆5 ↕4 🍸5

Once a quiet fishing town, Corralejo is now the most populous and versatile tourist town on Fuerteventura, making it the beating heart of the island. It's a great place to set up camp whether you're looking for nature, culture, sport, nightlife or sun. It has the island's most vibrant nightlife and biggest assortment of restaurants and bars, as well as sport and shopping facilities.

The nature is especially impressive – with the dunes of Corralejo Natural Park, the island of Lobos in the east, nice beaches for both sunbathers and surfers, and a handful of volcanoes to the south, as well as, of course, Lanzarote just across the water to the north.

B **LAJARES** ☆5 ↕4 🍸5

To the north of Fuerteventura, a few minutes south of Corralejo, is the village of Lajares, in a valley surrounded by hills and volcanoes. Given its central location between the beaches of the north, it nowadays hosts a vibrant community of expats and surfers, but the centre of the village remains quite small with a few good places to eat. When you're based here, you're 15 minutes from the beaches of El Cotillo, 20 from the surf in Playa Blanca, 15 from the restaurants and bars in Corralejo and 15 from kiting in the Corralejo Natural Park. If you like nature, this is potentially a better place to stay than Corralejo while still keeping all options in sight. North of the village is Volcán Calderón Hondo, which could become part of your morning running routine.

C **EL COTILLO** ☆4 ↕2 🍸4

In the north-west of Fuerteventura, 30 minutes from Corralejo, are the famous white sandy beaches of the fishing town of El Cotillo. It has a quieter and spacier vibe than Corralejo, and its turquoise water is almost unmatched anywhere on the island. It's the perfect place for a beach day out at Playa Castillo or Playa Concha, the latter voted one of the island's prettiest beaches on TripAdvisor. Nearby you'll find the El Tostón lagoons and lighthouse. If you like crafts and jewellery, the Friday artisanal market on Friday is a treat.

D **LA OLIVA** ☆2 ↕2 🍸2

The village has a market and arts centre, as well as accommodation, restaurant-bars, pizzerias and good bus services to Lajares and Corralejo. It's not really a place to stay, as there is not much to see apart from the 18th-century Casa de los Coroneles which served as a residence for the military governors is and is now a museum and art centre.

E **PUERTITO DE LOS MOLINOS** ☆5 ↕1 🍸2

Puertito de los Molinos is a small fishing village in the mid-west with a population of less than 20. Visit this small place for the excellent food served at its restaurants, a wonderful beach that is perfect for surfing, and a magnificent sea cave that can be visited only at low tide.

F **BETANCURIA** ☆5 ↕5 🍸2

Located in a valley in the centre of the island, in a mountain range, Betancuria used to be the capital of the island and the entire Canary Islands, after being founded in 1404 by the Frenchman Jean de Béthencourt from whom it takes its name. After a raid by pirates in 1593, the capital was razed to the ground before being rebuilt and remaining the capital of Fuerteventura until 1834.

Nowadays, it's a charming village with some nice streets to stroll, busy during the days and quiet in the evenings. There are some entertainment facilities – bars, restaurants, shops, etc. but it's no city so don't expect any nightlife. It lies on the GR131 in between two hills with some great viewpoints so it might be a good starting place for a hike.

One of the most beautiful places to visit in Betancuria is the Iglesia de Santa María de Betancuria, constructed in the Gothic style in the 15th century, before being successively remodelled in the Mudéjar, Renaissance and Baroque styles over the following centuries. The plaza directly in front of the church is one of the loveliest places to wile away the time in town. The hidden gem that is the Ermita de las Peñitas is nearby for those brave enough to undertake the hike.

G PÁJARA ☆ 2 ↕ 2 🍷 2

Pájara can be a welcoming stop during your hike or road trip through the vast midlands of Fuerte. The town is old but suffered some damage in the 16th century. Today it offers some, but not much, accommodation, a bank with ATM, restaurant-bars, shops and bus services.

H LA PARED ☆ 3 ↕ 2 🍷 2

Built in the 1980s, La Pared is not strictly a village but more 'a place to stay'. It rather weirdly combines a wide central avenue in the centre with very little surrounding it apart from a couple of small resorts and detached holiday homes. We nonetheless recommend it not because of any charm, but as a calm and quiet gateway to the beaches and ocean views loved by surfers, but also to the desert vastness of Istmo de la Pared.

I COSTA CALMA AT SOTAVENTO ☆ 3 ↕ 2 🍷 3

The counterpart of La Pared on the east, Costa Calma along the Sotavento Lagoon offers dozens of resorts and buzzing hospitality attracting tourists and kite/wind surfers. It doesn't have charm or quiet, but it's conveniently close to the turquoise wonders of Sotavento.

J MORRO JABLE ☆ 4 ↕ 4 🍷 5

The fishing town of Morro Jable is the southern alternative to Corralejo. With its similar mix of famous beaches – the central Playa del Matorral, the Playa de las Coloradas in the west and the Playa de Butihondo in the north, towards the Jandía beach resort – and the narrow streets of the old town filled with restaurants makes it a great attraction for many tourists. The Morro Jable lighthouse – the tallest in the Canary Islands – is a spectacular sight, while the town's proximity to nature makes it a great base for hikers as well, with the GR131 passing close by.

↑ LOBOS

FARO DE PUNTA MARTIÑO ↱

PLAYA DE LA CONCHA, LOBOS ISLAND

PUERTITO DE LOBOS

VOLCÁN CALDERÓN HONDO, 278M

PLAYA DE JARUBIO

↰ PUERTITO DE LOS MOLINOS

PLAYA DE GARCEY ↴

↰ MONTAÑA TINDAYA

IGLESIA DE NUESTRA SEÑORA DE LA CANDELARIA, LA OLIVA ↴

↰ MOLINO DE TEFÍA

DIDIER ↴

↰ FRANK

MOLINA DE TEFÍA ↴

MIRADOR MORRO VELOSA

ERMITA DE LAS NIEVES

⮤ MIRADOR DEL RISCO DE LAS PEÑAS, GR132 CROSSING FV-30

THE STATUES OF GUANCHE KINGS GUISE AND AYOSE ⮧

MONTAÑA CARDÓN, 694M

GR131, BARRANCO DE PECENESCAL, SOTAVENTO DE JANDÍA

SOTAVENTO LAGOON

PLAYA DE SOTAVENTO DE JANDÍA, GR131, RISCO DEL PASO

PICO DE LA ZARZA, 807M
ROQUE DEL
COFET
PLAYA DEL COFETE

PUNTA DE JANDÍA

CASA WINTER

↰ GR131, PUNTA DE JANDÍA

PUNTA DE JANDIA LIGHTHOUSE ↴

27.75237°
N

15.5959°
W

↱ Island 3 / 7
Gran Canaria

1,560km²
851,231 residents

3

⟶ BARRANCO DE TIRAJANA
27.871864 °N / 15.521910 °W

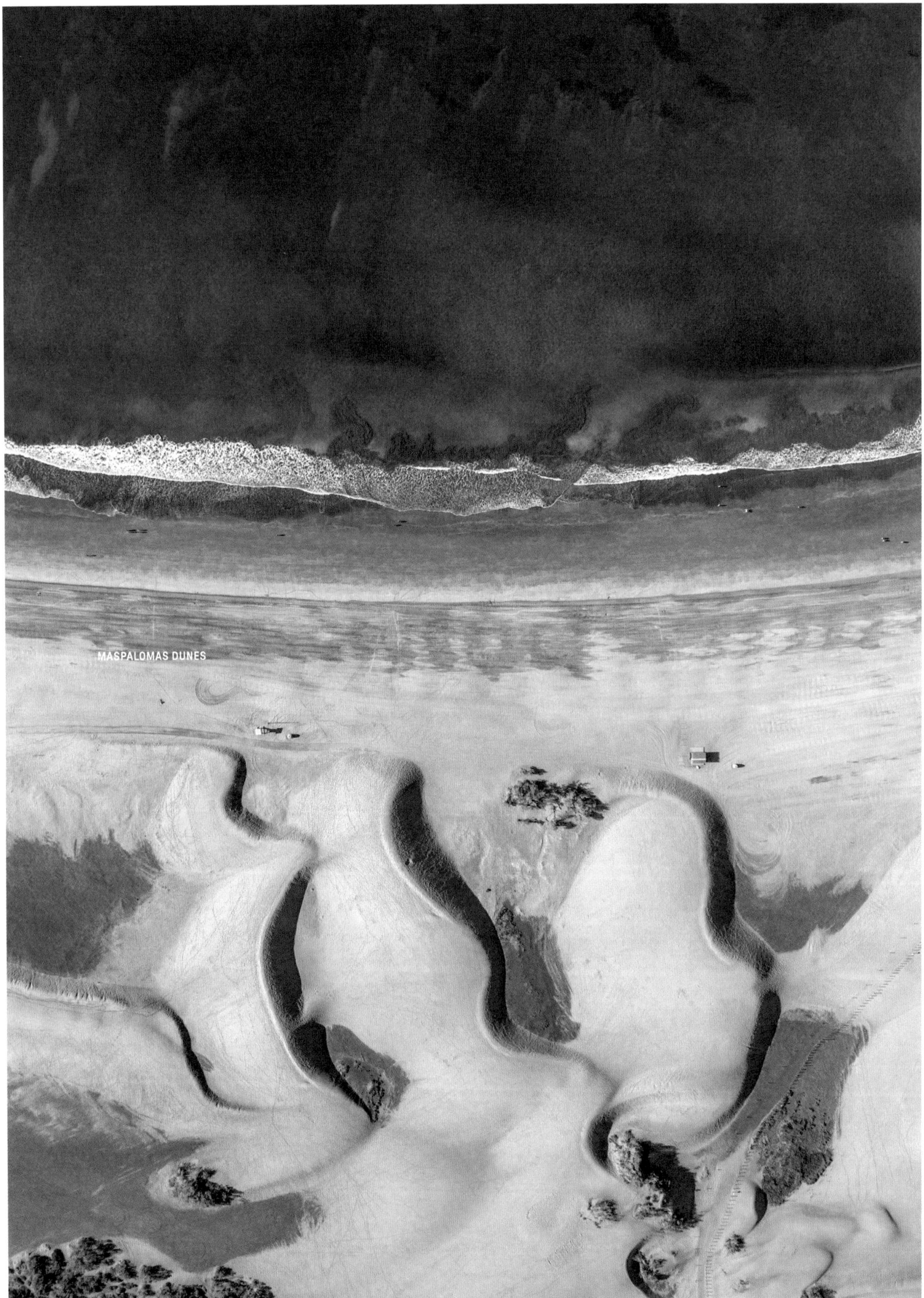
MASPALOMAS DUNES

↳ Welcome to Gran Canaria, the 'micro-continent' that offers a diverse abundance of both nature and culture. Nature lovers will head to Roque Nublo, a huge red rock bang in the middle of the island that might make you think you were in Texas or New Mexico, or to the subtropical, lush canyons and ravines that stretch inland from the beaches, and to the pine forests and cliffs of Tamadaba or the fairy-tale dunes of Maspalomas.

Culture vultures will take a stroll in the 15th-century historic centres of Las Palmas, Arucas and Teror, or discover whitewashed inland villages deep in the palm-filled valleys or quaint fishing villages. Rock and roll and sunbathing are on offer in Maspalomas, one of the most notorious nightlife and holiday destinations in Spain.

Gran Canaria
The Miniature Continent

Coastline: 236km
Highest point: 1,949m

BARRANCO DE LAS VACAS

The ‘Miniature Continent’, thanks to the variety of climates and landscapes, from white sandy beaches and dunes to green ravines and valleys in which nestle picturesque villages.

↳ Gran Canaria is an almost perfectly round dot in the middle of the Canaries, with the two highest peaks, Pico de las Nieves and Roque Nublo, right in the middle. Its terrain is rougher and much more elevated than those of its neighbours to the east. It looks almost as if a giant hand has crumbled a round piece of paper and tried to smooth it out again, leaving an erratic relief running inwards towards the centre. Dozens of canyons rise from the beaches to the elevated inland. The central highlands prevent rain-carrying clouds from entering the south, making the north more cloudy and green and the south more arid and sunnier. Let’s follow the circular island clockwise, starting with the largest cities of Las Palmas, Arucas and Teror in the north, at 12 o’clock. At 6 o’clock is Maspalomas, the leisure capital of the island, from which beautiful canyons radiate. At 7 o’clock is the charming coastal town of Mogán, the ‘Little Venice’ of the island, and at 10 o’clock are the Tamadaba Natural Park and Puerto de las Nieves.

Gran Canaria
↳ Introduction

HOW TO GET AROUND

The island's population is mostly spread out on the fringe between Arucas and Las Palmas in the north and Maspalomas in the south. The airport is in the mid-east, between Las Palmas and Maspalomas. The port of Las Palmas serves (in addition to the Spanish mainland) the eastern Canary Islands – Fuerteventura and Lanzarote – while Puerto de las Nievas is the gateway to Tenerife, both 2-hour-plus trips. The first thing you need to know is that it's hard to cover distance on this island, especially in the centre, because of the curvy canyons and the elevation. There is a highway running from Mogán to Agaete, the GC1 and GC2, covering three-quarters of the island's almost perfectly circular shape. Several roads radiate inland from the highway – allow one hour to drive from the beach to the centre. In the remaining quarter of the island, the roads are tough – winding as well up and down – so not for the faint-hearted.

WHERE TO STAY

Most tourists stay in Maspalomas owing to its abundance of accommodation and hospitality and its proximity to other highlights. The inlands are rather uneventful. If you like buzzing city life, pick Arucas or Las Palmas. If you appreciate beaches and panoramic views, Maspalomas, Mogán or Puerto de las Nieves are good picks.

BEACHES

The biggest beach is the black sand city beach of Playa de las Canteras in Las Palmas, a playground for local surfers. If you want to exchange city life for a more holiday-ish vibe, Playa del Inglés is your pick, likely the most famous (and infamous) in the Canaries. If you want to avoid the crowds, the western and northern parts of the island are better picks, with the remote beaches of Gui Gui, Faneroque or Guayedegra topping the lists of the hidden gems.

THREE-DAY STAY

Day 1 – City, culture and charm
Spend the morning in Las Palmas with a stroll along the Playa de las Canteras, followed by La Vegueta. Head to Caldera Bandama for dazzling views. Lunch in a Monte Lentiscal vineyard bodega. Go to the Bandama golf course, or grab some culture at the historical Fortaleza de Ansite or in the charming village of Fataga. Remember, you can't do it all. Finish the day with a sunset stroll through or around the Maspalomas Dunes and pick one of the many restaurants in the town.

Day 2 – Canyons and rocks
Breakfast and morning stroll in Mogán, a 30-minute drive from Maspalomas. Head for the canyons on the GC200 and continue on the GC605, after a short detour to the Azulejos de Veneguera if you have time. Take a picnic at Presa de las Niñas and enjoy the peace. Pick one of the hikes of the book to discover the midlands

Day 3 – Tamadaba
Make your way to the Mirador del Balcon for the most spectacular viewpoint on the island. The oceanside GC200 provides one of the most spectacular drives in the world. Lunch at El Risco and take a hike into the Tamadaba valley. After the exercise, enjoy a well-deserved swim at the remote Playa de Faneroque or Playa de Guayedra. Finish your day at Puerto de las Nieves.

GRAN CANARIA

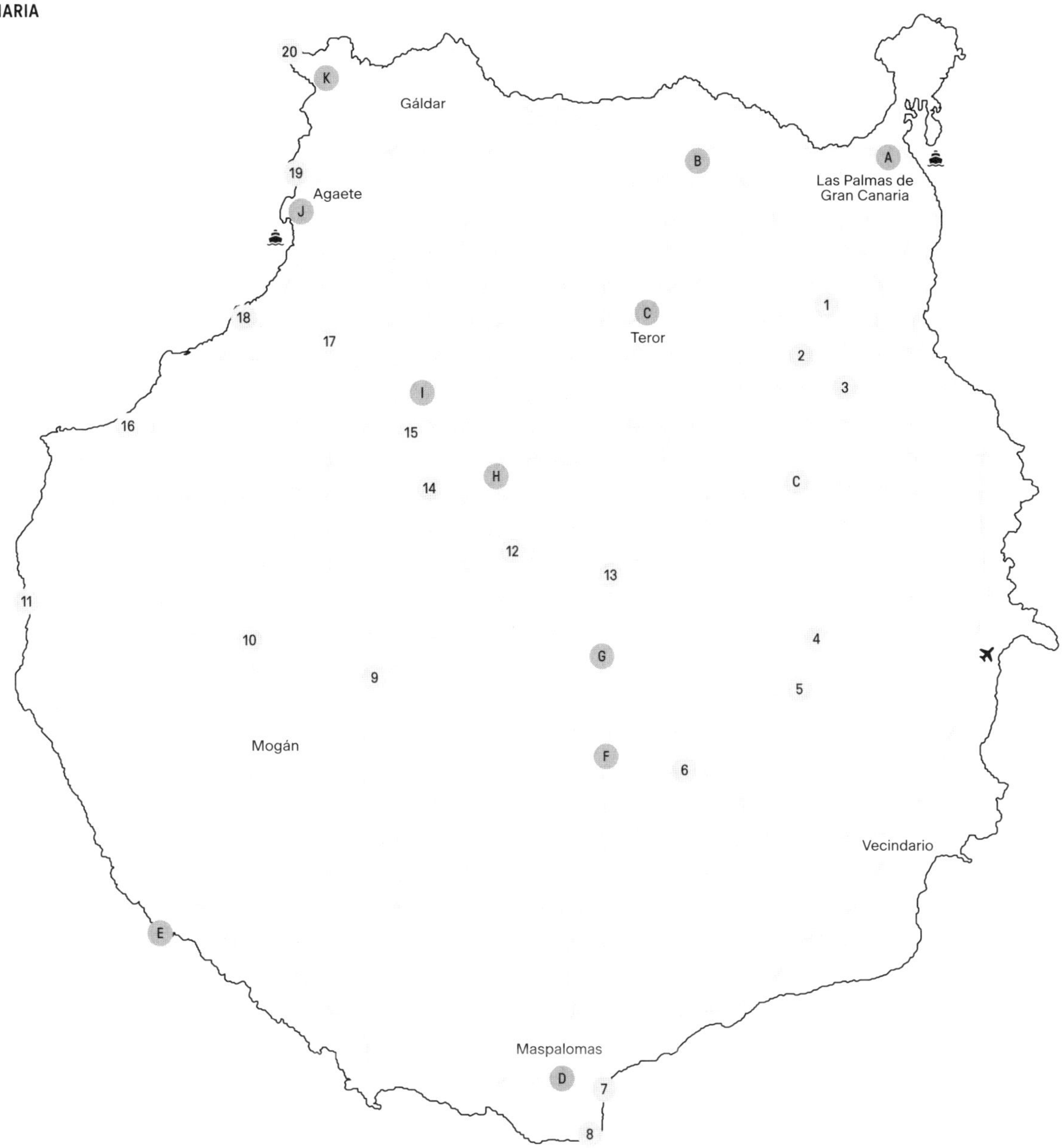

EXPLORE / HIGHLIGHTS

1 Jardín Botánico Viera y Clavijo
2 Monte Lentiscal Vineyards
3 Caldera de Bandama
4 Barranco de Guayadeque
5 Barranco de las Vacas
6 La Fortaleza de Ansite
7 Playa del Inglés
8 Maspalomas Dunes
9 Presa de las Niñas
10 Fuente de los Azulejos
11 Playa de Gui Gui
12 Roque Nublo
13 Pico de las Nieves
14 Roque Bentayga
15 La Cilla Viewpoint & Restaurant
16 Mirador del Balcón
17 Tamadaba Natural Park
18 Playa del Faneroque
19 Playa del Juncal
20 Faro Punta Sardina

STROLL / HIGHLIGHTS

A Las Palmas
B Arucas
C Teror
D Maspalomas
E Puerto de Mogán
F Fataga
G Tunte
H Tejeda
I Artenara
J Agaete & Puerto de las Nieves
K Playa de Sardina del Norte

MIRADOR DEL BALCÓN

Gran Canaria
↳ Key Facts

WHEREABOUTS	Name	Gran Canaria
	Origin of name	Named Canaria by the Roman writer Pliny the Elder as it contained 'vast multitudes of dogs of very large size'. The connection to dogs is retained in the coat of arms
	Nickname	The 'Miniature Continent', thanks to the variety of climates and landscapes, from white sand beache sanddunes, to lush green ravines and valleys dotted with pictures que villages
	Key towns and villages	Teror, Mogán, Fataga
DEMOGRAPHICS	Population	851,231 people, 40% of the Canary Islands, 2nd in rank
	Capital	Las Palmas de Gran Canaria (pop. approx. 377,000)
	Biggest cities	Las Palmas, Arucas, Maspalomas
INFRASTRUCTURE	Commercial Airport	Gran Canaria Airport (LPA), located in the middle of the eastern coastline
	Commercial Ports	Port of La Luz, Las Palmas, east – weekly ferry route to Cádiz, Spanish mainland Port of Las Nieves, Agaete, west – Fred Olsen ferry to Santa Cruz de Tenerife
	Agriculture	Grains and sugarcane
GEOGRAPHY	Size	1,560km², 3rd in rank
	Highest point	Pico de las Nieves (1,949m)
	Dimensions	Roughly circular, 50km in diameter
	Coastline	236km, of which 60km beach
	Origin	Formed in three cycles: the Old Cycle – 80% of the island formed starting 14 million years ago; the Roque Nublo cycle, 4 million years ago; 3rd cycle, starting 2.8 million years ago and ongoing, with last eruptions some 2,000 years ago
HISTORY	500 BC	Populated by the North African people known to the Romans as Canarii
	1483	Conquest by the Crown of Castile under Queen Isabella I after a campaign lasting five years, beginning in 1478 with the founding of Las Palmas
	1492	Christopher Columbus anchors to repair one of his ships during his first expedition to the Americas

Gran Canaria
↳ Where to Hike

OVERVIEW

The trails here offer a dramatic change in scenery from the earlier stages, exchanging barren plains for curvy canyons. The GR131 is just one of the many options in this hiking paradise, so it's worth considering alternatives. Beware, though, as you will find serious elevation on most of the trails. Stages 15 and 19 connect the high inlands with the coastal area. Stages 16, 17 and 18 wander through extensive upland pine forests and mountain passes and are comprised of steep single trails.

TERRAIN

Apart from Stage 15, which tries in vain to leave behind the buzzing urban surroundings of Maspalomas, most stages are off-road. Most of the trail is made up of paths with no or limited access to roads. None of the trails is especially technical but the gradient and remoteness mean you have to come prepared. The terrain is steeper, less accessible and more demanding than on the previous two islands, so plan carefully. There are often pine trees to find shade under, but you can be exposed to the sun, especially on the summits.

WHICH STAGE TO PICK

The five stages offer plenty of choice, a diversity of nature and stunning views. We don't recommend Stage 15 as much of it is on busy roads, especially close to Maspalomas. Stage 16 and 17 are climb stages with steep gradients in the midlands, with the latter showing off the impressive Camino de Santiago and views of Roque Nublo, making it a must on the island. Stage 19 offers a similarly demanding gradient with incredible views over the cliff coastline and the town of Agaete.

ELEVATION MAP

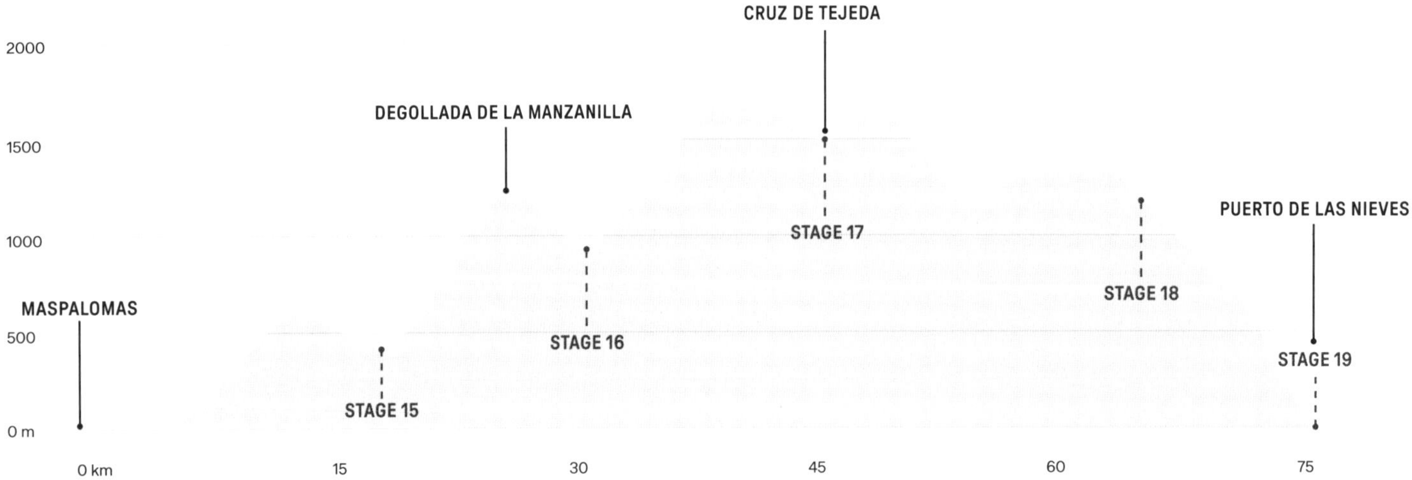

Gran Canaria
↳ Hikes Overview

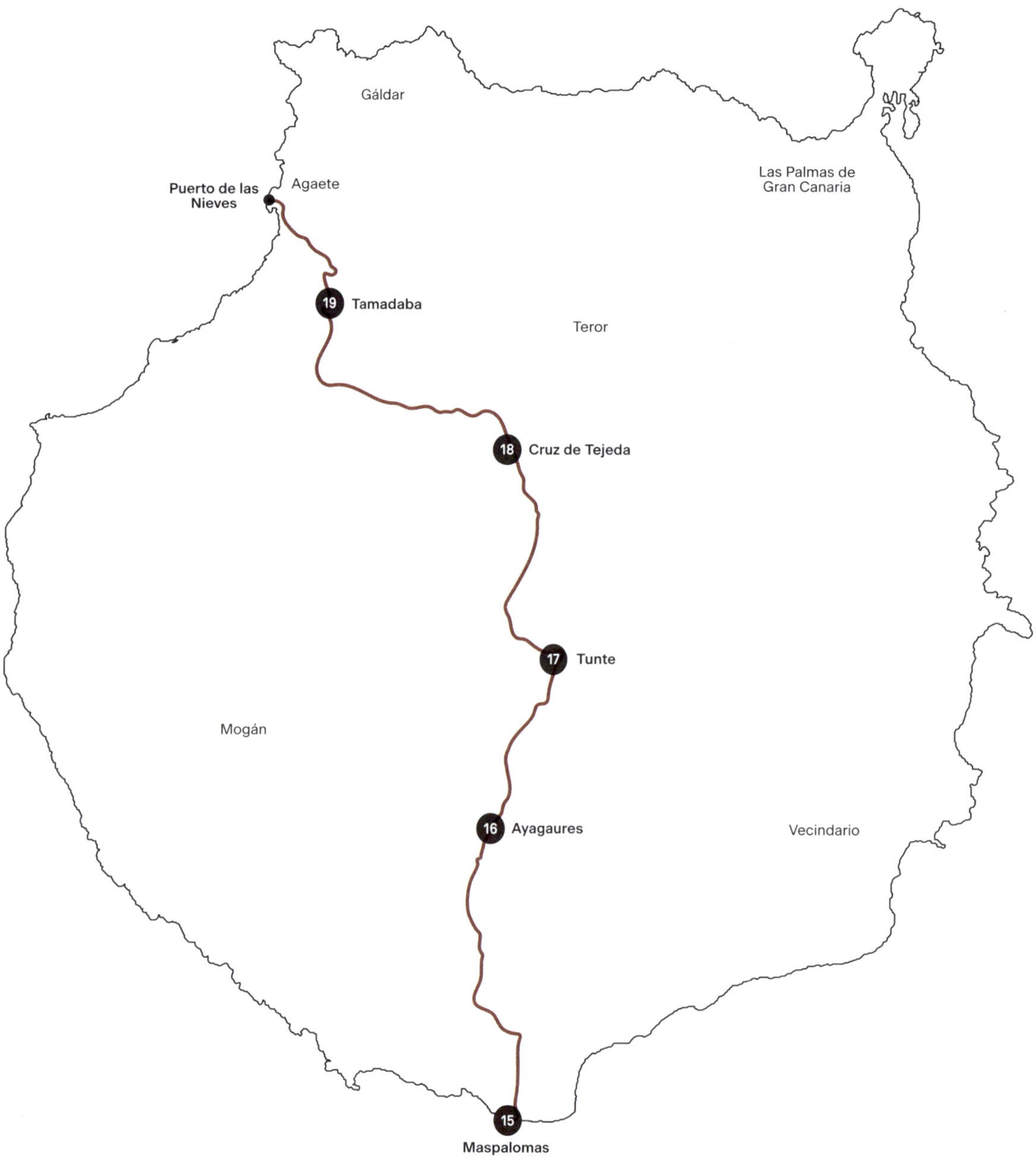

STAGE 15

MASPALOMAS TO AYAGAURES

Leaving Maspalomas, the trail climbs towards Mirador de Ayagaures along mostly asphalted, often busy roads.

Recommendation: 1 / 4
Technicality: 1 / 4
Facilities: 4 / 4
Type: GR131

Distance 18km **Ascent** 530m **Decent** 220m **Asphalt** 72%

Most of the track follows either dirt roads or roads, making it less attractive for hardcore nature lovers. The first 5km, starting at the lighthouse of Maspalomas, take you out of the resort of Maspalomas parallel to the Barranco de Fataga, a dry riverbed.

The next 10km are on an often busy road, making the hike somewhat unpleasant and dangerous. After Montaña la Data the road winds upwards to Mirador de Ayagaures, after which a U-curved road descends towards the artificial lake.

STAGE 16

AYAGAURES TO TUNTE

Mountain stage along a mule path through pine forest to reach a spectacular mountain pass, before a technical descent.

Recommendation: 3 / 4
Technicality: 3 / 4
Facilities: 1 / 4
Type: GR131

Distance 12.5km **Ascent** 900m **Decent** 320m **Asphalt** 24%

The first real mountainous stage in which an old mule path climbs through rugged territory, passes by a dam through old pine forests, to reach a spectacular mountain pass called the Degollada de la Manzanilla. After there is a short technical descent, passing spiky rock formations, towards Tunte, referred to as San Bartolomé de Tirajana. The hike is entirely along single trails, with no access to roads or towns. Spectacular views guaranteed over both the barranco with the Atlantic behind and later over the Tunte valley.

STAGE 17

TUNTE TO CRUZ DE TEJEDA

Mountain stage in the central highlands of the islands, mostly along cobbled paths built along the ravines, with stunning views of Roque Nublo towards the end.

Recommendation: 4 / 4
Technicality: 3 / 4
Facilities: 2 / 4
Type: GR131

Distance 15.5km **Ascent** 1,020m **Decent** 400m **Asphalt** 6%

Leaving Tunte, a cobbled path climbs through a pine forest towards the high mountains. Towards the peak the gradient gets more impressive and the vegetation scarcer with the path forming impressive S-curves squeezed against the rocky walls. On reaching the summit, or *cumbre*, in the last part, hikers once again encounter a pine forest, providing welcome shade. Here the path runs parallel to roads towards the strategic gap of Cruz de Tejeda, with stunning views of Roque Nublo and Roque Bentayga.

STAGE 18

CRUZ DE TEJEDA TO TAMADABA

Exchanging the highest points of the island for gentle valleys, the trail makes low-gradient descents along dirt or asphalt roads.

Recommendation: 2 / 4
Technicality: 1 / 4
Facilities: 2 / 4
Type: GR131

Distance 17.5km **Ascent** 750m **Decent** 1,060m **Asphalt** 11%

Although there is more descent than ascent, don't underestimate this stage. The high mountains and impressive views give way to gentle valleys en route to the town of Artenara. A lot of the route passes along dirt or asphalt roads.

STAGE 19

TAMADABA TO PUERTO DE LAS NIEVES

Spectacular views on the cliffed coastline around Agaete along a steep technical descent.

Recommendation: 3 / 4
Technicality: 3 / 4
Facilities: 3 / 4
Type: GR131

Distance 10.5km **Ascent** 50m **Decent** 1,250m **Asphalt** 10%

The final stage of the trek across Gran Canaria sees a sustained, steep descent from the forested uplands of Tamadaba onto increasingly arid slopes with low grassy vegetation and stunning views on the cliffs surrounding Agaete. The final vertical drop needs your attention and can get technical. No access to roads along the trail but plenty of facilities in Puerto de las Nieves.

MASPALOMAS DUNES

Gran Canaria
↳ To Explore

1 **JARDÍN BOTÁNICO VIERA Y CLAVIJO** ☆ 3 ⇨ 4 🍷 3

The Jardín Botánico Viera y Clavijo showcases the island's green and lush identity and is home to about 500 plant species, both endemic and imported such as succulents and cacti. The statue at the entrance is of José de Viera y Clavijo, the Spanish botanist who founded the garden. Today there is a library and laboratories on site.

2 **MONTE LENTISCAL VINEYARDS** ☆ 4 ⇨ 4 🍷 5

If you like to hop between vineyards to do some late-afternoon wine tasting, the vineyards of Monte Lentiscal, in the north, not too far from Las Palmas, are a great place to go.

The vineyards are located near the Caldera de Bandama so you can combine your trip with a stroll along the crater or with a game of golf. Several endemic grape varieties are grown, including Listán Negro and Listán Blanco, giving the wines a unique taste.

Recommended wine houses, or bodegas, include the following: Los Lirios – one of the oldest on Gran Canaria – and El Volcán.

3 **CALDERA DE BANDAMA (569M)** ☆ 5 ⇨ 2 🍷 3

Caldera de Bandama is a giant volcano crater located in the north of Gran Canaria, the largest on the island. The 1,100m-diameter and 200m-deep crater, formed by a collapse, not an eruption, is an impressive sight. You can walk both around the crater or descend into its depths along a fairly technical trail. The name 'Bandama' originates from the Flemish merchant Daniel Van Damme who was the first to explore the crater when planting a vineyard on its fertile soils. The British explorer Charles Edwardes described it as the 'most perfect Crater in the Canaries'. The place is chock-full of history because, on the flanks of the old volcano, you can find the oldest 18-hole golf course in Spain. From the top of Pico de Bandama you can enjoy a spectacular view over Las Palmas and the surrounding area.

4 **BARRANCO DE GUAYADEQUE** ☆ 5 ⇨ 3 🍷 3

In the south and east of Gran Canaria, you will find canyon after canyon carving their way through the landscape, giving the landscape a tropical, almost South American atmosphere. The Barranco Guayadeque is one of the longest ravines on the island and can be seen along a 10km road that rises towards a famous viewpoint at its end. Along the way, you'll find a number of famous restaurants housed in caves with wonderful food and views: Vega, Tagoror, La Era, El Centro and Guayadeque. There are several hiking opportunities.

5 **BARRANCO DE LAS VACAS** ☆ 3 ⇨ 2 🍷 2

Here you will find the rock formations known as the Tobas de Colores, which resemble Antelope Canyon in the USA or Las Grietas in Lanzarote. It's a small place so it tends to get overcrowded and parking is limited.

6 **LA FORTALEZA DE ANSITE** ☆ 5 ⇨ 2 🍷 5

Located in the south of Gran Canaria, along the GC65 and close to the town of Fataga and is one of the most important archaeological sites in Gran Canaria. Formed by three large rocks – Fortaleza Grande, Fortaleza Chica and Titana – it was here that the native islanders surrendered to the Castilian army led by Pedro de Vera at the close of the five-year conquest. Legend has it that the defeated native leaders threw themselves off the cliffs shouting, 'Atis Tirma', which means 'Glory to the sacred mountain'. It's not clear whether this actually happened, but radiocarbon dating and engravings in the caves indicate habitation up to 800 years ago. Nowadays, you can visit the many features and fortifications that make up the site – including living quarters, food storage areas and burial areas connected by a network of tracks.

7 PLAYA DEL INGLÉS ☆4 ⇨5 🍷5

This is the place where the magic happens, offering sand and sun by day and bars and clubs by night. Playa del Inglés, in Maspalomas, is one of the biggest holiday complexes not only in Gran Canaria but the whole of Spain, offering shopping malls – with the Yumbo Centre and Kasbah the biggest – hotels and (fast food) restaurants, making it the perfect destination for party crowds and families. Built in the 1960s, the resort boasts a 3km-long beach north of the Maspalomas Dune Natural Reserve.

8 MASPALOMAS DUNES ☆5 ⇨2 🍷3

Maspalomas is Gran Canaria's most famous natural landmark, featured on postcards and in travel guides. This pristine dune landscape provides a stark contrast with the mass tourism of Playa del Inglés. We're talking archetypal dunes of the kind you see in the movies, the sands coming from across the ocean, blown from the African mainland. The dunes stretch over a 3km-long L-shape from Meloneras in the south, where you find the lighthouse of Maspalomas, to Playa del Inglés, in the north-west. As the dunes are a fragile ecosystem, threatened by the swell of tourism nearby, it's important to follow one of the three walking routes.

9 PRESA DE LAS NIÑAS ☆4 ⇨3 🍷1

This large artificial lake is located in the Monumento Natural del Roque Nublo at an altitude of 900m. The lack of rainfall in the Canaries has made the locals expert in preserving the scarce water resources. As a result, you can find 140 water reservoirs in Gran Canaria, with Presa de las Niñas, close to Tejeda in the south of the island, being one of the prettiest ones. It's a great place for day out with the family. While there are no food facilities, you'll find a car park, toilets and picnic tables as well as great hiking. It's surrounded by the typical pine trees of the island, some of which are more than 400 years old.

10 FUENTE DE LOS AZULEJOS ☆4 ⇨2 🍷1

In the south-west of the island, Fuente de los Azulejos is like a large mural painted onto the rocks, close to Mogán. Suddenly, deep in the Barranco de Veneguera – on the GC200 between Mogán and La Aldea de San Nicolás – an unusual rock formation appears with a rainbow palette of joyful colours ranging from turquoise blue to orange-red, the result of oxidation. Its name means 'Fountain of Tiles', referring to the colourful azulejo tilework of Portugal. There is a very small parking facility at 27.92402, -15.72732 with room for not much more than three cars, marking the beginning of a hiking trail.

11 PLAYA DE GUI GUI ☆4 ⇨1 🍷1

Playa Gui Gui (variously spelled Güigüi, Güi güi, Guguy, Guigui or Güy-güy) is definitely the remotest beach on the island. Not only is there a long drive from the main populated areas along winding mountain roads – 1.5 hours from Las Palmas and 1 hour from Maspalomos – to reach the beach you also need to undertake a 5km hike with 500m of elevation.

A serious hike on a single trail, it is located in the most desolate part of the island. To get there pass the village of Tasartico, drive towards the Playa de Tasartico and park your car along the road at 27.92248, -15.80843. An unassuming single trail climbs away from the car park, and this is where you need to get started. The trail is not always clear, so if after 10m there's no clearly trodden path, retrace your steps and look for it again. The hike is strenuous but not too technical.

12 ROQUE NUBLO (1,813M) ☆5 ⇨2 🍷2

Roque Nublo is probably the symbol of the island. The 67m monolith stands proud in the centre of the island and is visible from far afield. The rock originated 4.5 million years ago during a volcano eruption and the consequent lava clouds gave it its exceptional hardness. The rock appears to stand alone but around are other remarkable formations such as the Roque La Rana and Roque La Fraile, somewhat reminiscent of a frog and a monk, respectively. You can reach Roque Nublo via a relatively short but steep 1km-plus hike from the car park at La Goleta.

13 PICO DE LAS NIEVES (1,949M) ☆4 ⇨4 🍷2

Pico de las Nieves is the highest point on the island and its mathematical centre. It's an incredible viewpoint which allows you to spot the nearby Roque Nublo (at 1,813 the second highest point), as well as the summit of Mount Teide on Tenerife (at 3,718m the highest point in Spain) and the Maspalomas Dunes.. Cyclists can ride up from sea level to the summit via two routes. The one from Maspalomas is 45km long with a cumulative elevation of 2,200m, an average gradient of 4 per cent and maximum gradient of 15 per cent. The one from Carrizal is shorter, 25km, but therefore much steeper with an average gradient of 7 per cent and a maximum of 19 per cent.

14 **ROQUE BENTAYGA (1,414M)** ☆ 4 ⚐ 3 🍷 2

Roque Bentayga is a rock formation and an archaeological monument, containing an *almogarén*, a sanctuary built by the indigenous Guanche people. It is easy to reach, as it is only a few hundred metres from the GC607.

On the mountain flank we find the aboriginal settlements of Cuevas del Rey and Roque Camello, made up of dozens of caves.

15 **LA CILLA VIEWPOINT & RESTAURANT** ☆ 5 ⚐ 4 🍷 5

This restaurant and viewpoint is carved into a cliff with a view of the neighbouring Roque Bentayga and Roque Nublo. You do not have to eat in the restaurant – a 50m tunnel allows you to reach the viewpoint just to enjoy the view – but its 150 seats offer a great opportunity to taste traditional local goat dishes and Artenara almond cake.

16 **MIRADOR DEL BALCÓN** ☆ 5 ⚐ 4 🍷 1

Sited on the scenic GC200 between La Aldea de San Nicolás and Agaete, the Mirador del Balcón is a spectacular viewpoint for daredevils who are unafraid of heights. The place – also called Anden Verde – probably has the best views of the island. From the trianglular platform, there are views over the blue of the Atlantic ocean, the silhouette of neighbouring Tenerife and Mount Teide and the Dragon's Tail, a series of cliffs on Gran Canaria's western coast.

Turning around you see the ravine of La Arena making its way up towards the centre of the island and the green valley of La Aldea where oranges are harvested.

17 **TAMADABA NATURAL PARK** ☆ 5 ⚐ 3 🍷 1

The Natural Park of Tamadaba is located in north-west Gran Canaria, in between Agaete in the north and La Aldea de San Nicolás, a 90-minute drive from the capital Las Palmas.

This region, declared a UNESCO Biosphere Reserve, covers 7,500ha and is the most untouched part of the island with a rich variety of landscapes, from forests of Canarian pine – an endemic, symmetrical species with a high resistance to fire – to the spectacular cliffs of its almost inaccessible coast and the many ravines that are typical of the island. It has many walking routes – the GR131 being one of them, making its way from Tejeda to Agaete, and is adjacent to the Parque Rural del Roque Nublo. The highest point, at 1,444m, is Pico de la Bandera.

18 **PLAYA DEL FANEROQUE** ☆ 4 ⚐ 2 🍷 1

The complete opposite of the famed Playa del Inglés, Playa de Faneroque is a black sand beach in the west of the island, close to Agaete, only accessible by foot via a 20 minute hike from a parking next to the GC-200 at coordinates 28.05965, -15.72968.

Your time on the beach is limited, literally, as the beach is only accessible at low tide with the danger of getting stuck, so please check the tide table in advance. It's nicknamed 'beach of the tractor', as there is an abandoned tractor on the sand which is actually a bulldozer being left behind when a local road, used to transport sand to a local cement factory, collapsed. This hidden gem is one of the most pristine beaches of the island and sits at the foot of the giant cliff of Faneque, located between El Risco beach and Guayedra beach. Because of its privacy, the place is often frequented by nudists.

19 **PLAYA DEL JUNCAL** ☆ 2 ⚐ 2 🍷 1

This deserted beach is in a rocky cove near Gáldar, at the end of the Barranco Juncal and is a good place for snorkelling.

20 **FARO PUNTA SARDINA** ☆ 2 ⚐ 4 🍷 1

This red-and-white active lighthouse marks the north-west extremity of the island.

ARTENARA

Gran Canaria
↳ To Stroll

A **LAS PALMAS** ☆ 5 ↕ 5 🍷 5

Home to half of Gran Canaria's population, Las Palmas is the biggest city on the Canary Islands, with 300,000 inhabitants in the city and 700,000 in the metropolitan area. Together with Santa Cruz de Tenerife it is one of the two capitals of the Canary Islands.

The Playa de Canteras is like a black sand version of Copacabana in Río, where you can stroll past local restaurants and charming bars offering Canarian tapas, such as papas arrugadas ('wrinkly potatoes'), local cheeses and pata de cerdo (ham hock). The area also boast one of Spain's largest shopping malls.

Culture lovers will want to know that Christopher Columbus himself lived in Las Palmas for a short period. At the Casa de Colón, you can marvel at old maps and take a peak at the man's diary.

The city can be divided into three main quarters: La Isleta peninsular in the north, the Playa de las Canteras towards the south, and in the south-east the old town of La Vegueta, whose origins date to the 15th century.
Stroll along traditional cobbled streets past pretty houses to Plaza de Santa Ana to see the town's main draw, the Cathedral of Santa Ana, along with the Museum of Sacred Art and the Casa de Colón, dedicated to the life of Christopher Columbus.

La Vegueta is also home to the Pueblo Canario, an interpretation of a traditional Canarian village, located on the south side of the Parque Doramas. The complex puts on Canarian folk performances, every Thursday and Sunday, and is also home to the Museo Néstor, one of the city's principal art galleries.

La Isleta is less well known but, with its narrow streets, old shops and bars, and the lively Plaza Ingeniero Manuel Becerra, overlooked by a lighthouse, is worth visiting. The Castillo de la Luz, the oldest fortress on the island, protects the narrow isthmus that connects the peninsula with the mainland.

B **ARUCAS** ☆ 5 ↕ 4 🍷 4

Arucas is located 12km from Las Palmas, in the north of the island, at an elevation of 600m. The city is synonymous with its cathedral, although this 60m-high miracle built out of black volcanic rock is technically not a cathedral, despite being the tallest church on the island and being referred to as such by the locals. It was built in a Neogothic style between 1909 and 1977 and is dedicated to St John the Baptist.

The 'cathedral' is far from being the only highlight, however: there is a rum distillery, open for visits and sampling; the Jardín de la Marquesa, an extensive botanical garden with tropical plants; the Casa de la Cultura, a traditional 17th-century Canarian home complete with dragon tree; and the Mirador de la Montaña de Arucas, which boasts not only a famous viewpoint over a fertile plain of banana plantations but also a Michelin-starred restaurant.

Outside the city, you'll find the Piedras la Cantera – a quarry open for visits – and on the rocky coastline several little beaches including the Playa de Bañaderos-El Puertillo and the Playa de San Andrés.

C **TEROR** ☆ 5 ↕ 4 🍷 4

Home to a population of 10,000, Teror, in the east of the island, is according to many the most beautiful town on the island. It is also the oldest town on the island with buildings dating back to 1692, many with the typical dark, wooden balconies. Its extensive historic centre is pedestrianized. It's a mid-sized town with a strong religious dimension, famous globally as a pilgrim destination for the Virgen del Pino – the Lady of the Pine Tree – patron saint of Gran Canaria, who is said to have appeared on the branch of a pine tree in 1481.

The Virgen del Pino's feast is celebrated on 8 September when people come from all over the island to venerate its patroness. Her shrine can be found in the basilica of Nuestra Señora del Pino. A typically Canarian market is held in front of the basilica every Sunday morning selling local delicacies such as chorizo sausages or sweets made by the local Cistercian nuns.

The nature around Teror is mountainous and lush. On offer are the Caldera del Pino Santo, the forested estate of the Finca de Osorio, the Parque Rural de Doramas, the Agujereada ('perforated') rock formation, and the deep valleys and canyons of Madrelagua, Pino and La Molineta.

D MASPALOMAS ☆ 5 ↕ 4 🍷 5

The holiday capital of the island comprises the beach resorts of Águila, Las Burras, San Agustín and Playa del Inglés – 17km of wide sandy beaches that attract beach lovers, party crowds and families, who come to enjoy the shallow waters and all- year sunshine, sheltered from Atlantic rains by the island's central mountains.

Apart from food and drink, wonderful nature is close by with the El Oasis and La Charca nature reserves, the latter home to the famous Maspalomas Dunes.

At the southern tip of Maspalomas's beaches – and the most southerly tip of the island – is the town's famous 55m lighthouse. Around it are many shops and restaurants.

E PUERTO DE MOGÁN ☆ 5 ↕ 4 🍷 5

Puerto de Mogán – called 'Little Venice' because of its canals, bridges and colourful houses – is a charming must-see fishing town with a little port at the foot of spectacular cliffs and close to the Barranco de Veneguera.

It offers a little bit of everything: the nearby beach – Playa de Mogán – and beach resorts, a charming town centre with lots of shops and restaurants, some historic buildings such as the church of San Antonio de Padua (built 1814) and the Molino Quemado, a 19th-century gofio mill, and the nearby mountains.

The newly renovated Parque Nicolás Quesada is a pleasant small park whose most notable feature are the five wall murals in the Rincón de Mima. From the port you can board a whale-spotting trip or do scuba diving.

F FATAGA ☆ 5 ↕ 3 🍷 2

On the southern slopes of the island, Fataga is one of the few whitewashed settlements in Gran Canaria, apart from Agaete in the north-west, Tufia in the east and Mogán in the south.

You can't leave this charming village – with its tiny, narrow streets lush with flowers, palm trees and pine trees – without visiting the church of San José or the old watermill.

The surrounding Fataga valley is nicknamed the 'Valley of the Thousand Palms' and can be explored on camel back. The valley is home to many diverse attractions, from the Degollada de las Yeguas viewpoint, with spectacular views of Maspalomas, to the Mundo Aborigen (Aboriginal World), which recreates an ancient Guanche village.

G **TUNTE** ☆ 2 ↕ 3 🍷 2

This mountain town offers a welcomed break for those on their way to Cruz de Tejeda. Tunte is the local name for San Bartolomé de Tirajana, capital of the San Bartolomé de Tirajana municipality, mostly known for its wine and olives. The Tirajanas winery is a great way to discover local farming.

H **TEJEDA** ☆ 2 ↕ 3 🍷 2

Tejeda is a village perched 1,050m high in the mountains, mostly known for the nearby viewpoint of Cruz de Tejeda, which at 1,500m is the highest pass on the island. This is the exact geographical centre of the circular island, a spot marked by a big stone cross. The pass is home to the famous Parador de Cruz de Tejeda, part of the Paradores hotel chain, as well as other bars and restaurants – useful stops if you are hiking one of the several walking trails that pass through here.

Don't get confused, the Cruz de Tejeda is not in the town itself, and while it's only 2km away 'as the crow flies', by car it's a 15-minute drive. Tejeda itself does not have a huge amount to offer but it's a great place for lunch during your trek through the mountains, with most of the restaurants and bars in the Calle Dr Domingo Hernández Guerra. For those in need of a bit of culture there's a museum devoted to the work of Abraham Cárdenes, a famous local sculptor, and the church of Nuestra Señora del Socorro, dating to 1921.

I **ARTENARA** ☆ 3 ↕ 2 🍷 2

Artenara is the highest village of Gran Canaria at 1,219m above sea level. The remote village is known for its caves. To the east of the village you'll find the chapel of the Virgen de la Cuevita, carved into the rocks, while to the west is the famous Mirador La Cilla, with dazzling views over the highlands. You guessed it: this, too, is built into the rock. The archaeological complex of Acusa, with its ancient cave houses, is not too far away either.

J **AGAETE & PUERTO DE LAS NIEVES** ☆ 4 ↕ 3 🍷 4

Puerto de las Nieves is one of Gran Canaria's most attractive seaside towns with whitewashed houses, blue window frames and a great pebble beach. Sadly, its famous Finger of God Rock collapsed during Tropical Storm Delta in 2005. The lack of the deity's finger doesn't make the town any less attractive, as the impressive cliffs towering out over the sea make for an amazing sight in themselves. The town is small in size but abundant in bars and restaurants close to the port.

Its twin town, Agaete, lies half a kilometre higher inland and is home to white houses and narrow streets but very few leisure activities. The Agaete Valley behind the town is one of the island's best. It's green and fertile and full of old Canarian houses, terraced fields and palm trees. You'll even find the only coffee plantation in Europe, the 200-year-old Bodega Los Berrazales.

Agaete comes alive every year for the Bajada de la Rama festival on 4 August. It's a huge, spectacular fiesta with about 50,000 people crammed into the square and narrow streets. In the morning everybody troops down the hill carrying branches. After a long pause for beer, rum and lunch, the procession continues down towards the sea at Puerto de las Nieves. Here everybody 'beats the sea' to appease the ancient goddess of rain.

K **PLAYA SARDINA DEL NORTE** ☆ 3 ↕ 2 🍷 3

Sardina del Norte beach is a beautiful coastal town located in the municipality of Gáldar, in the north of Gran Canaria. Here you can enjoy its spectacular coves and beaches, dive, fish, practise water sports, and enjoy delicious Canarian food overlooking the sea.

VIEW ON MASPALOMAS & EL TEIDE

FORTALEZA DE ANSITE

DEGOLLADA DE LA MANZANILLA, TUNTE

RUTA DE LA PLATA

ARRIVING AT CRUZ DE TEJEDA

ROQUE NUBLO

↰ SUNSET ON ROQUE NUBLO AND ROQUE BENTAYGA

ROQUE NUBLO, SEEN FROM CRUZ DE TEJEDA ↴

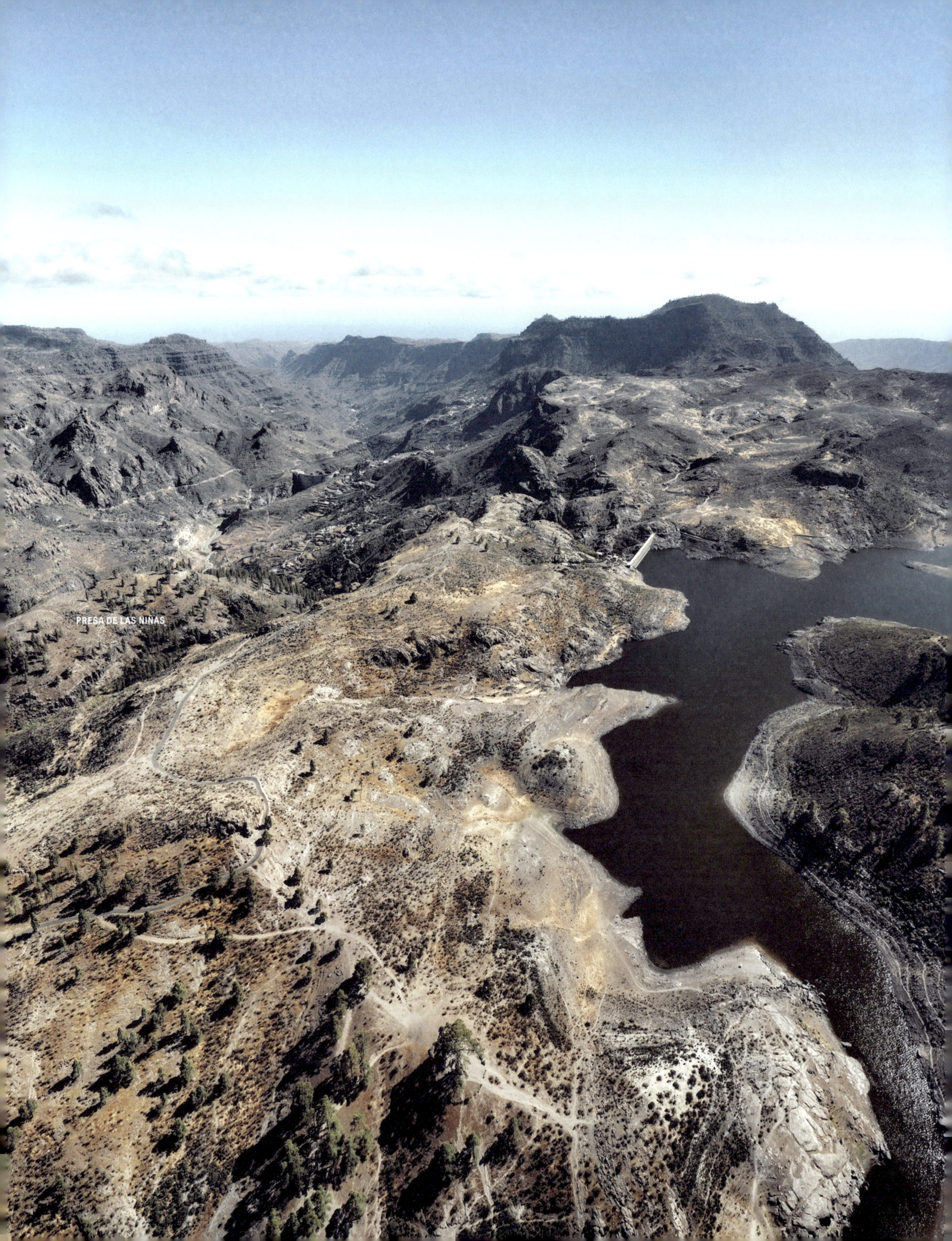
PRESA DE LAS NIÑAS

ROQUE FANEQUE

↰ EL RISCO, TAMADABA

PLAYA DE GUAYEDRA ↴

MIRADOR DEL BALCON

GC200 FROM LA ALDEA TO AGAETE

28.3632°
N

↱ Island 4 / 7
Tenerife

2,034km²
917,841 residents

4

→ LOS GIGANTES
28.2744° N / 16.8562° W
HEIGHT 600M

↳ Welcome to Tenerife, the biggest and best-known island of the seven Canaries. It's the monarch of the archipelago in many ways, with the 3,718m-high Mount Teide dominating the surroundings. None of the islands can demonstrate such a rich diversity of climates and vibes. The dense jungle forests of Anaga or Masca look like as though they have been transported from the Brazilian coast, the pine forests in the midlands take you to Canada, and the Parque Nacional del Teide might double for Mars in a movie.

There are towering cliffs circled by marine wildlife, resorts with white sand beaches and a buzzing nightlife, vibrant cities famous for their annual festivals, and forgotten villages in the midst of the mountains. All these treasures are up for grabs yet have to be shared with the 6 million people who flock the island every year. Luckily, it's big enough and you can choose whether to hide away from the crowds or immerse yourself in them.

Tenerife
Island of Eternal Spring

Coastline: 344km
Highest point: 3,718m

Island of Eternal Spring, attracting people from around the world who come for its gentle, balmy climate.

↳ One might compare Tenerife with an isosceles triangle, tilted 45 degrees off north to the right. It has three big national parks: the exotic jungle of succulents and laurel in the Parque Rural de Anaga in the eastern corner; the pine forests and arid, red Martian landscape of the Parque Nacional del Teide in the centre; and the mountains of the Parque Rural de Teno, with the famous village of Masca, in the western angle, dropping to the sea and the towering cliffs of Los Gigantes. Most tourists congregate in the south-west, flocking to the luxury upscale resorts and golf courts in Adeje and to the more mass-market Playa de las Americas and Los Cristianos nestled in the right angle. Most locals live up north in the metropoles of Santa Cruz de Tenerife, with its port, and San Cristóbal de la Laguna, with its university and colonial houses, on the fringes of the Anaga park. The more adorable villages are found on the north-western side, with the vineyards of Icod de los Vinos and the charming houses of Garachico as the main attractions.

FARO DE ANAGA

Tenerife
↳ Introduction

HOW TO GET AROUND

There are two airports, one in the south, close to Los Cristianos, and one in the north, next to San Cristobál and Santa Cruz, so make sure to check which you are landing at before your departure. The same is true for the ports. Ferries connect either from Los Cristianos, for the western islands, or from Santa Cruz, for the eastern islands. Both ports also connect to each other. There is a main road that follows the coast except in the fringes of Anaga and Teno where settlements are served by smaller, winding roads.

The most western and eastern extremities are only accessible by foot. The Parque Nacional Teide, one of the most visited parks in the world, can be reached by road via Vilaflor.

WHERE TO STAY

If you like relaxed beach life with lots of options, you want to base yourself between Adeje and Los Cristianos where the majority of hotels are. The Adeje resorts are more luxurious while those around the Playa de las Americas are more mass-market. Surfers look for the more laid-back atmosphere of El Médano, while 'normal' city life is found up in the north-east at San Cristóbal and Santa Cruz. Charming villages and vineyards are found in the north-west of the island.

BEACHES

With 67km of beach there is an abundance of attractive coastline in Tenerife. In the west is the Playa de la Arena, a small black volcanic sand beach overlooked by the town and promenade.

Further south are the fashionable beaches of Adeje – Playa del Duque and Playa de Fañabé. The most famous beaches still further south are the Playas de las Americas, de las Vistas and de los Cristianos, all with a buzzing nightlife and plenty of restaurants. A rocky stretch of coastline separates these tourist beaches from the Playa el Médano loved by kite surfers.

Close to the capital is the black sand Playa de las Arenas, protected by a jetty from the waves, but it's the Playa de las Teresitas with its white sand that is one of the most beautiful and enjoyable. On the north side of the island, the coastline is mostly rocky, but you can find smaller beaches such as Playa de Benijo.

THREE-DAY STAY

Day 1 – The east
Start the day with a hike from Benijo to the remote Faro de Anaga. Have lunch in San Cristóbal and marvel at the colourful streets. Spend the night in Santa Cruz after visiting its magnificent auditorium and/or relaxing on the Playa de las Teresitas.

Day 2 – El Teide
If you want to watch the sunrise from Mount Teide, you need to get up very early as the hike will take 3–5 hours. Alternatively, take the cable car, and walk the last few metres to the top and grab the view from Pico Viejo (you will need to apply for a free summit access permit well in advance of your trip). Lunch in the Parador de las Cañadas hotel before taking a postprandial stroll around Roques de García. Spend the afternoon in the Masca Valley and the marvellous Barranco de Masca. If you are fond of some villagey charm, you can grab dinner at Garachico or Icod de los Vinos.

Day 3 – The south-west
Take a boat tour around Los Gigantes to marvel at the lofty cliffs and the marine wildlife. If you'd rather stay dry, pick one of the golf courses, preferably Buenavista or Abama. Enjoy a fancy lunch at the Ritz or another Adeje restaurant and relax for the rest of the afternoon before the sunset.

TENERIFE

EXPLORE / HIGHLIGHTS

1 Anaga Rural Park
2 Bosque Encantado
3 Faro de Anaga & Roque Bermejo
4 Roques de Anaga
5 Playa de Benijo
6 Roque de Taborno
7 Path of the Senses
8 Playa de las Teresitas
9 Auditorio de Tenerife Adan Martin
10 Pirámides de Güímar
11 Teide Observatory
12 Teide National Park
13 Pico del Teide
14 Pico Viejo
15 Roques de García
16 Mount Guajara
17 Dragon tree, Icod de los Vinos
18 Teno Natural Park
19 Punta de Teno Lighthouse
20 Los Gigantes
21 Playa de la Arena
22 Playa del Duque
23 Barranco del Infierno
24 Roque del Conde

STROLL / HIGHLIGHTS

A Taganana
B Chinamada
C Santa Cruz de Tenerife
D San Cristóbal de la Laguna
E Puerto de la Cruz
F El Médano
G Playa de las Americas
H Icod de los Vinos
I Garachico
J Masca
K Los Gigantes
L Adeje

TEIDE NATIONAL PARK

Tenerife
↳ Key Facts

WHEREABOUTS	Name	Tenerife
	Origin of name	The Indigenous peoples of La Palma referred to neighbouring Tenerife with the words *teni* ('mountain') and *ife* ('white'). The letter 'r' was added later by the Spanish
	Nickname	The Island of Eternal Spring, attracts tourists from all over the world with its all-year-round balmy temperatures
	Key towns and villages	Masca, Taganana, El Médano, Icod de los Vinos, Garachico
DEMOGRAPHICS	Population	917,841 people, 43% of the Canary Islands, 1st in rank
	Capital	Santa Cruz de Tenerife (pop. approx. 205,000)
	Biggest cities	Santa Cruz de Tenerife, San Cristóbal de La Laguna, Los Christianos
INFRASTRUCTURE	Commercial Airport	Tenerife North Airport (TFN), San Cristóbal de La Laguna Tenerife South Airport (TFS), El Médano, busiest
	Commercial Ports	Port of Santa Cruz de Tenerife, serving islands to the east Port of Los Cristianos, serving capitals of islands to the west
	Agriculture	Agriculture is centred in the north with tomatoes and bananas along the coast, and potatoes, tobacco and maize in the drier central zones.
GEOGRAPHY	Size	2,034km², 1st in rank
	Highest point	Mount Teide (3,718m)
	Dimensions	Long triangular shape with length of 80km and width at widest part of 50km
	Coastline	342km, 67km beaches
	Geologic origings	Seven million years ago, three distinct island volcanoes emerged, giving rise to what are now the Anaga, Teno and Adeje. Two millions years later, volcanic activity created the massive stratovolcano, Teide, in the centre, which led the separate islands to merge, forming the largest of the Canary Islands.
HISTORY	End of 14th century	The nine children of Tinerfe the Great split Tenerife into nine *menceyatos*, or kingdoms, corresponding to the present-day municipalities.
	1464-1496	Tenerife is the last island to be conquered by the Spanish.
	27 March 1977	The deadliest accident in commercial aviation history. Two Boeing 747s collided at Los Rodeos Airport (now Tenerife North Airport), causing 583 fatalities.

Tenerife
↳ Where to Hike

OVERVIEW

Tenerife is the largest of the Canaries, with the most diverse landscapes and the largest offer of hiking trails of all the islands. It's also by far the island with the highest elevations, a fact that contributes to the variety of climates and landscapes. From east to west, there are four major sections on the trail: the Parque Rural de Anaga in the east (A1, A2, A3); the pine forested midlands towards the Parque Nacional del Teide (20, 21); the Teide park trails (22A, 22B, 22); and the descent to Los Cristianos (23, 24, 24B).

TERRAIN

The terrain differs materially from section to section. Anaga offers technical single trails through jungle and rugged cliffs with the ocean nearby. The pine midlands offer broad tracks through dense forests with Mount Teide looming in the distance. The Parque Nacional del Teide, towering over the island, is a reddish Martian landscape with no vegetation across, where the single trail climbs up and down. The descent leaves behind the petrified lava for, first, pine forest and then scrubland as the trail approaches the coast.

WHICH STAGE TO PICK

Both the Anaga and Teide parks are UNESCO World Heritage Biosphere Reserves, but each of a completely different kind. Anaga has tropical, Amazonian vibes while Teide offers an extra-terrestrial experience. You shouldn't leave the island without at least exploring one of those parks, with stages A1, A2, 22A or 22B highly recommended. The trails in Teide require specific preparation, so read the relevant section carefully.

ELEVATION MAP

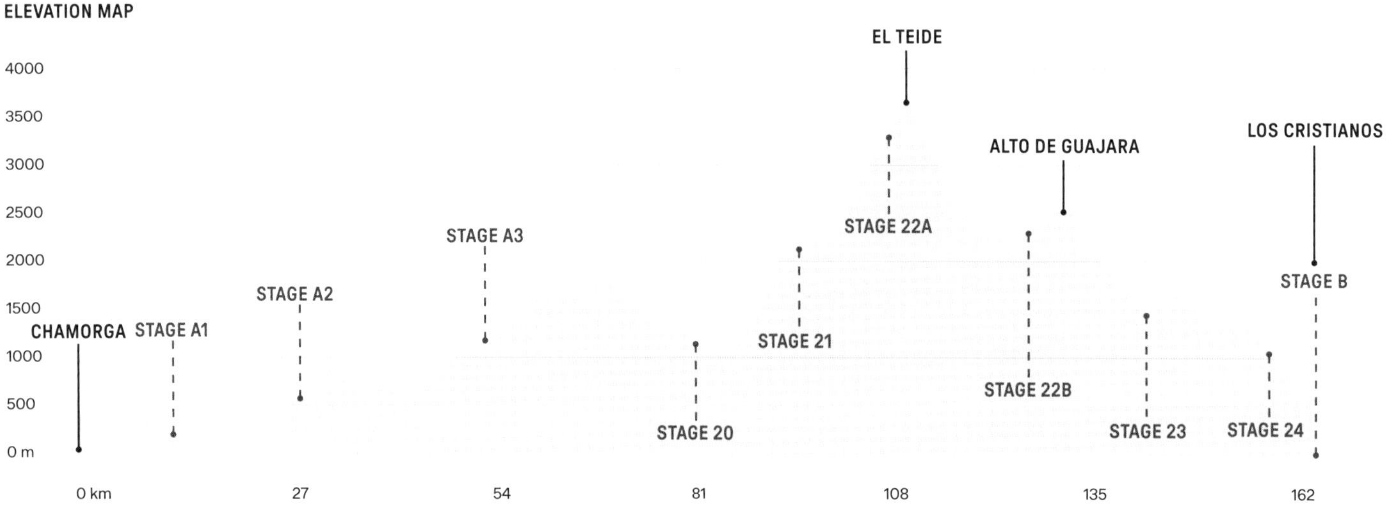

Tenerife
↳ Hikes Overview

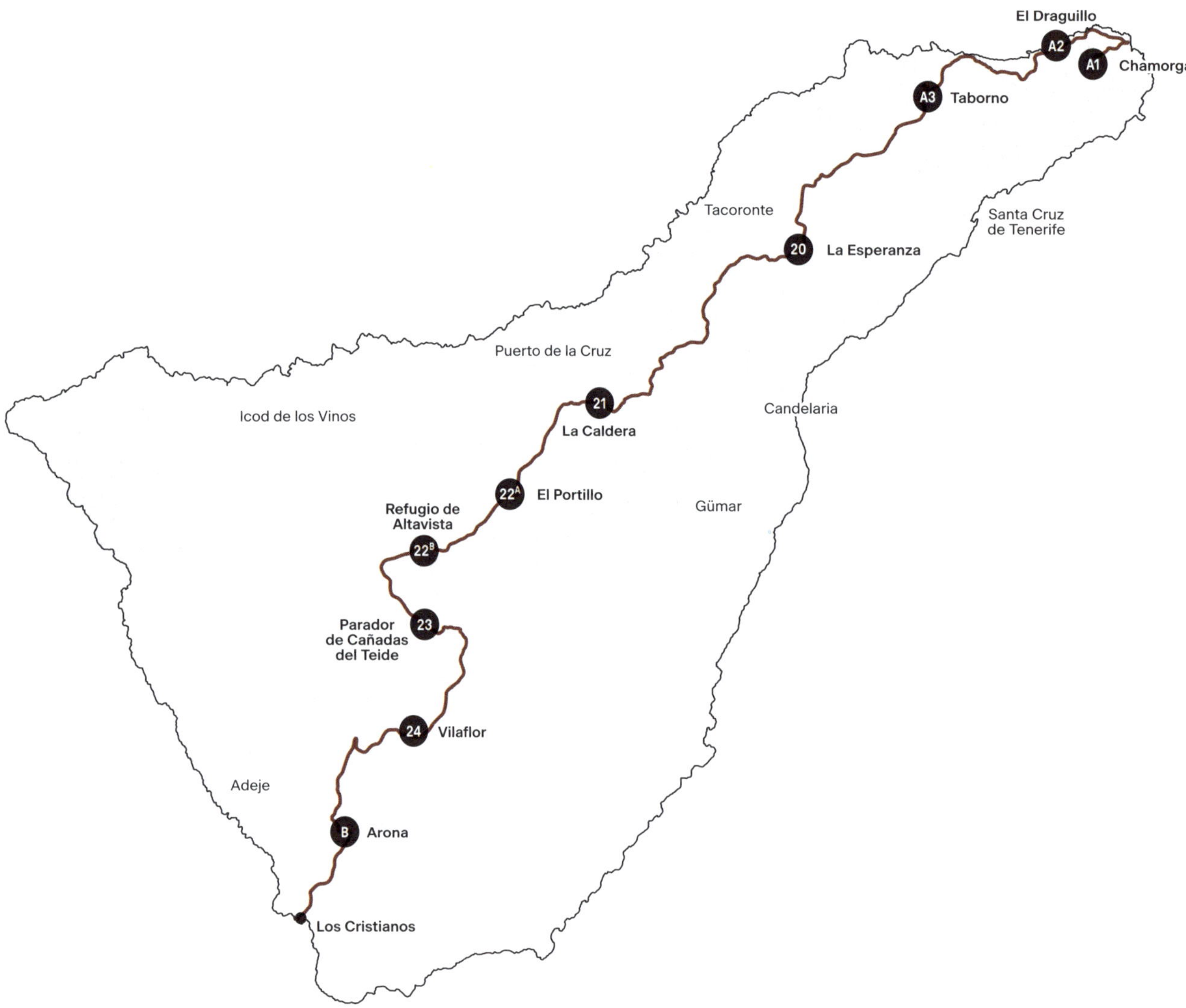

STAGE A1 **CHAMORGA TO EL DRAGUILLO**

Distance 10.4km **Ascent** 670m **Decent** 940m **Asphalt** 0%

Non-GR131, technical trail in Anaga with incredible views of the Roques de Anaga, Faro de Anaga and the secluded beach of Roque Bermejo.

Recommendation: 4 / 4
Technicality: 4 / 4
Facilities: 1 / 4
Type: GR131

To reach the eastern extremity of Tenerife, you have to start in Chamorga, the last place accessible by car before you set off along a single trail through the jungle. After 3–4km of technical descent you end up at the end of the world and the black sand beach of Roque Bermejo. The winding path to the Farode Anagais a legendary one with an incredible view. After the lighthouse, you turn either left or right. The left-hand path is the GPX route and the safest option. The right-hand path is the one we chose, but was, during our visit, poorly maintained and exposed to the cliff edge – even if the views are incredible.

STAGE A2 **EL DRAGUILLO TO TABORNO**

Distance 18km **Ascent** 1,360m **Decent** 950m **Asphalt** 22%

Non-GR131, technical trail in Anaga along cliffs with ocean view and through dense jungle with a high off-the-beaten-track vibe.

Recommendation: 3 / 4
Technicality: 4 / 4
Facilities: 2 / 4
Type: GR131

The first part of the trail passes the villages of Playa de Benijo and Taganana with an incredible asphalt section up to the Mirador Risco Amogoje, before returning to the cliffs above the roaring ocean. After this, the trail heads inland, covering steep, often very technical and dense jungle terrain as it makes its way through a ravine to Taborno. Most of the trail is remote and unreachable by any sort of vehicle. Be careful.

STAGE A3 **TABORNO TO LA ESPERANZA**

Distance 24km **Ascent** 1,040m **Decent** 730m **Asphalt** 42%

Long stage with the first part in dense forests, with some parts hard to find. Second part is partly urban or in nature with a view of the area of San Cristóbal.

Recommendation: 2 / 4
Technicality: 3 / 4
Facilities: 3 / 4
Type: GR131

This long stage has two faces. From Taborno to the town of Las Mercedes, the trail passes through dense moist forest with limited surrounding views. At Las Mercedes come the first views over the magnificent San Cristóbal de la Laguna valley with the towering Mount Teide in the background. From then on, the trail travels the low green hill ridges looking over San Cristóbal. The last 7km is all on road, part of which is 700m on the busy two-lane TF152 highway, and so not recommended. We only traced the last part to connect La Esperanza with the Anaga part of the island.

STAGE 20 **LA ESPERANZA TO LA CALDERA**

Distance 29.5km **Ascent** 1,650m **Decent** 1,360m **Asphalt** 5%

On of the longest and least accessible stages through pine forests in Tenerife midlands, slowly approaching the Teide.

Recommendation: 3 / 4
Technicality: 2 / 4
Facilities: 1 / 4
Type: GR131

This is a very long stage, without any obvious way to shorten it. The first part is easy, along broad forest tracks and paths. In the second half, the roads become single trails winding through ravines, offering more technicality and excitement. Often, you can see Mount Teide peering through the trees. The finish at La Caldera offers picnicking facilities and public transport in the form of buses, but no hospitality. Be well prepared.

STAGE 21 **LA CALDERA TO EL PORTILLO**

Distance 13.5km **Ascent** 1,090m **Decent** 240m **Asphalt** 2%

Another climbing stage through pine forest, shorter but steeper than the last one, arriving at the Parque Nacional del Teide at 2,000m above sea level.

Recommendation: 3 / 4
Technicality: 3 / 4
Facilities: 2 / 4
Type: GR131

This segment begins amid dense forest, and although there are occasional glimpses of lower, cultivated terrains, it primarily ascends among the towering trees. The landscape is laced with numerous paths and tracks that weave across the slopes, making it important to stay alert to the GR131 signposts and markers. As the day progresses, the trail eventually breaks free from the forest cover, revealing stunning vistas of the magnificent Teide park. With a 1,000m-plus ascent on a short track of 14km, this is one of the steepest stages on the whole route.

STAGE 22A	EL PORTILLO TO REFUGIO DE ALTAVISTA	**Distance** 11.5km **Ascent** 1,250m **Decent** 20m **Asphalt** 0%

Climb to the highest point in Spain at sunrise and get rewarded with stunning views over Tenerife and the surrounding islands.

Recommendation: 4 / 4
Technicality: 3 / 4
Facilities: 1 / 4
Type: GR131

This stage leads from El Portillo at 2,032m to the refuge hut at Altavista at 3,270m. From there, another 2km takes you to the lower station of the Mount Teide cable car, at 3,533m. The Teide summit is at 3,718m. Along with 22B, it's the most demanding stage. The high altitude can take its toll, so it's recommended that you stay in the area the day before. You need to time and prepare yourself well. The trail from the lower cable car station to the summit can be accessed only with a permit, which must be reserved months in advance. If you reach the summit before 9am, you do not need a permit, but you will need to start the ascent at El Portillo at 5am at the latest. Last but not least, the refuge hut at Altavista is small and often closed, so do your research if you want to spend the night there.

STAGE 22B	ALTAVISTA TO PARADOR DE CAÑADAS DEL TEIDE	**Distance** 13km **Ascent** 450m **Decent** 1,570m **Asphalt** 0%

Descent from Mount Teide on the west flank, passing the wonderful Pico Viejo and the Roques de García.

Recommendation: 4 / 4
Technicality: 4 / 4
Facilities: 1 / 4
Type: GR131

The GR131 uses this stage as the descent from Teide. If you take out the Altavista–cable car section, you'll notice that the cable car–Parador section is steeper than the 22A, and makes for a worthy alternative way to climb Mount Teide. This route passes the Pico Viejo, an old volcano with an impressive crater, and just before the end, the Roques de García, prior to arriving at the parador hotel, where you can eat and/or spend the night.

STAGE 23	PARADOR DE CAÑADAS DEL TEIDE TO VILAFLOR	**Distance** 15.5km **Ascent** 380m **Decent** 1,100m **Asphalt** 0%

Descent stage leaving the Parque Nacional del Teide with great views over the island's west coast.

Recommendation: 3 / 4
Technicality: 3 / 4
Facilities: 2 / 4
Type: GR131

A rugged climb from the parador kicks off the stage which exits the national park via Alto de Guajara, Tenerife's third highest peak. A fairly technical winding descent leads to a remarkable straight stretch through volcanic black sand, an experience you will not forget. After this, easier forest paths lead to the village of Vilaflor, at 1,400m above sea level, where you can find some facilities.

STAGE 24	VILAFOR TO ARONA	**Distance** 18km **Ascent** 450m **Decent** 1,260m **Asphalt** 22%

Downhill climb in two legs, one through pine forests and ravines, the latter with open views over the approaching coastline.

Recommendation: 3 / 4
Technicality: 3 / 4
Facilities: 2 / 4
Type: GR131

The last leg of the Tenerife stretch of the GR131 is mostly downhill. The path meanders through pine forests around the ravine of Barranco del Rey, before descending towards Ifonche. From there on, the vegetation becomes scrubbier and the views wider, circling around the striking Roque Imoque peak. As you make your way downwards, you'll navigate steep and craggy slopes adorned with ancient agricultural terraces, leading to the quaint town of Arona. From here, there are bus connections to Los Cristianos.

STAGE B	ARONA TO LOS CHRISTIANOS	**Distance** 8.5km **Ascent** 0m **Decent** 620m **Asphalt** 82%

Non-GR131 track whose only function is to get you to Los Cristianos. Not recommended.

Recommendation: 1 / 4
Technicality: 1 / 4
Facilities: 3 / 4
Type: GR131

We only planned this track to complete the coast-to-coast path from east to west. The track is the shortest way from Arona, the end of the GR131 on Tenerife, to Los Cristianos, where you can stay the night or take the ferry to another island. We don't recommend this stage unless you are determined to cover all the islands.

PLAYA DE LAS AMERICAS, LOS CRISTIANOS

Tenerife
↳ To Explore

1 **PARQUE RURAL DE ANAGA** ☆ 5 ⇨ 2 🍷 1

The Parque Rural de Anaga, in Tenerife's north-eastern tip, earned UNESCO Biosphere Reserve status in 2015. This mountainous region boasts craggy peaks, deep ravines, and the island's largest laurel forest, home to unique plant species. Formed by a volcanic eruption 7–9 million years ago, Anaga is Tenerife's oldest part. Visitors can dine in ancient cave dwellings, hike through lush forests, and swim in natural pools or at pristine beaches. Key attractions include Faro de Anaga, Roque Taborno, Benijo beach, the Enchanted Forest, but one must-see is the dramatic coastal views in the north. With only around 2,500 residents across 26 small towns within its 15,000ha expanse, Anaga offers a serene escape for nature enthusiasts, just an hour's drive from Santa Cruz de Tenerife. You can get more information at Centro de Visitantes del Parque Rural de Anaga in Cruz del Carmen or stay the night at the lodge of Montes de Anaga.

2 **BOSQUE ENCANTADO** ☆ 4 ⇨ 2 🍷 1

The Bosque Encantado (Enchanted Forest) in La Laguna is a mystical destination on Cordillera Dorsal's mountain ridges. The mist-shrouded forest offers a unique micro-climate and diverse vegetation. There are several hikes of 2–8km in length with no loops, featuring slippery trails and lush plant life. While scenic views are limited due to the thick vegetation, there are occasional glimpses of the northern coastal villages of Almáciga and Benijo.

Accessible from the TF123 with ample parking, this forest is a must-visit for a serene, otherworldly experience in Tenerife. Visitors require a free permit, which should be applied for months in advance.

3 **FARO DE ANAGA & ROQUE BERMEJO** ☆ 4 ⇨ 1 🍷 1

The Faro de Punta de Anaga marks the most eastern part of Tenerife. Built in 1864, it is one of the oldest working lighthouses in the Canary Islands and definitely one of the most remote and atmospheric. Perched on a cliff in the middle of the jungle, overlooking the remote beach and village of Playa de Roque Bermejo, with no decent road within a 3km radius, it is accessible only via a technical trail. This trail begins in tranquil Chamorga, at the heart of Anaga Forest, one of Tenerife's most scenic hikes. Chamorga offers easy roadside parking. Follow PR-TF6.1 for 2.8km along a narrow rocky path. At Casas de Tafada, take the left-hand path up to the lighthouse or take a right if you want to dip your feet in the ocean. As you pass the occasional house in the jungle, you may well wonder how many times a year the inhabitants escape this green wilderness and visit 'civilization'.

4 **ROQUES DE ANAGA** ☆ 4 ⇨ 1 🍷 1

The Roques de Anaga, or Roques de Chinamada, are a group of distinctive rock formations located in the Anaga park. They are characterized by their tall, needle-like spires and rugged cliffs, creating a dramatic and picturesque landscape, reminiscent of a dragon's back emerging from the sea.

The basaltic Roques de Anaga are the result of millions of years of volcanic activity, through processes such as lava flows, volcanic eruptions, and subsequent erosion by wind and water. The best way to get there is to drive to the village of Benijo and then park up as far east beyond there as you can. From the last parking opportunity – the closest you'll get – it's a 2.5km hike.

5 **PLAYA DE BENIJO** ☆ 3 ⇨ 3 🍷 1

The Playa de Benijo is one of the most secluded and pristine beaches in Taganana, a charming town in the Anaga region. It shares its black volcanic shores with two neighbouring bathing areas, El Roque de las Bodegas and Almáciga. To reach this coastal gem from, Santa Cruz, travellers embark on a road with breathtaking views over the surrounding rolling hills.

6 **ROQUE TABORNO** ☆2 ⇨2 🍷1

Roque de Taborno, nicknamed 'Tenerife's Matterhorn', is a thumb-shaped rock that rises 706m above sea level on the north coast of the Anaga Peninsula.

7 **PATH OF THE SENSES** ☆3 ⇨3 🍷1

The Path of the Senses, located in Cruz del Carmen, within the Parque Rural de Anaga, follows an ancient 'royal road' that once connected the villages of Anaga and La Laguna. A part of this historic path has been restored to offer a sensory journey through the heart of the forest along a short, user-friendly trail suitable for all. Along the way information panels help to attune your senses – touch, smell, sight and hearing – to the surrounding nature. Some sections invite you to listen to the forest's sounds, while others encourage tactile exploration of laurel forest tree trunks. It's perfect for those wanting to connect with nature and explore new island spots without requiring extensive experience or physical preparation.

There are three distinct paths on offer:
1. Awaken Your Senses: Experience the forest's humidity and scents on a 340m wheelchair-accessible route. Length: 340m. Difficulty: Low.
2. Be Amazed: A circular path with stone-cut steps, a bridge and a high runway. Length: 544m. Difficulty: Low.
3. Discover Hidden Secrets: An uphill, stepped circular route leading to the Llano de los Loros viewpoint. Length: 1,272m. Difficulty: Low to medium.

8 **PLAYA DE LAS TERESITAS** ☆5 ⇨5 🍷5

Situated in the town of San Andrés within Santa Cruz de Tenerife, this 1km beach was created in the 1970s, replacing a volcanic sand beach. The beach was expanded using golden sand imported from the Sahara Desert, providing more space for beachgoers. To create a tranquil environment, a breakwater dam was constructed to calm the crystal-clear waters. Today, Las Teresitas beach is, alongside Playa de las Américas, one of the most bustling in Tenerife. With its serene, transparent waters, golden sands, and numerous beachfront cafés and bars, it has become a popular destination for families. With every amenity on hand, it guarantees a delightful day at the seaside.

9 **AUDITORIO DE TENERIFE ADÁN MARTIN** ☆5 ⇨5 🍷4

The Auditorio de Tenerife Adán Martín, known as the Auditorio de Tenerife, is a renowned architectural and cultural icon in Santa Cruz de Tenerife, designed by architect Santiago Calatrava, who also built the Oculus in New York and (with Félix Candela), the City of Arts and Sciences in Valencia. It's celebrated for its avant-garde design, featuring a distinctive wave-like roof. Others says it resembles the sail of a ship. As a major cultural hub, it hosts classical music, opera, ballet, theatre and contemporary music events, serving as the home of the Tenerife Symphony Orchestra.

10 **PIRÁMIDES DE GÜÍMAR** ☆4 ⇨4 🍷4

The Pirámides de Güímar, located in the south-east of Tenerife, is an enigmatic site featuring six rectangular step pyramids, of unclear origins. The highest is 12m tall. Theories about their builders and purpose vary. It's most commonly believed that they are the result of 19th-century farmers stacking stones uncovered while ploughing, but other theories have been proposed. The Güímar Valley was once a spiritual centre for the Guanches, Tenerife's original inhabitants. Norwegian anthropologist Thor Heyerdahl discovered that these pyramids, made of lava rock rather than regular stones, align astronomically. At the summer solstice, by standing on the platform of the largest pyramid, you can witness a double sunset as the sun sets behind a nearby mountain peak, reappears briefly, and then sets behind a neighbouring one. The 6.5ha site was opened to the public in 1988 and is today an archaeological park housing a museum, viewpoint, walks and garden. The Mirador de Don Martín offers a splendid view of the surroundings. Another point of interest is the Volcán de Güímar, a volcano with a crater that reaches an impressive depth of 60m. Lastly, there is the unique Jardín Venenoso, which houses over 70 poisonous plant species from around the world.

11 **TEIDE OBSERVATORY** ☆4 ⇨4 🍷3

Stargazers and cosmic geeks will marvel at the sight of a bunch of weirdly shaped white buildings popping out of the ochre-coloured slopes of Mount Teide. The Observatorio del Teide is a part of the Teide National Park, providing, at 2,390m above sea level, exceptionally clear and stable atmospheric conditions, which are essential for precise astronomical observations. The telescopes based there such as the Vacuum Tower Telescope (VTT), the Swedish Solar Telescope (SST) and the GREGOR solar telescope are on a mission to uncover the Sun's deepest secrets, including solar magnetism, solar flares and solar oscillations. While the observatory is mostly used by professionals, there's a visitor centre where you can get a sneak peek into the starry world beyond, including guided tours.

12 **PARQUE NACIONAL DEL TEIDE** ☆5 ⇧5 ♀3

The Parque Nacional del Teide is the largest national park in the Canary Islands, covering 190km^2 (18,990ha). With around 3 million visitors annually, it's also the most frequented national park in Spain. Its crowning feature is Mount Teide (see below). The park has paved roads, two visitor centres, restaurants, many panoramic viewpoints, a large network of hikes, and two contrasting accommodation options, the Parador de Las Cañadas del Teide and the Altavista mountain hut, which lies at 3,270m above sea level. The first includes a famous training camp for professional athletes because of its altitude and the surrounding roads. During our stay there we ran into two Grand Tour winners and a few Olympic medallists. The mountain hut is not always open, so plan carefully.

There is one visitor centre in El Portillo, while the other is inside the parador. In 2007 UNESCO recognized the park as a World Heritage Site.

Las Cañadas del Teide, a colossal caldera, is a circular rocky wall, 17km in diameter and 25km long, in the middle of the park. It originated 198,000 years ago through a massive landslide, its towering walls reaching a height up to 600m, at the Guajara Pass.

The Teide Park has a wealth of volcanic features, with hundreds of cones, hardened lava flows and caves. And let's not forget the rich flora and fauna, including numerous endemic species found exclusively on the Canary Islands or even solely within the park.

In spring, don't miss the splendid red bugloss (*Echium wildpretii*), whose thousands of tiny deep-red flowers form efflorescences that can reach up to 3m high. Another unique species is the Teide violet, the park's emblem, which grows only above 2,500m. Spotting one is a rare and fortunate sight.

As for the wildlife, keep an eye out for tiny creatures like the Canarian lizard, Delalande's gecko, the Gran Canaria skink and Corsican mouflon.

13 **PICO DEL TEIDE (3715M)** ☆5 ⇧2 ♀1

The highest point in Spain is not on the mainland but on one of the Canary Islands. At 3,718m, it's not only the highest peak on Spanish soil, but also the third highest volcano in the world, when measured from the ocean floor, after Mauna Kea and Loa, two peaks in Hawaii. Your trip to Tenerife is not complete without planting your flag on its summit and marvelling at the sight of the four surrounding islands – Gran Canaria, La Palma, El Hierro and La Gomera – as well as the view over Tenerife itself.

There are two ways to get there, by foot or by cable car. The lower station of the lift is at 2,356m and the upper station at 3,555m, covering the elevation in less than 8 minutes. At the top, you're still quite a few steps away from the summit. The hike isn't easy but definitely worth it. Take note that you need to register on the National Parks website – www.reservasparquesnacionales.es – to acquire an access permit. You should ideally do this more than two months before.

If you don't have a permit or like a challenge, then you could hike up – but you'll need to get up early: no permit is required if you get to the summit before 9am. There are two routes, both along the GR131, both 13km long and both starting at 2,200m above sea level. The eastern route starts at El Portillo and the western at the parador. On the eastern side, you could spend the night at the Altavista mountain refuge, although its opening times can be haphazard. On average plan a 5 hour ascent, wear protective clothes and take sufficient carbs and water.

14 PICO VIEJO (3,104M) ☆ 4 🪧 2 🍷 1

Close by, slightly to the south-west of Mount Teide, you'll find a spectacular crater: the 3,104m-high Pico Viejo, boasting an 800m-diameter crater, once home to an impressive lava lake. This is the second-highest volcano in the Canary Islands. The hike from the lower cable car station to the Pico Viejo Viewpoint, known as Hiking Route 12 and referred to as Montaña Chahorra, is excellent and relatively easy, essentially serving as a viewpoint itself.

As the sun sets or rises, the surroundings take on vibrant hues, leaving no one untouched by its beauty. The last historical eruption in the Pico Viejo area occurred in 1798. This eruption lasted a whopping 3 months and gave rise to the Las Narices del Teide (Noses of Teide), the craters that spewed lava during this historic event, located in the western foothills of Pico Viejo. As you stroll along the Pico Viejo trail, you can admire the solidified lava flow from this eruption at a distance.

15 ROQUES DE GARCÍA ☆ 4 🪧 3 🍷 3

The Roques de García are a set of unique rock formations south of the Pico del Teide. They are very accessible being close to the Mirador de la Ruleta, a few hundred metres from the parador. This 'flock' of rocks with different shapes and forms are the result of millions of years of erosion that split the large Las Cañadas volcanic caldera into two craters. Over time, the rock formations – the most famous in Tenerife – have absorbed various volcanic materials from an immense ancient volcano that existed prior to Mount Teide, taking on their distinctive red colour.

The 217m Roque Cinchado is probably the most remarkable, widely known as the Finger of God or the Stone Tree due to its tree-like shape. It is so iconic that it was chosen to appear on the back of the now-defunct 1,000-peseta banknote. Other rock formations are La Catedral and La Cascada, as well as smaller structures such as El Burro, Torrotito and Roque Blanco.

16 MOUNT GUAJARA (2718M) ☆ 5 🪧 4 🍷 1

Mount Guajara, at 2,718m, is the highest point within the park and the third highest peak in Tenerife. If you want to hike up, it's advised to park at the parador and do the remaining 5km on foot along the GR131. From Guajara, you have a great view over Las Cañadas del Teide, El Pico del Teide and the slopes dropping down by an elevation of almost 3,000m to Playa de las Americas in the south.

17 DRAGON TREE, ICOD DE LOS VINOS ☆ 4 🪧 5 🍷 4

The Dragon Tree of Icod de los Vinos, also known as the Drago Milenario, is one of the most famous landmarks on the island. *Dracaena draco*, commonly known as the dragon tree, is a rare and unique species of tree, characterized by its thick, palm-like trunk and clusters of long, narrow leaves that resemble dragon's scales. Another explanation for its name is the blood-red rubbery sap that flows when you cut into its trunk.

This type of tree used to be very common around the Mediterranean, but ancient climate changes and ice ages have brought about its decline in areas other than on Tenerife.

This particular tree, the Drago Milenario, is estimated to be over a thousand years old, making it one of the oldest living things on the island. It is approximately 16m high and has a circumference of about 20m. This tree has deep cultural and historical significance for the people of Tenerife: it is often considered a symbol of the island, is featured on the municipal coat of arms of Icod de los Vinos, and is protected by various laws and regulations, including UNESCO World Heritage status.

According to local legend, the dragon tree sap has healing properties and over centuries has been used for various medicinal purposes, as well as in the mummification of corpses, as a hair dye, and in wood varnish, especially for violins. The tree was also considered sacred by the Guanche people.

18 PARQUE RURAL DE TENO ☆ 3 ⇨ 2 🍷 2

Hiking through the Parque Rural de Teno is like walking on an island within an island. This mountain range, rising over 1,300m, covers the entire western tip of Tenerife and is almost entirely surrounded by the sea. In fact, Teno was originally a small isolated island that only later, along with other islands, formed what is now known as Tenerife. The relative geographical isolation of its ravines and narrow valleys has helped to preserve the biodiversity, architecture and unique customs that have largely been lost in the Tenerife of mass tourism.

While traversing the Parque Rural de Teno, you can enjoy lush laurel forests on Monte del Agua, beautiful thickets of cactus-like plants in the monumental ravine of Masca or enjoy ocean views at the island's most westerly point, Punta de Teno, in the shade of its remote lighthouse. The close relationship between nature and the local mountain population is one of the themes highlighted in the park's visitor centre located in the village of El Palmar. There, you can find information about the 13 well-marked hiking trails in the park and the best places to purchase local products.

19 PUNTA DE TENO LIGHTHOUSE ☆ 3 ⇨ 2 🍷 2

Protected by its lighthouse, Punta de Teno is a rocky headland, marking the north- western tip of Tenerife. From this cinematic location in the Teno Park you can observe Los Gigantes cliffs, a bit further to the south.

To get there, take the TF445, following the coastal road from the centre of the town of Buenavista del Norte. To reach Punta de Teno, you can drive (at certain times), hike or take a bus. Technically, you can't drive to the end of the headland, as car access is restricted, which makes the Punta de Teno delightfully uncrowded during the day.

20 LOS GIGANTES ☆ 5 ⇨ 4 🍷 3

Los Gigantes, or 'The Giants', are among Tenerife's most awe-inspiring natural wonders. Situated on the western coast of the island, these colossal rocky walls rise dramatically from the sea, reaching heights of up to 600m in some places. Stretching for approximately 15km from the port of Los Gigantes to Punta de Teno, the westernmost point of Tenerife, they form a breathtaking basalt wall of volcanic origin. For the ancient Guanches, the original inhabitants of Tenerife, Los Gigantes held a special significance. They referred to the formation as the 'Wall of Hell' or the 'Wall of the Devil', in the belief that it marked the end of the world.

There are several ways to marvel at the grandeur of Los Gigantes. First, the Archipenque Viewpoint allows you to admire not just the cliffs, but also the Punta de Teno lighthouse, and you may even get a glimpse of the neighbouring island of La Gomera. Second, a three-hour hiking trail from the village of Masca in Buenavista takes you through the Barranco de Masca ravine to the beautiful Playa de Masca where there is a unique view of Los Gigantes. To return, you can either hike back again or take a boat that offers a captivating view of the cliffs. Third, the Punta de Teno, at the north-western tip of Tenerife, serves as both the endpoint of the Los Gigantes and an excellent vantage point from which to admire this monumental rock wall.

21 **PLAYA DE LA ARENA** ☆4 ⇨5 🍷5

Playa de la Arena, located on the south-western coast of Tenerife, is a hidden gem among the island's many beautiful beaches. Translating to 'Beach of Sand', it lives up to its name with its pristine volcanic black sand.

Nestled in the tranquil resort town of Puerto de Santiago, Playa de la Arena offers a more relaxed and family-friendly atmosphere compared to some of Tenerife's busier beaches, with waters known for their cleanliness and safety, making it a popular choice for swimming and sunbathing. The backdrop of dramatic cliffs adds to the beach's charm, and there are just enough restaurants, shops and amenities on hand not to be overwhelming.

22 **PLAYA DEL DUQUE** ☆4 ⇨5 🍷5

Playa del Duque is a luxurious beach located in Costa Adeje, on the southern coast of Tenerife, and is renowned for its pristine golden sands, crystal-clear waters, and a sophisticated atmosphere with upscale hotels, stylish promenades, and lush gardens, setting it apart from many other beaches on the island.

The calm and gentle waters of Playa del Duque make it an ideal spot for swimming and paddling, suitable for families with children. While it's not a hub for water sports junkies, you can still find some activities like jet-skiing and parasailing nearby. There are plenty of upscale amenities such as water parks and golf courses, as well as other beautiful beaches close by such as Playa de Fañabé and Playa de Torviscas.

23 **BARRANCO DEL INFIERNO** ☆4 ⇨2 🍷1

Barranco del Infierno, or 'Hell's Gorge', is a captivating natural wonder located in the western part of Tenerife near Adeje, a remarkable ravine offering visitors a half-day hike through a diverse and ever-changing landscape.

You'll find yourself surrounded by towering mountain slopes, with cacti clinging to steep rock walls. The path eventually descends into the heart of the ravine, where a waterfall cascades down from a narrow crevice, plummeting some 200m.

Barranco del Infierno is a protected natural area with strict visitor limits, with a maximum only 200 visitors per day, making it advisable to make advance reservations. The hike spans approximately 6km and takes about half a day to complete. Please note that the trail may sometimes be temporarily closed due to the risk of rockfalls, so it's essential to check for up-to-date information at www.barrancodelinfierno.es.

24 **ROQUE DEL CONDE** ☆4 ⇨2 🍷1

Roque del Conde, a rocky plateau located near Playa de las Americas, is a popular hiking destination on Tenerife. The ridge extends northwards, encompassing rock formations like Los Riscos, Roque de los Brezos and Roque Imoque, all of which were once volcanic plugs. Nestled at its base to the west lies Barranco del Infierno, one of the island's most renowned canyons. Often, the trails leading to Roque del Conde traverse yet another of these canyons, the Barranco del Rey.

What sets Roque del Conde apart are the breathtaking panoramic views it offers, which stretch across the vibrant tourist towns along the island's south-west coast. While the mountains above are frequently cloaked in trade wind clouds, Roque del Conde often remains as a solitary outpost beneath the fog. You can reach the summit via a 2.5km hike from Las Casas. Roque del Conde is a popular destination among paragliders, owing to its strategic position on the lee side of the island, providing shelter from the prevailing trade winds. The name 'del Conde' pays homage to one of the marquesses of Adeje, within which area the Roque del Conde is located.

Tenerife
↳ To Stroll

A **TAGANANA** ☆4 ↕2 🍷2

Taganana is a picturesque hamlet nestled within the Parque Rural de Anaga. This charming village is not only blessed with stunning natural surroundings but also has historic importance as one of the first settlements established by the Spanish conquistadors on the island.

It has two culturally important sites: the Iglesia de Nuestra Señora de las Nieves (Church of Our Lady of the Snows), one of Tenerife's oldest churches, and the Ermita de Santa Catalina (St Catherine's Shrine). In the church, among many other artworks, is a famous triptych showing the Adoration of the Kings, painted by a 16th-century Flemish artist.

To reach Taganana from the north, you cross the forest of Las Mercedes, one of the oldest in Europe, along winding roads that descend through rugged ravines. The El Bailadero Viewpoint offers a photogenic panorama of the area. The heart of the village is the Plaza de Nuestra Señora de las Nieves, a peaceful square where locals gather in the shade of laurel trees. The white houses of Taganana contrast beautifully with the lush green mountains.

B **CHINAMADA** ☆3 ↕1 🍷1

Chinamada is a lesser-known hamlet situated in the north of Tenerife, in the Anaga massif. It's not a widely known destination, but is unique for its 'troglodyte community' of some 30 cave houses. Despite the unconventional housing, the residents enjoy modern comforts, as all cave houses are have electricity. Come for the charm, though not for lunch or dinner, as there is only one restaurant.

C **SANTA CRUZ DE TENERIFE** ☆5 ↕4 🍷4

Situated on the north-eastern coast, Santa Cruz de Tenerife – usually referred to simply as Santa Cruz – is the capital city of the province of Santa Cruz de Tenerife and one of the two capital cities of the Canary Islands. It serves as the cultural, economic and political centre of Tenerife and the Canary Islands as a whole, hosting a wide range of cultural events and festivals throughout the year of which the Carnival of Santa Cruz de Tenerife is the most famous. This is one of the world's largest and most extravagant carnivals, taking place every February and featuring colourful parades, elaborate costumes, music and dancing.

The Tenerife Auditorium, designed by architect Santiago Calatrava, is a symbol of the city. Santa Cruz is surrounded by nature, offering several urban beaches, including Playa de las Teresitas and Playa de las Gaviotas, the latter a popular spot for surfing and water sports. The city is home to beautiful parks like Parque García Sanabria, a lush botanical garden featuring sculptures and tropical plants, and Parque de la Granja, an urban park with playgrounds and walking paths. Calle Castillo is a popular shopping street lined with boutiques, department stores and markets.

As the capital, Santa Cruz is well connected, having a port and an international airport, Tenerife North Airport.

D **SAN CRISTÓBAL DE LA LAGUNA** ☆5 ↕5 🍷5

San Cristóbal de La Laguna, commonly known as La Laguna, is a historic city located in the northern part of the island as well as the first city established in the Canary Islands and the only one designated as a UNESCO World Heritage Site. The city's layout, which dates back to the 15th century, includes a pedestrian-friendly historic centre, whose linear streets boast an array of colonial- style buildings characterized by pastel-coloured facades, stone porticoes, and interior courtyards graced with wooden balconies.

Notable sites include the Neoclassical cathedral, the Church of Christ, the Nava and Salazar palaces, and the Santa Catalina and Santa Clara monasteries. La Laguna is home to the University of La Laguna (Universidad de La Laguna), one of the oldest universities in Spain, which adds a vibrant and youthful atmosphere to the city. It's thanks in part to its 30,000 students that the city has such a lively nightlife. Apart from being a cultural and culinary hotspot, it's a great base for exploring the Parque Rural de Anaga to the east or the Parque Nacional del Teide to the west.

E PUERTO DE LA CRUZ ☆ 4 ↕ 3 🍷 4

Puerto de la Cruz is a picturesque coastal town located on the northern coast and one of the island's most popular tourist destinations, known for its charming atmosphere, historic sites, beautiful beaches and subtropical gardens. Puerto de la Cruz boasts several beautiful beaches, including Playa Jardín – designed by the famous Canarian artist César Manrique and renowned for its black volcanic sand and lush gardens – Playa Martiánez and Playa San Telmo.

One of the town's most famous attractions is Loro Parque, a world- renowned wildlife park and conservation centre. Visitors can see a wide variety of animals, including parrots, dolphins, killer whales and more. The town is also home to the Jardín Botánico de Puerto de la Cruz, a botanical garden with a vast collection of tropical and subtropical plants from around the world. It's a tranquil place to explore and learn about exotic flora. Puerto de la Cruz has a charming historic quarter with narrow streets, colonial architecture and picturesque squares. Plaza del Charco is the central square, surrounded by cafés and restaurants, making it a great place to relax and people-watch.

F ELMÉDANO ☆ 4 ↕ 2 🍷 4

El Médano is located on the southern coast, renowned for its stunning beaches, particularly Playa El Médano, which is one of the island's most famous spots for water sports and windsurfing. Beyond Playa El Médano, you can also explore other nearby beaches like Playa de Leocadio Machado and Playa de la Tejita.

El Médano is considered one of the top windsurfing and kitesurfing destinations in Europe. The consistent trade winds make it an ideal spot for these sports, and there are numerous rental shops and schools in the area if you want to learn or improve your skills.

The town is surrounded by natural beauty, including the iconic Montaña Roja (Red Mountain), a volcanic cone that adds to the unique landscape. There are also walking and hiking trails in the nearby Montaña Roja Nature Reserve, offering breathtaking views of the coastline. El Médano has retained a relaxed, laid-back atmosphere, making it a favourite spot for both locals and visitors looking for a more authentic and less crowded experience. It is conveniently located near Tenerife South Airport.

G PLAYA DE LAS AMERICAS ☆ 4 ↕ 4 🍷 5

Playa de las Américas, often simply referred to as Las Américas, is a vibrant and bustling seaside resort located on the southern coast of Tenerife. Since its creation in the early 1960s, it has evolved into one of the largest and most famous tourist areas on the island. It now offers a wide range of accommodation, including hotels and apartments to suit various budgets. Situated between the towns of Los Cristianos and Costa Adeje, Playa de las Américas is connected to them via a promenade, where you can enjoy a leisurely stroll with numerous opportunities for refreshments along the way. It's a shopper's paradise and famed for its lively nightlife scene, with the Veronicas Strip, a 1km stretch lined with nightclubs and restaurants. If you're looking for a tranquil retreat, this may not be your ideal destination. Golf enthusiasts will find Golf Las Américas, an 18-hole golf course, right in the heart of the resort.

H ICOD DE LOS VINOS ☆ 4 ↕ 3 🍷 4

Icod de los Vinos is a charming town located on the north-western coast of Tenerife, known for its rich cultural heritage, historic architecture and, most notably, the famous Dragon Tree. Like La Laguna, the town's historic centre features well-preserved colonial architecture, including traditional houses with wooden balconies. San Marcos church, dating back to the 16th century, is an important religious and architectural landmark. The town's name, 'de los Vinos', refers to its historical connection to wine production, so unsurprisingly visitors can explore local wineries and taste wines produced in the region.

Near Icod de los Vinos, you can find the Cueva del Viento. About 17km long, it is one of the largest lava tubes (pyroducts) in the world. Guided tours are available for those interested in exploring this underground geological wonder.

The town hosts various festivals throughout the year, of which the best known is the Feast of San Andrés in November, when locals and visitors participate in wine-related activities and customs.

I GARACHICO ☆ 5 ↕ 3 🍷 4

Garachico, situated in the north-west, is regarded as one of the most beautiful towns on the island. Its charm lies in its picturesque historic quarter, declared an Asset of Cultural Interest in 1994, as well as the surrounding natural beauty characterized by palm trees and banana plantations set into a steep volcanic terrain.

Founded in the late 15th century by a Genoese banker, Garachico quickly rose to prominence as the island's busiest commercial port. Its docks played a crucial role in the trade between Europe and the Spanish colonies in America, handling shipments of local wine and sugar. However, in 1706, the nearby Trevejo volcano, also known as the Arenas Negras volcano, erupted, devastating a significant part of the village, including its valuable port, which was buried under lava. Modern-day Garachico is a testament to resilience, having emerged from the ashes of destruction.

Exploring Garachico offers a glimpse into the bygone era of the Canary Islands. The town's historic centre, of cosy dimensions, is a treasure trove of architectural heritage from the 16th and 17th centuries. It stands as one of the best-preserved and most representative historical and artistic centres in the Canary Islands. A visit to Garachico can also include excursions to landscapes such as Caleta de Interián, the Chinyero Volcano, and the cliffs of La Culata, offering a harmonious blend of history and nature.

J MASCA ☆ 5 ↕ 2 🍷 2

Masca is a picturesque mountain village located in the north-west of the island, known for its breathtaking natural beauty and unique setting within an ancient volcanic crater, making it one of the most authentic and remote villages on Tenerife. Its rugged natural surroundings and the challenging access contributed to its isolation for many years. The village sits at around 700m above sea level, nestled among steep cliffs and dramatic rock formations, creating a captivating and otherworldly landscape.

The fertile soil in the crater allowed Masca to thrive agriculturally, producing some of Tenerife's finest onions, potatoes and garlic. Masca recently gained widespread recognition as the starting point for the popular hiking trail through the Barranco de Masca, which takes approximately 6 hours and offers stunning views of the ravine and on the Gigantes cliffs.

The discovery of the Barranco de Masca by tourists has brought an increase in visitors to the area, leading to changes in the village's character, but it remains relatively quiet, and the growth in tourism has resulted in improved dining options.

K **LOS GIGANTES** ☆4 ↕3 🍷4

This picturesque village is located on Tenerife's sunny west coast, known for its stunning natural beauty and unique attractions, with the Los Gigantes cliffs dominating the northern side of the village.

Los Gigantes is an excellent destination for outdoor enthusiasts. It offers fantastic opportunities for diving and dolphin- and whale-watching, with over 28 species of cetaceans in the nearby waters. There are sea safari trips that depart from the harbour.

The underwater part of the cliffs teems with marine life, making it a popular spot for divers. There are numerous diving centres where visitors can explore this vibrant submarine world.

Above water the town offers a more tranquil and serene atmosphere compared to other resorts, priding itself on its abundant sunshine – it can boast more hours of sunshine than any other part of the island. While Los Gigantes may not have extensive sandy beaches, it does offer a small resort beach with black sands situated next to the small harbour.

L **ADEJE** ☆4 ↕3 🍷5

Adeje is a lively municipality located on the south-west coast of the island, known for its beautiful beaches, luxury resorts, and a wide range of leisure and entertainment options.

It's home to several stunning beaches, including Playa de Fañabé, Playa del Duque and Playa de la Pinta. These beaches boast golden sands and crystal-clear waters, making them ideal for sunbathing, swimming and water sports.

Known for its high-end luxury resorts and hotels that offer top-notch accommodation, spa facilities and fine dining, Adeje attracts visitors seeking a luxurious and relaxing vacation.

One of the standout attractions in Adeje is Siam Park, a world-renowned water park that consistently ranks among the best in the world. It features thrilling water slides, a lazy river, a wave pool, and a variety of attractions suitable for visitors of all ages.

Adeje is also home to Golf Costa Adeje, an 18-hole champion-ship golf course with beautiful views of the ocean and surrounding landscapes.

FARO DE ANAGA

ROQUES DE ANAGA

↰ ROQUES DE ANAGA (L) AND ROQUE DE LAS ANIMAS AND TAGANANA (R)

MIRADOR RISCO AMOGOJE ↴

SAN CRISTÓBAL DE LA LAGUNA

↰ GARACHICO

MONTAÑA DE EL PALMAR, TENO RURAL PARK ↴

OBSERVATORIO ASTRONOMICO DEL TEIDE

VIEW FROM EL TEIDE SUMMIT ON LAS CAÑADAS DEL TEIDE

↰ ROQUES DE GARCÍA

PICO VIEJO ↴

PATH FROM EL TEIDE SUMMIT TO THE CABLE CAR STATION ↗

↰ MASCA

DRAGO MILENARIO, ICOD DE LOS VINOS ↴

LOS GIGANTES

28.4829° N

17.8512°
W

↱ Island 5 / 7
La Palma

708km²
82,671 residents

5

⟶ ROQUE DE LOS MUCHACHOS
28.7547° N / 17.8850° W
HEIGHT 2,426M

CUMBRE VIEJA NATIONAL PARK

↳ Welcome to La Palma, the perfect blend of stunning natural beauty and fascinating cultural heritage. It offers a rich palette of colours: black volcanic ridges, the lush green of the banana plantations and pine forests, and the turquoise blue of its pristine beaches and natural pools. The Caldera de Taburiente, the massive crater that dominates the island, and its peak, the Roque de los Muchachos, is a stargazing heaven towering permanently above the clouds. During the day it is a hiking paradise, offering magical views over the ocean and valleys. Tucked away from the big resorts but still accessible, 'La Isla Bonita' offers a diverse idyll for stargazers, sunbathers, hikers and food lovers alike.

La Palma
La Isla Bonita

Coastline: 166km
Highest point: 2,426m

BARRANCO DE LAS VACAS

La Isla Bonita – a tranquil paradise with lush green forests, black volcanic ridges and pristine beaches

↳ La Palma has the shape of an upside-down teardrop. At this tip we find the Fuencaliente Lighthouse and salt marshes and from here the Cumbre Vieja volcanic ridge runs towards northwards to the island's centre. On the east of this widest part of the 'tear' sits the capital, Santa Cruz de La Palma, almost mirrored by the towns of Tazacorte and Los Llanos in the west.

These cities and towns are in the most populous regions of the island and the cultural and political centres. The interior is dominated by a massive 10km-diameter crater and a 2,000m elevation drop with a lush valley of forests and banana plantations at its centre. The crater starts in the west at Playa de Tazacorte and runs towards Mirador El Time, over Roque de los Muchachos, the highest point at 2,426m, before circling east and then south, back to the Cumbre Vieja. It shields the valley of Llanos de Ariadne where you find the natural pools of La Fajana and Charco Azul and the lush forests like Bosque de los Tilos.

TAZACORTE, LOS LLANOS DE ARIDANE

La Palma
↳ Introduction

HOW TO GET AROUND

Boats and planes land in the east, close to the capital Santa Cruz de la Palma. La Palma is the smallest island to accept international flights, so finding a flight here from Europe will be harder than finding one for Tenerife. Boat connections can be found to La Gomera, Tenerife and Gran Canaria. La Palma features the second highest elevation of the Canaries, so car trips will take longer.

There is a tunnel under the 2,000m wall of stone connecting Santa Cruz with the Los Llanos valley, making this connection relatively efficient. The northern part, with the famous Charzo Azul, is harder to reach while a trip south to Fuencaliente is relatively straightforward.

WHERE TO STAY

Most accommodation is to be found either in the east, around the capital of Santa Cruz de la Palma, or in the west, in the Los Llanos de Aridane municipality. We would probably recommend the western side of Los Llanos as it has a pleasant open feel with easy access to hikes and viewpoints and to the beaches around Tazacorte. Because the 2,000m-high Cumbre Vieja ridge stop rainclouds coming from the east, it also enjoys the island's best climate. Further down on the west coast, there is Puerto Naos or the Teneguía resorts for those looking for a laid-back beach holiday.

BEACHES

While La Palma may not have as many beaches as some other Canary Islands, it compensates for this with its natural beauty and quieter, more laid-back atmosphere.

Most of the beaches are to be found on the western and southern sides of the island. Playa de Tazacorte and Puerto Naos in the west are among the most popular destinations on the island, both featuring long dark volcanic sand beaches and promenades with restaurants, shops and a good choice of accommodation.

Playa de Charco Verde and Playa de la Zamora lie further to the south and are small pristine beaches bordered by banana plantations. Playa de Echentive on the western side of the island's southern tip is wild and remote. On the eastern side are the popular resorts of Los Cancajos with a scattering of natural black volcanic beaches.

The true gem and must-see beach lies to the north of Santa Cruz de la Palma. Playa de Nogales is a beautiful beach known for its dark volcanic sand and dramatic cliffs. It's popular for surfing and offers a more secluded experience. Further north, you have the natural pools of Charco Azul and La Fajana as pristine turquoise-blue alternatives.

TWO-DAY VISIT

Day 1
Arrive in Santa Cruz de la Palma. Have lunch in Santa Cruz or somewhere by the water and then drive all the way south. Once there, hiking along the Ruta de los Volcanes is a must, making your way through the black lava sand and the pine forests with stunning views over the surrounding volcanos, calderas and islands. Head back to the valley of Llanos de Aridane for a sunset view from the Mirador El Time or on the beach of Tazacorte. Dine in Llanos de Aridane.

Day 2
What about an early rise to see the sunrise from the island's highest point, the Roque de los Muchachos? Descend (a part of) the GR131 from here all the way to the sea, a 2400m vertical drop hike if done entirely. Spend the afternoon relaxing close to the water at either Charco Azul or Playa de Nogales, both must-sees. Enjoy dinner and spend the night in Santa Cruz de la Palma.

LA PALMA

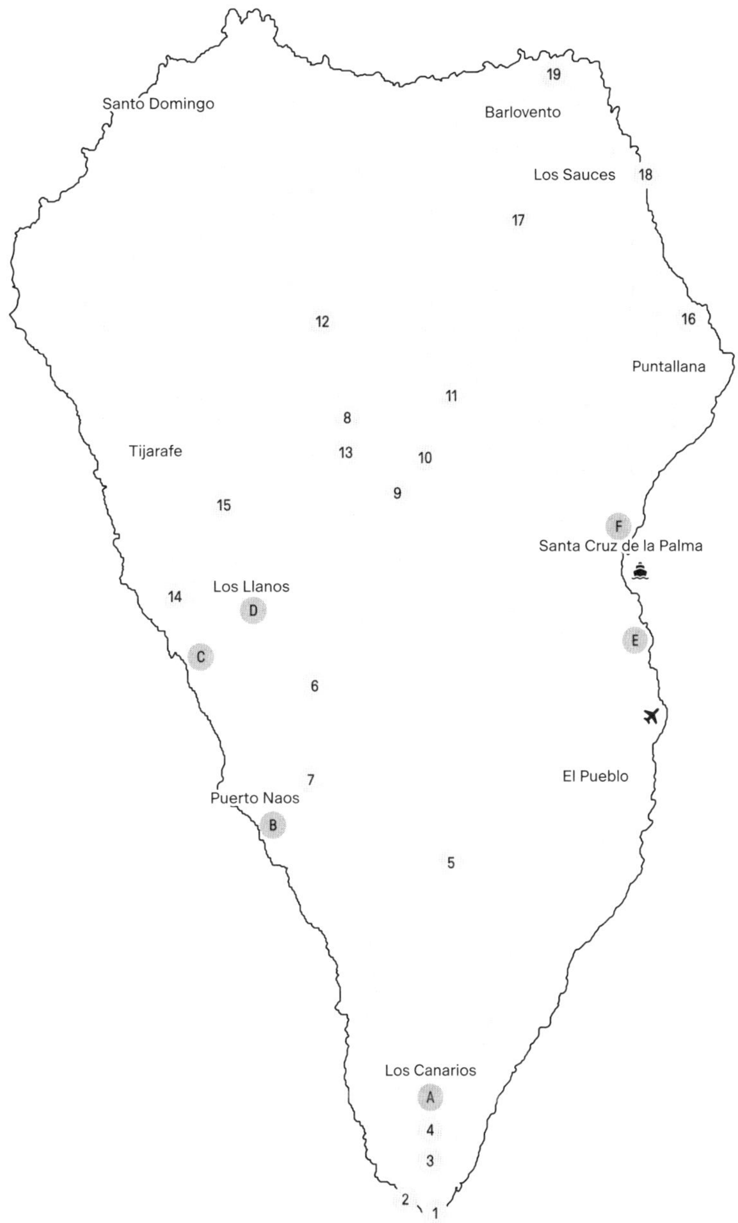

EXPLORE / HIGHLIGHTS

1 Fuencaliente Lighthouse & Salinas
2 Playa de Echentive
3 Volcán Teneguía
4 Volcán de San Antonio
5 Cumbre Vieja National Park
6 Tajogaite & Eruption Area
7 Cueva de las Palomas
8 Caldera de Taburiente
9 Mirador de La Cumbrecita Viewpoint
10 Refugio Punta de los Roques
11 Pico de la Nieve
12 Roque de los Muchachos
13 Cascada de los Colores
14 Mirador El Time
15 Torre del Time
16 Playa de Nogales
17 Bosque de los Tilos
18 Charco Azul Natural Pools
19 La Fajana Natural Pools

STROLL / HIGHLIGHTS

A Los Canarios
B Puerto Naos
C Tazacorte
D Los LLanos de Aridane
E Los Cancajos
F Santa Cruz de la Palma

La Palma
↳ Key Facts

WHEREABOUTS	Name	The full name is San Miguel de La Palma, usually abbreviated to La Palma
	Origin of name	Named for its palm trees and in honour of St Michael by the Spanish conquerors
	Nickname	La Isla Bonita – 'The Beautiful Island' – for its rich flora and fauna
	Key towns and villages	Playa de Tazacorte, Los Canarias, Puerto Naos
DEMOGRAPHICS	Population	82,671 people, 4% of he Canary Islands, 5th in rank
	Capital	Santa Cruz de la Palma (pop. approx. 16,000)
	Biggest cities	Santa Cruz de la Palma, Los Llanos de Aridane, Tazacorte
INFRASTRUCTURE	Commercial Airport	La Palma Airport, Santa Cruz de la Palma (SPC) – island flights to Tenerife and Gran Canaria and major European countries
	Commercial Port	Port of Santa Cruz de la Palma – ferries to Los Cristianos, Cadiz, San Sebastián de la Gomera, Las Palmas, Santa Cruz de Tenerife, Puerto del Rosario, Arrecife
	Agriculture	Bananas grown throughout the island, mostly on the western side around Los Llanos de Aridane. Bird of paradise flowers, oranges, avocados and grapes
GEOGRAPHY	Size	708km², 5th in rank
	Highest point	Roque de los Muchachos (2,426m)
	Dimensions	Teardrop shaped, 40km in length, 26km in width at broadest point
	Coastline	166km, 20km beach, 30 beaches
	Origin	About a half a million years ago, the Volcán Taburiente collapsed causing a giant landslide, forming the Caldera de Taburiente. There have been eight eruptions since records began, there have been eight eruptions, all along the Cumbre Vieja ridge, the latest in 2021
HISTORY	1493	Conquest of La Palma by Alonso Fernández de Lugo, who defeated Tanausu, the last Guanche king on the island
	1985	Launch of the Roque de los Muchachos observatory after 15 years of international work, hosting many telescopes from the UK, the Netherlands, Spain and other countries
	September 2021	Latest eruption of the Cumbre Viejo ridge in the valley of Los Llanos de Aridane causing €1 billion of damage to the economy

La Palma
↳ Where to Hike

OVERVIEW

'La Isla Bonita' is a hikers' paradise, offering trails over volcanoes, through pine forests and along towering ridges, all with incredible views over the island's valleys and surrounding islands.

The GR131 starts in the southern tip and makes its way up on the volcanic ridge of the Cumbre Vieja during Stage 28 and 27. Stage 29 circles the Caldera de la Taburiente ridge which dominates the centre of the island. Stage 30 drops vertically from the highest peak, the 2,426m Roque de los Muchachos, to sea level at the lively Puerto de Tazacorte.

TERRAIN

Variety is the name of the game here, as we move from loose black sandy soils in the south to rocky single trails in the centre. La Palma has the second highest peak of the Canaries, and because the island is the third smallest, the gradient here is the steepest across all the islands. Better bring your climbing shoes!

WHICH STAGE TO PICK

All four stages are great, offering unique landscapes and incredible views. Stage 27 is short and convenient, compared to the other, longer, more demanding stages. It's accessible, yet still offers great views with two notorious adventures en route.

If we had to pick one, it would be Stage 28 because of its unique appearance and the remarkable volcanoes. Stage 29 is a ridge hike through the island's highest terrain. Stage 30 offers the biggest vertical drop of the Canaries.

ELEVATION MAP

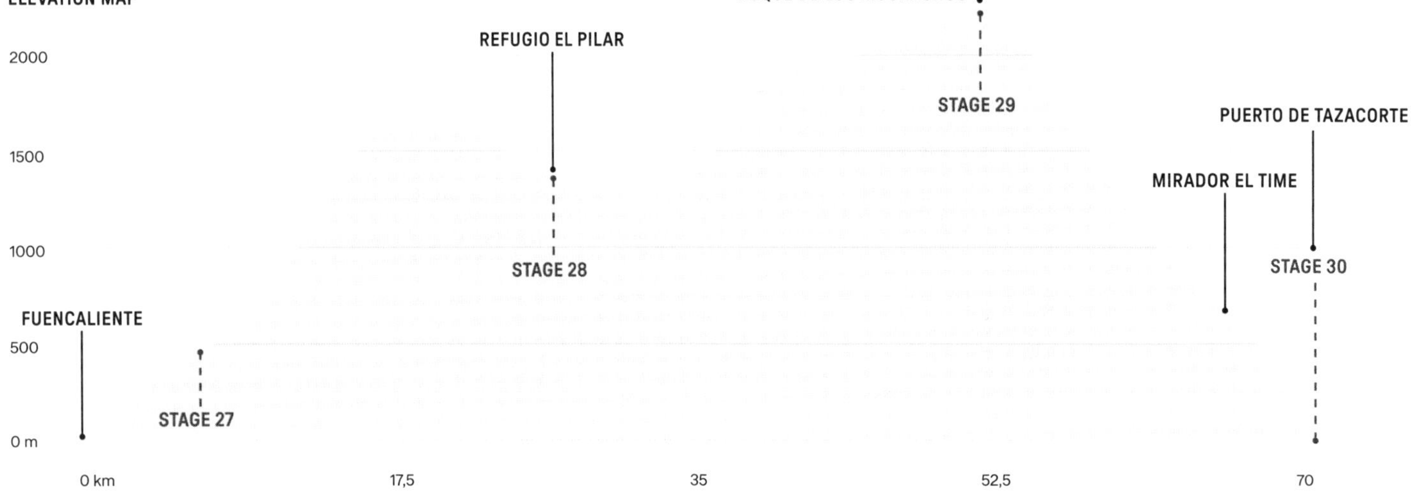

GR131, CUMBRE VIEJA NATIONAL PARK

La Palma
↳ Hikes Overview

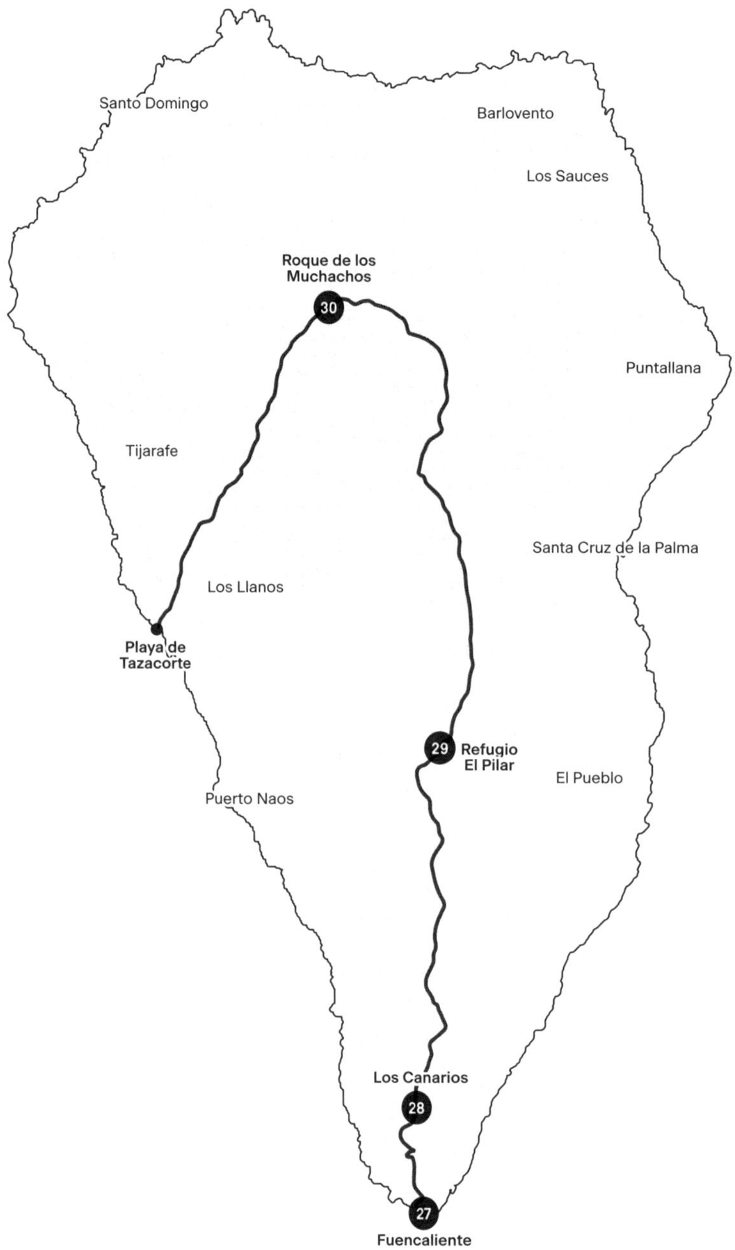

STAGE 27

FUENCALIENTE TO LOS CANARIOS

Distance 7km **Ascent** 710m **Decent** 0m **Asphalt** 14%

Climbing route from the tip of the island along volcanic gravel roads with open views over the ocean through volcanic landscapes.

Recommendation: 3 / 4
Technicality: 2 / 4
Facilities: 2 / 4
Type: GR131

This hike, though brief, comes highly recommended. The area around the Faro de Fuencaliente is rich in sights, featuring not just one but two lighthouses and traditional salt flats (*salinas*). The route ascends through stark, desolate lava flows, scattered with ash – an environment where plant life barely manages to survive. Along the way, the path takes you past two prominent volcanoes, Volcán Teneguía and Volcán de San Antonio, before reaching the stage's endpoint at Fuencaliente.

STAGE 28

LOS CANARIOS TO REFUGIO EL PILAR

Distance 17.5km **Ascent** 1,450m **Decent** 720m **Asphalt** 3%

Indispensable stage on the Cumbre Vieja volcanic ridge amid black volcanic ash, volcanoes and lush green pine forests.

Recommendation: 4 / 4
Technicality: 2 / 4
Facilities: 1 / 4
Type: GR131

This part of the GR131 is known as the Ruta de los Volcanes, carving its way through pine forest and black seas of volcanic ash and dirt on the Cumbre Vieja, an active volcanic ridge. This track is a must for its unique scenery of volcanoes, green pines and black soils as well as stunning views over the surrounding islands and shores. It's a completely inaccessible stage with a serious gradient, so come prepared. The El Pilar refuge hut offers shelter, but little else.

STAGE 29

REFUGIO EL PILAR TO ROQUE DE LOS MUCHACHOS

Distance 27km **Ascent** 1,880m **Decent** 900m **Asphalt** 1%

Ridge hike traversing the highest peaks of the island, rounding the Caldera de la Taburiente to reach the island's highest peak.

Recommendation: 3 / 4
Technicality: 3 / 4
Facilities: 2 / 4
Type: GR131

This stage is challenging and lengthy, further compounded by its remote nature and the absence of convenient access or amenities. The route initially follows the forest-laden spine of the Cumbre Nueva, then ascends sharply through a pine forest. It continues across a series of rugged peaks, navigating the ridge of the Caldera de la Taburiente, and culminates at the island's highest peak, the Roque de los Muchachos. It's essential to be well prepared for this trek. Arranging a taxi pick-up in advance is advisable.

STAGE 30

ROQUE DE LOS MUCHACHOS TO PUERTO DE TAZACORTE

Distance 18km **Ascent** 1,440m **Decent** 100m **Asphalt** 18%

Downhill stage with stunning views, passing through a pine forest, and ending with a spectacular zigzagging drop to the coast.

Recommendation: 3 / 4
Technicality: 3 / 4
Facilities: 2 / 4
Type: GR131

This stage includes breathtaking views from Roque de los Muchachos before embarking on relatively straightforward trails that lead past several nearby peaks. This stage is mostly steep downhill, with a few minor climbs. It begins on open mountain slopes, transitions through forests, and then winds down through terraced farmlands. The journey concludes with a spectacular zigzagging path carved into a cliff, leading you right to the seaside at Puerto de Tazacorte. This is of the longest descents in Europe. With a 2,500m drop in only 17km, the gradient is on average almost 15 per cent.

La Palma
↳ To Explore

1 **FUENCALIENTE LIGHTHOUSE & SALINAS** ☆ 5 ⇨ 4 🏆 2

The Faro de Fuencaliente and Salinas de Fuencaliente mark the southern tip of La Palma. There are in fact two lighthouses: the new lighthouse is the one painted in red and white stripes, while the old one has been recently restored and is open to the public.

The Salinas de Fuencaliente, or salt flats, are an integral part of the area's cultural and economic history, having been in operation for centuries, dating back to the time of the Guanche people who inhabited the Canary Islands before the arrival of the Spanish. Just as in Lanzarote and Fuerteventura, salt is eva-porated from sea water, leaving behind salt crystals. The salt is then harvested and processed in a grid of rectangular saltpans, creating a striking mosaic against the blue backdrop of the ocean.

Visitors can explore the salt flats and learn about the salt production process in the visitor centre or on guided tours.

A part of the GR131 known as the Camino del Sal – the Salt Path – begins here, stretching from the lighthouses through the black moonlike landscape to the Volcán de Teneguía and Volcán de San Antonio. If you'd rather relax, visit the nearby Playa de Echentive.

2 **PLAYA DE ECHENTIVE** ☆ 4 ⇨ 4 🏆 2

Located in the south of La Palma, Playa de Echentive is one of the island's youngest beaches, formed only in 1971 after an eruption of Volcán Teneguía. It's part of the Monumento Natural Volcanes de Teneguía and is located in stunning, pristine black natural surroundings.

There are a couple of natural pools nearby, perfect for a relaxing dip when the sea is too rough. It's a small beach, 275m long, easily accessible by car and a good place for people looking for peace and quiet. There are no facilities at all, so come prepared.

3 **VOLCÁN TENEGUÍA (428M)** ☆ 5 ⇨ 2 🏆 3

In 1971, Volcán Teneguía made the global headlines when it dramatically erupted, unleashing massive volumes of molten magma, covering a significant portion of La Palma's southern region with lava and volcanic ash. It also gave rise to a new and intriguing tourist attraction, as the unique lava flows created by Volcán Teneguía and its close neighbour Volcán de San Antonio, which erupted in the 18th century, were designated as a National Monument.

The visitor centre is located a short ten-minute drive from the town of Los Canarios. Visitors can explore the area by camel or by hiking.

One route leads to the summits of Volcán de San Antonio and Volcán Teneguía via the expansive vineyards of Fuencaliente. There are awe-inspiring views from the towering Teneguía summit, where you can also experience the warmth emanating from the volcano. Another route, part of the GR131 trail, takes you down to the Salinas de Fuencaliente, at the southern tip of the island.

4 **VOLCÁN DE SAN ANTONIO (653M)** ☆ 5 ⇨ 2 🏆 3

The Volcán de San Antonio is a relatively young volcano, with its most recent eruption in 1677. The volcano is near the town of Fuencaliente, a little further north than the Teneguía volcano. Both are part of the active Cumbre Vieja volcanic ridge, which runs along the southern half of the island.

There are well-marked hiking trails that lead to the summit of the volcano (see the section on the Volcán Teneguía above). Near the volcano, there is a visitor centre that provides information about the geological history of the area, the 1677 eruption, and the volcanic processes that have shaped La Palma.

5 CUMBRE VIEJA NATIONAL PARK ☆ 5 ⇨ 1 🏆 1

This volcanic ridge boasts nearly 30 craters, stretching from the centre to the south of the island. All volcanic eruptions on La Palma originated in the Cumbre Vieja, making it a focal point of volcanic activity. The natural park covering the area was created in 1987.

The pine forest that blankets a significant portion of the park contrasts with the dark earth, creating an impressive landscape. There's a trail known as the Ruta de los Volcanes (Route of the Volcanoes) which traverses the park from north to south, a must-do when on La Palma. Note that the itinerary is not suitable for vehicles, and its steep slopes and remoteness make the hike challenging, though worthwhile for its unique views of La Palma and the neighbouring islands.

What's more, it is the only place in Spain where, within a matter of hours, you can touch rocks dating back to the 16th, 17th, 18th, 19th and 20th centuries. It also represents some of the youngest terrain in the Canary Islands. Over the past 600 years, dating back to 1430, there have been seven documented eruptions in the Cumbre Vieja ridge similar to the one in 2021. The lava tongues from most of these previous eruptions flowed down the western slopes of Cumbre Vieja,with many reaching the sea and forming platforms that expanded the island's surface.

The eruption that added the most new land occurred in 1949, originating from Volcán de San Juan and creating fertile soils that have provided an ideal foundation for banana trees, which thrive best at sea level.

6 TAJOGAITE & CUMBRE VIEJA ERUPTION AREA ☆ 4 ⇨ 3 🏆 3

Between 19 September and 13 December 2021, the Cumbre Vieja ridge witnessed the longest recorded volcanic activity on the island. This eruption originated from five new vents, unleashing a sea of molten lava that flowed across the Cabeza de Vaca area, on the western slopes of the island.

The lava flow covered an extensive area, spanning over 1,000ha, nearly 2 per cent of the island. At its widest point, the flow was 3.5km, extending 6.2km to reach the ocean. The eruption prompted the evacuation of 7,000 people, resulted in the destruction of 3,000 buildings, and led to the loss or disappearance of 80km of roads and 179 banana plantations – producing a total economic loss of €900 million.

The town of Todoque was entirely engulfed and obliterated by the advancing lava. The eruption was accompanied by numerous daily earthquakes, reaching 5.1 on the Richter scale.

Fortunately, thanks to diligent prevention and evacuation efforts, there were no casualties directly attributed to the volcanic eruption. Some 50ha of new land was created owing to the eruption, and a vote was held to name the new volcano in 2022. It was named Volcán de Tajogaite, in reference to the Guanche name for the Montaña Rajada.

From the Mirador El Time or on the Ruta de los Volcanes, you have a good view of the area with the Volcán de Tajogaite.

7 CUEVA DE LAS PALOMAS ☆ 4 ⇨ 3 🏆 3

The Palomas lava tube is a remarkable cave-like volcanic formation created in 1949 following the eruption of Volcán de San Juan.

This lava tube is some 800m long and is best experienced by taking a guided tour, for which you have to wear all the necessary safety gear. Before embarking on your adventurous exploration of the lava tube, visit the Caños de Fuego Interpretation Centre.

8 **CALDERA DE TABURIENTE** ☆5 ⇨3 ♀2

The centre of the island is dominated by a massive crater, the Caldera de Taburiente, a huge erosion crater. It has a diameter of 10km and its walls rise 2,000m above the caldera floor, which is at sea level. The highest point is the Roque de los Muchachos on the northern wall, accessible by road and home to the telescopes of the Roque de los Muchachos Observatory, located near the summit.

To the south-west, the caldera slopes down to the sea along the Barranco de Las Angustias, through which the Río de Taburiente flows during the winter.

In the south-east, the crater rim connects to the Cumbre Nueva mountain ridge, which, together with the southern Cumbre Vieja, forms the backbone of the island. During the Spanish conquest of the islands in the 15th century, the caldera served as the last stronghold for the Guanches, the former inhabitants of the archipelago. The Parque Nacional Caldera de Taburiente is one of four national parks in the Canary Islands, designated thus in 1954.

9 **LA CUMBRECITA** ☆5 ⇨5 ♀1

Opposite the Roque de Los Muchachos, on the south- eastern crater rim, you'll find the La Cumbrecita viewpoint, offering fantastic views of the caldera, and reachable by car from the visitor centre near El Paso. Due to limited parking, access is regulated, and reservations need to be made in advance.

10 **REFUGIO PUNTO DE LOS ROQUES** ☆3 ⇨1 ♀1

This refuge lodge located on the GR131 is a great place to stay overnight if you want to get out, enjoy the unspoiled nature and peace and quiet, and are looking to complete the GR131's circuit of the Caldera de Taburiente. There is place for 20 people but don't expect luxury as there are no shower facilities and you have to bring your own sleeping bag.

11 **PICO DE LA NIEVE (2,239M)** ☆4 ⇨1 ♀1

This remote summit, marked by a wooden cross, is on the GR131 between Punto de los Roques and Punto de la Cruz. It is only accessible by trail and overlooks the Caldera de Taburiente.

12 **ROQUE DE LOS MUCHACHOS (2,426M)** ☆5 ⇨4 ♀1

Roque de los Muchachos is the highest point on La Palma and the second-highest peak in the Canary Islands, surpassed only by Mount Teide on Tenerife. It's renowned as one of the finest places on Earth for stargazing as its distance from the continent means there is minimal light pollution. Other winning factors are La Palma's low population density and unique climate resulting in clouds forming at relatively low altitudes, typically 1,000– 2,000m above sea level. The highest parts of the island therefore offer clear, pristine night skies nearly all year round.

The Roque de los Muchachos is home to the largest astronomical observatory in the northern hemisphere, and to as many as 13 telescopes, attracting scientists from around the world. During the day visitors can tour, by making an advance reservation, the Astrophysical Observatory of Roque de los Muchachos. The observatory is easily accessible by car.

13 **CASCADA DE LOS COLORES** ☆5 ⇨2 ♀2

Cascada de los Colores is a remarkable waterfall that shimmers red and gold. It's a hidden gem within the protected landscape of the Barranco de las Angustias, situated on the outskirts of the renowned Parque Nacional Caldera de Taburiente. The red and gold colours originate from algae and the iron from a wall built in the 1960s to protect the caldera from water erosion. Drive from Los Llanos de Caldera to the parking area (28.68563, -17.90978) at the base of Barranco de las Angustias, from where you have a 8km hike to the waterfall.

GR131, CAMINO DEL SAL, FUENCALIENTE

14 MIRADOR EL TIME (513M) ☆ 5 ⇨ 5 🏆 5

The Mirador El Time, at almost 700m, offers one of the most spectacular vistas over the island and the Aridane Valley, with its lush banana plantations. The view is dissected by the deep Barranco de las Angustias, which reaches the shore at the charming Tazacorte harbour. Situated along the LP1 highway, Mirador El Time is an ideal spot to pause for a coffee, tortilla or barraquito, during your exploration of western La Palma.

For the more adventurous traveller, there's the option of reaching Time on foot via a steep 3km cobbled path, part of GR131 that zigzags its way up from the old Tazacorte pier along the coastline.

15 TORRE DEL TIME (1,160M) ☆ 2 ⇨ 4 🏆 1

This remote viewpoint lies in the middle of the caldera's western ridge. Don't confuse this with the popular Mirador El Time, a few hundred metres lower.

This less popular one has not much to show for itself, but the view of the caldera is incredible and it could serve as an intermediate starting point for a hike if you don't want to climb the whole way up from sea level.

16 PLAYA DE NOGALES ☆ 5 ⇨ 3 🏆 2

Playa de Nogales is a beautiful beach located in the northern part of the island, known for its rugged and natural beauty with unique black volcanic sand and towering surrounding cliffs.

It's a popular spot for surfing. To access Playa de Nogales, visitors have to descend a winding path from the cliffside. All this adds to impression that this is a remote, special place. The 600m beach doesn't have any restaurants or shops, so come prepared.

17 BOSQUE DE LOS TILOS ☆ 4 ⇨ 2 🏆 1

The lush and enchanting Bosque de los Tilos is an ancient laurel forest located in the north-east of the island. It is a UNESCO Biosphere Reserve as it's considered one of the last remaining laurel forests in Europe. Bosque de los Tilos offers visitors a network of hiking trails of which the Ruta del Agua (The Water Route) is the most famous, taking you through a series of tunnels and aqueducts that were historically used for transporting water.

At the entrance to the forest, you'll find the Los Tilos Visitor Centre, which serves as an information hub for visitors on the forest's ecology, wildlife and history as well as providing maps and guides for hiking in the area.

18 CHARCO AZUL NATURAL POOLS ☆ 5 ⇨ 4 🏆 4

Charco Azul is a series of stunning natural pools created in the volcanic rocks along the coastline, forming inviting, crystal-clear swimming areas. Charco Azul, which translates to 'Blue Pool' in English, is photogenic as the turquoise colour of the water provides a stark contract with the black volcanic rock.

The area is surrounded by lush vegetation and tropical plants, making it a picturesque spot to relax, and there are walkways and stairs that lead down to the pools, providing easy access. There are picnic areas and places to relax in the shade as well as nearby restaurants and cafés where you can enjoy local cuisine.

19 LA FAJANA NATURAL POOLS ☆ 5 ⇨ 4 🏆 4

The La Fajana pools are similar to the Charco Azul ones with the added bonus of a cave-like lava tube. Visitors can explore the cave and view the geological formations inside. Both spots feature blue natural pools against the backdrop of black volcanic rock and lush green vegetation. La Fajana is situated slightly further to the north, on the north-eastern tip of the island.

La Palma
↳ To Stroll

A **LOS CANARIOS** ☆^{3} ↕^{2} 🍷^{3}

Los Canarios, also known as Fuencaliente de La Palma, is a charming village located on the southern tip of the island, known for its proximity to volcanic activity, including the Volcán Teneguía.

It's the perfect base for hiking, either north on the Ruta de los Volcanes over the Cumbre Vieja or south on the Camino del Sal, to the Faro de Fuencaliente.

The region around Los Canarios is also known for wine production, with local vineyards producing wines unique to La Palma and using a number of varieties including the renowned Malvasia. It's not a touristy place but it does have a few restaurants, offering a relaxed, authentic experience.

B **PUERTO NAOS** ☆^{3} ↕^{2} 🍷^{3}

Puerto Naos is a popular coastal resort town located on the west coast, known for its beautiful beach, pleasant climate and vibrant atmosphere. Playa de Puerto Naos features dark volcanic sand and calm, clear waters, making it an ideal spot for swimming, sunbathing, and water sports.

The beach is equipped with sunbeds and umbrellas for visitors' comfort. The beachfront promenade, known as the Paseo de los Tilos, stretches along the coastline, and is lined with a variety of restaurants, cafés and shops.

The town has a range of hotels, apartments and holiday rentals, and the calm waters and consistent breezes make Puerto Naos a suitable location for water sports.

C **TAZACORTE** ☆^{5} ↕^{2} 🍷^{5}

Tazacorte is a charming town on the west coast of the island, known for its picturesque setting, traditional colourful Canarian houses, pleasant climate, and a mix of natural beauty and historical charm.

Playa de Tazacorte, one of the most popular beaches on the island, features dark volcanic sand and calm, clear waters, with plenty of restaurants in which to enjoy a relaxing seafood lunch washed down with a beer.
The area is famous for its banana plantations, stretching across the landscape, some offering guided tours. Tazacorte has a small but active fishing harbour where you can watch local fishermen at work.

The town is the perfect gateway for hikes like the GR131 to Mirador El Time or along the Barranco de las Angustias.

Last but not least, Tazacorte is known for its breath-taking sunsets over the Atlantic, which can be enjoyed from the beach or the nearby cliffs.

D **LOS LLANOS DE ARIDANE** ☆^{5} ↕^{4} 🍷^{5}

Los Llanos de Aridane is the second largest town of La Palma, situated in the west of the island, in the middle of the Parque Nacional Caldera de Taburiente, making it an excellent base for exploring this natural wonder.

The town centre features a mix of historic and modern architecture with a good variety of shops, restaurants, and cafés, making it popular with both residents and tourists. Plaza de España is one of the main squares and a hub for events and gatherings.

The town has several cultural attractions, including the Church of Los Remedios and the Museo Arqueológico Benahoarita, which provides insights into the island's Indigenous culture and history.

E **LOS CANCAJOS** ☆ 5 ↕ 4 🍷 5

Los Cancajos is a picturesque village on the east coast, just 5km from the island's airport, making it easily accessible for travellers arriving on La Palma. One of the key attractions of Los Cancajos is its promenade and beautiful beach area, where the dark volcanic sand contrasts with the lush green landscape.

It's a popular destination for scuba diving. The village offers opportunities for scuba diving classes and guided dives, allowing visitors to discover the rich marine life and vibrant coral reefs.

F **SANTA CRUZ DE LA PALMA** ☆ 5 ↕ 4 🍷 5

Santa Cruz de La Palma, referred to simply as Santa Cruz, is the island's capital. Located on the east coast, it is a charming, historic city known for its colonial architecture and maritime heritage. The centre features narrow cobblestone streets, colourful colonial buildings with wooden balconies, and charming squares. Its main street, Calle Real, is lined with shops, cafés and restaurants. The Plaza de España is the picturesque heart of Santa Cruz with a beautiful fountain, palm trees and historic buildings, including the Palacio de Salazar, which houses the Museo Insular devoted to the history and natural history of the island. Santa Cruz has a strong maritime tradition that can be explored in the Museo Naval.

PLAYA DE ECHENTIVE

↑ FUENCALIENTE LIGHTHOUSE & SALINAS

GR131, FUENCALIENTE ↓

FARO DE FUENCALIE

PLAYA DE ECHENTIVE
VOLCÁN TENEGUÍA

↰ GR131, CUMBRE VIEJA NATIONAL PARK

A VIEW OF TENERIFE & LA GOMERA ↴

↰ VOLCÁN TAJOGAITE, WHICH ERUPTED IN 2021

LA CALDERA DE TABURIENTE ↴

CHARCO AZUL

GR131, LA CALDERA DE TABURIENTE

GR131, ROQUE DE LOS MUCHACHOS

TELESCOPIOS
MAGIC I-II

↰ DESCENT FROM MIRADOR EL TIME TO EL PUERTO DE TAZACORTE

GR131, MUCHACHOS TO MIRADOR EL TIME ↴

PLAYA DE TAZACORTE

28.1134°
N

17.1325°
W

↱ Island 6 / 7
La Gomera

370km²
21,503 residents

6

→ ROQUE DE AGANDO
28.1053° N / 17.2136° W
HEIGHT 1,250M

↳ Welcome to La Gomera, the greenest and most exotic island of the seven, with a lush, subtropical vibe. Its round shape and erratic hilly landscape with canyons and ridges may be reminiscent of Gran Canaria, but the moss, palm trees and mists also bring to mind the South or Central American jungle, with the Roque de Agando as the tropical pièce de résistance. Colourful hillside villages sitting beside banana plantations, unique volcanic rock formations and pristine beaches are the local treasures. This is a paradise for nature and sunshine, so don't expect buzzing city life or wild party scenes. The capital, San Sebastián de la Gomera, is a small town but with a rich history, as it's famously the last stop Christopher Columbus made before sailing across the Atlantic and discovering the Americas, thereby winning the island its nickname La Isla Colombina.

La Gomera
La Isla Colombina

Coastline: 100km
Highest point: 1,487m

La Isla Colombina, named after Christophe Columbus setting foot here as last stopover before discovering America

↳ La Gomera is a round-shaped island with many irregular highlands and ravines criss-crossing the rocky mountains. Most of the terrain, especially the north, is covered with lush laurel, palm and banana vegetation. The biggest towns sit on the circumference of the circle, close to the sea, some of them with a rich history in the banana trade. In the east, San Sebastián, the capital, connects the island with the world. Hermigua and Agulo in the north-east are known for their green valleys, and Valle Gran Rey in the west features a tropical ravine, protected as a UNESCO Biosphere. The vertical drop from the highlands in the centre – rising to 1,487m at Alto de Garajonay – gives rise to spectacular views from the many viewpoints, notably Mirador de Abrante and Mirador El Palmarejo, respectively overlooking the east and west coasts. The coastline is home to many spectacular beaches, often secluded and protected by towering cliffs.

La Gomera
↳ Introduction

HOW TO GET AROUND

Boats arrive on the east of the island, at San Sebastián de la Gomera, sailing from La Palma and Tenerife. There is an airport in the south close to Playa Santiago, but is used only for inter-island flights. Roads are in good condition, though there is no complete circular highway around the island. The main road, the GM200, departs from San Sebastián towards Roque de Agando and from there connects to either Valle Gran Rey in the west or Hermigua and Vallehermoso in the east. It's a scenic road, curving along the highest plateau on the island passing by the Roque Agando. Other places are reached by the hairpin roads that wind through the ravines and slopes towards the coast. San Sebastián is the only passenger port, but the little port in Valle Gran Rey offers boat trips for whale watching and the like.

WHERE TO STAY

There are probably three main hubs to stay. The first one is conveniently near the capital, San Sebastián de la Gomera, where you will also find a parador. If it's nature and peace you want, you will probably prefer to base yourself in the Hermigua valley in the east or Valle Gran Rey in the west. Both are lush green valleys full of banana and palm trees with houses on the slopes facing towards the sea. Hermigua is a wide valley and a great base for the many nearby beaches and also sits closer to Parque Nacional de Garajonay and the higher midlands. The town of Valle Gran Rey sits at the foot of steep cliffs, right next to the sea. If you like beach life, water sports or scuba diving, this is probably your best bet.

BEACHES

La Gomera has 90km of coastline, so there is something for everyone. The beaches of Valle Gran Rey in the west are perhaps the most popular, offering the best spot to catch the sunset. You'll find bars and restaurants nearby, which is more the exception on La Gomera. Further south is the Playa de Santiago whose calm waters are protected by a jetty, close to the town. In the capital are the urban beaches Playa de San Sebastián and Playa de La Cueva, and a bit further away the black sands of Playa de Ávalo.

Further east, you find the beaches of Playa de la Caleta, Playa Hermigua, the calm Playa del Medio and Playa de Vallehermoso, the latter with a charming bar. Rounding the clock, you find Playa de Alojera, a beach next to a little village at the end of a ravine, one of our favourites.

TWO-DAY STAY

Day 1
A morning hike on the GR131 before sunrise towards the highlands of the island is truly unforgettable. When the sun rises, the silhouette of Mount Teide, visible from the trail, will be bathed in liquid gold. An alternative is the hike to the top of Fortaleza de Chipude. After this morning exercise, make your way to the Hermigua valley, where you can enjoy lunch at the Mirador de Abrante (making a reservation might be sensible). Before or after, take half an hour's stroll through Agulo. After lunch, it's beach time on Playa de la Caleta, Hermigua or Vallehermoso (there are bars on the second two). Head back inland for a dazzling view from Mirador Alojero. Spend the night in Valle Gran Rey.

Day 2
Start the day with a hike in Barranco de Arure or with a boat trip departing from Puerto de Valle Gran Rey, where you can watch whales or visit Los Órganos, a natural wonder in the cliffs. Have lunch at the César Manrique viewpoint El Palmarejo (again, it's best to make a reservation). Spend the afternoon either on the marvellous beaches of Valle Gran Rey or on the golf course in Playa Santiago. Have dinner in San Sebastián before heading home or staying overnight in the parador.

LA GOMERA

EXPLORE / HIGHLIGHTS

1 Playa de Ávalo
2 Roque de Agando
3 Garajonay National Park
4 Mirador de los Roques
5 Alto de Garajonay
6 Fortaleza de Chipude
7 Parque Natural Majona
8 Roques de Pedro y Petra
9 Playa Hermigua
10 Mirador de Abrante
11 Roque Cano
12 Presa de la Encantadora
13 Playa de Vallehermoso
14 Monumento Natural de los Órganos
15 Playa de Alojera
16 Mirador de Alojera
17 Mirador El Palmarejo & Valle Gran Rey
18 Barranco de Arure

STROLL / HIGHLIGHTS

A San Sebastián de la Gomera
B Playa Santiago
C Hermigua
D Agulo
E Vallehermoso
F Valle Gran Rey
G Chipude
H Alajero

34

La Gomera
↳ Key Facts

WHEREABOUTS	Name	La Gomera
	Origin of name	Earliest references to the island are found in Spanish and Portuguese texts. Some suggest the name isderived from the Latin word gomor, meaning 'a heap' or 'pile', referring to the island's mountainous terrain
	Nickname	La Isla Colombina, named after Christophe Columbus setting foot here as last stopover before discovering America
	Key towns and villages	Valle Gran Rey, Hermigua, Agulo, Chipude, Alojera, Playa de Santiago
DEMOGRAPHICS	Population	21,503 people, 1% of the Canary Islands, 6th in rank
	Capital	San Sebastián de la Gomera (pop. approx. 10,000)
	Biggest cities	San Sebastián de la Gomera
INFRASTRUCTURE	Commercial Airport	Aeropuerto de la Gomera (AMZ), Playa de Santiago, in the south of the island
	Commercial Ports	La Gomera port
	Agriculture	Bananas
GEOGRAPHY	Size	370km2, 6th in rank
	Highest point	Alto de Garajonay (1,487m)
	Dimensions	A rough circle, 22km in diameter
	Coastline	100km, 15km beaches, mostly small secluded beaches of black volcanic sand or pebbles. No large white sand beaches
	Origin	Twelve million years of age, created by the accumulation of material emitted during different eruptive periods. Volcanic activity has occurred over the last 12,000 years on all islands except for La Gomera, the oldest of the Canary Islands
HISTORY	Silbo Gomero	La Gomera's inhabitants' ancient way of communicating across deep ravines by means of a whistled speech called Silbo Gomero, which can be heard two miles away
	6th Sept 1492	Christopher Columbus departs San Sebastián de la Gomera, replenished with supplies of water and sugarcane, en route to the Americas
	1498	Third and last stop of Columbus on La Gomera

La Gomera
↳ Where to Hike

OVERVIEW

La Gomera is significantly smaller than its neighbours to the north and the east. Nonetheless, it is a surprising paradise for hikers with plenty of remote beaches connected to the ravines and canyons and tropical forests of the high midlands. The GR131 makes an L-shape connecting the east with the north, passing through the landmarks of Roque de Agando and Alto de Garajonay and ending at the secluded Playa de Vallehermoso. Stage 25 is the climb stage from sea level to Chipude, a well-known mountain town. Stage 26 drops back to sea level through jungle towns and dense forest and close by a dam.

TERRAIN

A large part of the island is covered in subtropical laurisilva forest, giving La Gomera a mystical and exotic vibe. The trail switches between asphalt and single trail, of which some parts can be steep and technical. There are views over the surrounding landscapes when there are breaks in the forest cover.

WHICH STAGE TO PICK

While the GR131 offers two stages to choose from, there are plenty of other hiking opportunities, especially in the valleys of Hermigua or the Valle Gran Rey or along the clifftop coast.

Sticking to the GR131, both stages are worthy of your time. We'd recommend doing Stage 25 as a sunrise hike so you can enjoy the view over to Mount Teide. Stage 26 offers some punchy descents with a great finish at the Playa de Vallehermoso, where you can enjoy a relaxing dip or a beer.

ELEVATION MAP

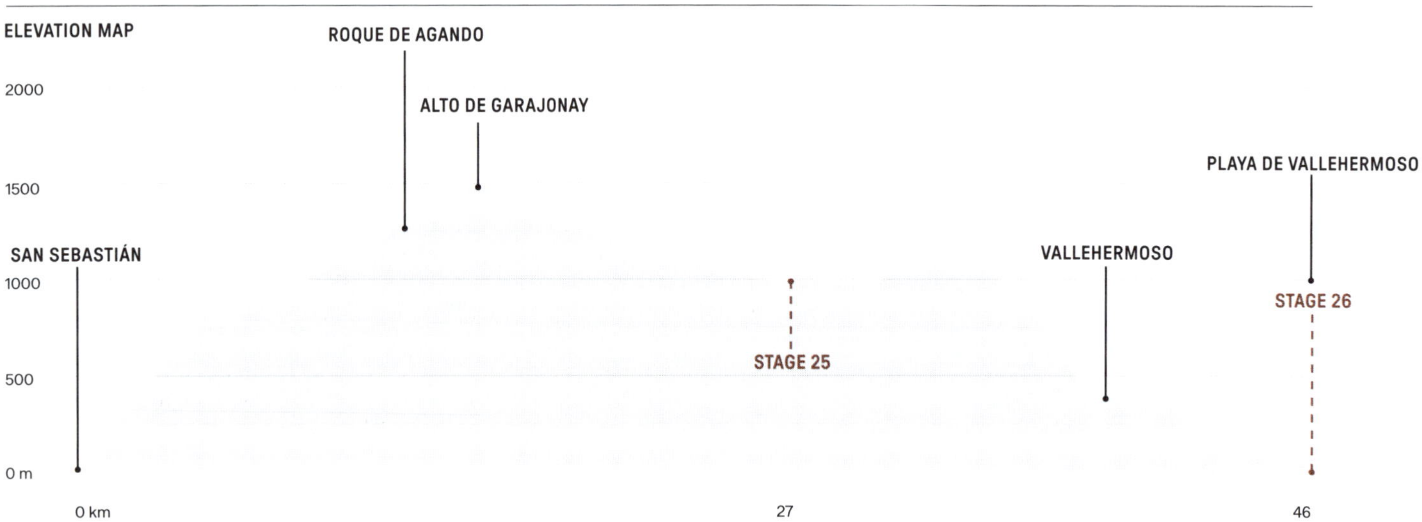

La Gomera
↳ Hikes Overview

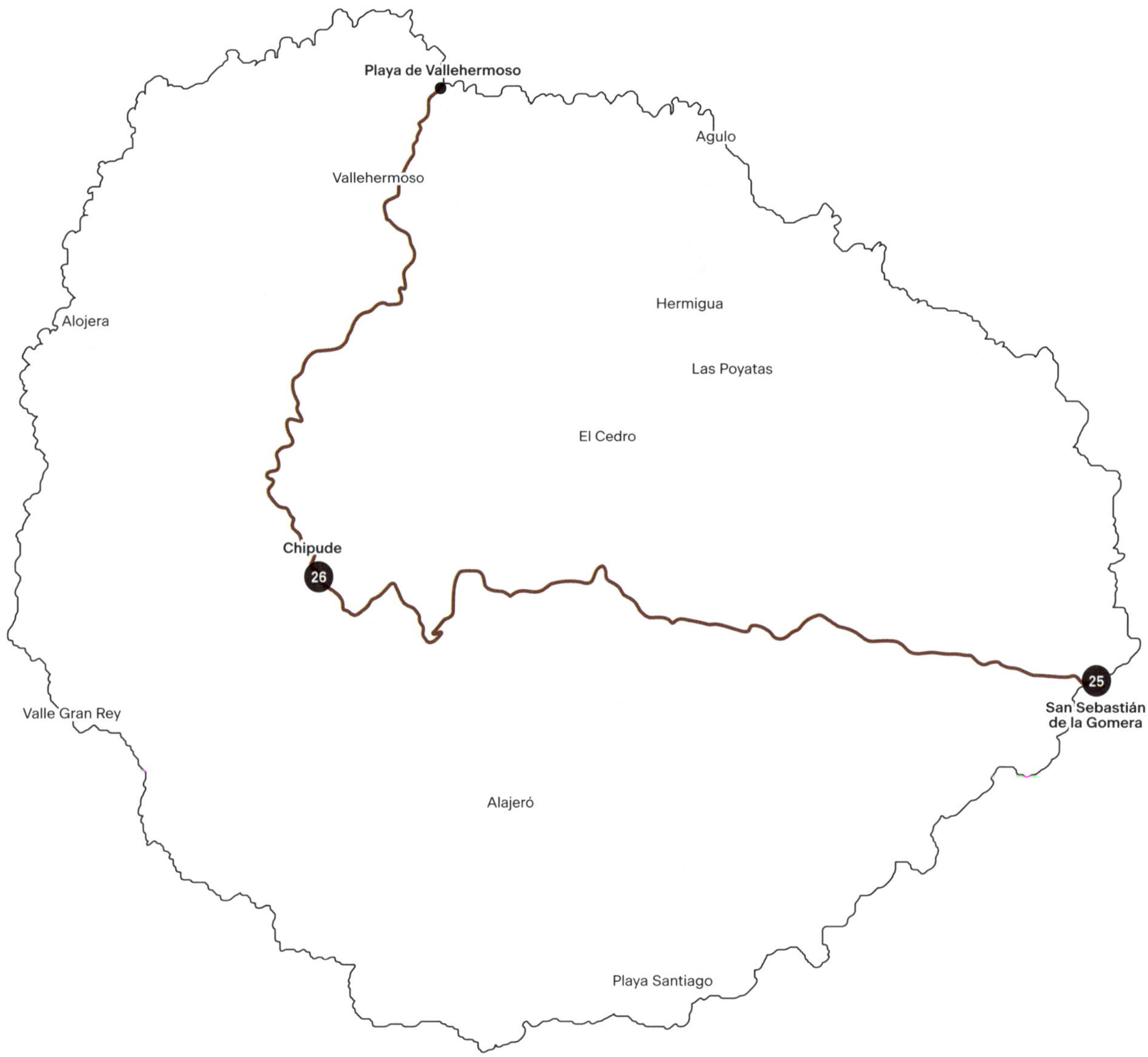

STAGE 25

SAN SEBASTIÁN DE LA GOMERA TO CHIPUDE

Distance 27km **Ascent** 1,960m **Decent** 880m **Asphalt** 19%

A long climb through terraced slopes to reach the Garajonay tropical forest ridge. After the Roque de Agando and Alto de Garajonay, we drop to Chipude.

Recommendation: 3 / 4
Technicality: 3 / 4
Facilities: 2 / 4
Type: GR131

The GR131 rises steadily from the coastal starting point at San Sebastián, aiming for La Gomera's high point, Alto de Garajonay.
Along the ascent, the trail traverses rugged hillsides with ancient terraces, leading up to denser forests. The path winds past the impressive Roque de Agando, then continues along a dense forested ridge, typical of the Parque Nacional de Garajonay, towards Alto de Garajonay at 1,487m above sea level. Connecting mountain trails and routes lead to Chipude.
Leaving San Sebastián at before the sun rises, allows for a spectacular view of the sun rising behind the El Teide silhouette, a scenery you won't forget.

STAGE 26

CHIPUDE TO PLAYA VALLEHERMOSO

Distance 18.5km **Ascent** 420m **Decent** 1,500m **Asphalt** 27%

Descent stage with mostly forest and jungle passages, passing by a dam and ending on the remote Playa de Vallehermoso.

Recommendation: 3 / 4
Technicality: 3 / 4
Facilities: 3 / 4
Type: GR131

Beginning at an elevated altitude, the GR131 meanders through villages, following the course of ravines before directly entering the laurisilva 'cloud forest'. It then descends for a while, with a technical challenge towards the end, eventually reaching the village of Vallehermoso.
From there, a straightforward walk through the valley leads to the trail's conclusion on the northern coastline.

La Gomera
↳ To Explore

1 **PLAYA DE ÁVALO** ☆ 2 · 3 · 2

This sheltered, semi-circular red-coloured beach is conveniently close to the capital, San Sebastián de la Gomera.

2 **ROGUE DE AGANDO** ☆ 5 · 1 · 1

The Roque de Agando is a striking and prominent landmark, a symbol of La Gomera's natural beauty and a testament to the island's volcanic past. Its impressive size and the lush greenery of its surroundings make it a must-visit for anyone travelling to the Canary Islands.

It's one of several monoliths in the Parque Nacional de Garajonay but definitely the most famous and visually impressive, standing 1,250m high. It's often associated with various local legends and stories, reflecting the island's cultural heritage.

3 **GARAJONAY NATIONAL PARK** ☆ 5 · 3 · 1

Parque Nacional de Garajonay is one of the four national parks in the Canary Islands. It covers 11 per cent of La Gomera and is renowned for its extensive and well-preserved laurisilva (laurel) forests. These ancient forests are remnants of the subtropical vegetation that covered much of Southern Europe and North Africa millions of years ago, but which is now only found in the Canaries, Madeira and the Azores. The year-round high humidity and mild temperature create an ideal environment for this type of vegetation which grows among a network of flowing streams that serve as the main water source for the island. Moss-covered laurel trees, rickety stepped paths and drifting mists create an enchanting atmosphere in these prehistoric forests.

There are a couple of hiking trails in the park, the GR131 being one of them. An easy but beautiful trail is the Cañada de Jorge, a 3km loop starting in Valle Gran Rey. Garajonay holds significant cultural importance, its name derived from the legend of Gara and Jonay, a story akin to Romeo and Juliet that's deeply rooted in the local culture, back to pre-Hispanic times.

4 **MIRADOR DE LOS ROQUES** ☆ 5 · 5 · 1

A bit further west, 300m from the Roque de Agando, along the GM200 road at x28.10905, -17.21462, there is a small parking area and viewpoint from where you can admire the Roque de Agando.

Another viewpoint, Mirador del Morro de Agando, 400m further along the GR131, provides another vantage point, this time accessible only on foot. If you continue the GR131 a little further still, there's an iconic bridge that crosses over the road.

5 **ALTO DE GARAJONAY (1,487M)** ☆ 4 · 5 · 1

The 1,487m Alto de Garajonay is the highest point on the island, towering above and named after the Parque Nacional de Garajonay. It's accessible by car via the GR131, providing a stunning 360-degree view over the area.

6 **FORTALEZA DE CHIPUDE (1,240M)** ☆ 5 · 1 · 2

La Fortaleza de Chipude, located in the south-west, is a remarkable geological and historical site. This eroded volcanic structure, often described as a 'table mountain', has a plateau at an altitude of 1,240m, standing about 500m above its surroundings, dominating the landscape.

The original inhabitants of the island regarded it as a sacred site, and used it as a refuge during the 15th-century Spanish invasion. At the base of La Fortaleza lies the village of Chipude, with a church dating back to the 16th century. Hikers can climb up to the summit from the parking spot at 28.10396, -17.27513 along the CV17 road. It's a 1km hike, the first few metres on the GR131, then a sharp right turn facing the rock.

This path, once moderately difficult, has been made more accessible with cut steps leading to the mountain's base, though climbing up the couloir itself remains challenging. A short, exposed traverse on top of the buttress leads to the Fortaleza plateau, suitable mainly for experienced hikers. Hikers are rewarded with spectacular views of the Parque Nacional de Garajonay and the surrounding barrancos (ravines).

7 PARQUE NATURAL MAJONA ☆ 3 ⇨ 2 ♀ 1

La Gomera's second largest park, the Parque Natural Majona, is located on the east coast and is great for walkers. Known as one of the wildest areas of the island it features 1,757ha of dense forests and deep ravines.

8 ROQUES DE PEDRO Y PETRA ☆ 3 ⇨ 1 ♀ 3

Roques de Pedro y Petra are two notable rock formations, looking like two giant bookends. They are volcanic formations known as phonolite plugs, formed when magma hardens within a vent of an active volcano to later become exposed over time as the surrounding softer rock erodes away.

These rock formations are steeped in local folklore: they are named after mythical characters and are associated with various legends that have been passed down through the generations on La Gomera. While the rocks themselves are not accessible for climbing, there are hiking trails in the vicinity.

9 PESCANTE DE HERMIGUA AND MIRADOR DE LA PUNTA ☆ 3 ⇨ 2 ♀ 3

The Pescante de Hermigua is an abandoned pier located at Playa de Hermigua, once used to facilitate the island's fruit exports, particularly tomatoes and bananas. Constructed between 1907 and 1908, using stone, iron and mortar, it went out of use when the port of San Sebastián was built in the 1950s.

The pier also housed offices and a warehouse, which were essential for managing the bustling traffic of goods. A significant player in this operation was the British company Fyffes, known for its expertise in constructing such facilities. Today, the structure stands abandoned and weathered by time, but it tells a rich story of La Gomera's trading history and highlights the island's pivotal role in the economic and industrial development during a significant period.

From the nearby Mirador de la Punta you have a great view over the Pescante and the fertile valley of Hermigua.

10 MIRADOR DE ABRANTE ☆ 5 ⇨ 5 ♀ 5

The Mirador de Abrante is a remarkable viewpoint that combines stunning views, architectural innovation and culinary delights. Perched 620m above sea level, the building features a 7m-long glass walkway that extends out from the cliff where you can marvel at the plummeting depths beneath your feet.

From this vantage point, you can take in the picturesque landscape of Agulo village, the vast expanse of the ocean, and even the island of Tenerife in the distance.

Apart from the stunning views, the viewpoint houses a restaurant that offers creative international dishes as well as delectable Canarian cuisine.

The building itself is an architectural gem, designed by José Luis Bermejo Martín. Its design harmoniously blends with the natural surroundings, making it not just a viewpoint but also a work of art.

11 ROQUE CANO ☆ 2 ⇨ 1 ♀ 3

Shaped like a giant spearhead, Roque Cano is another example of the volcanic formations known as phonolite plugs, similar in appearance to Roque de Agando and Roque de Pedro y Petra. You can't reach the top without a harness and ropes, but there are plenty of hikes nearby if you have adventure in mind.

12 PRESA DE LA ENCANTADORA ☆ 3 ⇨ 4 ♀ 3

The Encantadora Dam is located close to Vallehermoso and is the largest reservoir on the island (750 million litres of water). It's a great place to enjoy a day in full contact with nature, especially if you're a birdwatcher, as it's a stopover for many migratory birds.

13 **PLAYA DE VALLEHERMOSO** ☆ 4 🪧 5 🍷 3

This spectacular secluded beach marks the end of the GR131. There's a restaurant and other facilities nearby. If this beach isn't remote enough for you, climb – at your own risk – the zigzagging path over the hill on the right (looking out at the ocean). On the other side you will find a smaller valley and the tiny Playa de Tamargada.

On the left (again facing the ocean) is another gem, the Castillo del Mar (Sea Castle), whose melodic nicknames include El Pescante and Empaquetadora de Platanos. This was a docking station built in 1890, for steam ships, making Vallehermoso the economic centre of La Gomera. On the lower floors of the 'castle', bananas were washed, weighed, measured, sorted and packed before being loaded into the ships' holds. On the upper floors of the castle were canons, ready to fire on any marauding pirates.

14 **MONUMENTO NATURAL DE LOS ÓRGANOS** ☆ 4 🪧 1 🍷 1

As the name suggests, the natural rock formation of Los Órganos resembles giant church organ pipes, made by the slow cooling of basalt magma. The natural organ stands 80m tall and 175m wide above the sea, although its actual height is 800m as most of the rock is hidden underwater. You can only see it from the sea, thanks to its position on a cliff face along the north shore in the most remote and inaccessible part of the island. There are boat trips offered from the port in Valle Gran Rey.

15 **PLAYA DE ALOJERA** ☆ 3 🪧 3 🍷 4

Playa de Alojera is a small, secluded, black volcanic beach on the island's western coast at the end of canyon, surrounded by a serene natural environment, making it a popular spot for both locals and visitors. It's part of the village of Alojera, known for its laid-back way of life and beautiful setting. The beach is relatively easy to access, though it may require a bit of a drive from the main towns on the island. Basic amenities like restaurants and bars are nearby, and the sea at Playa de Alojera is generally calm, making it a good spot for swimming.

16 **MIRADOR DE ALOJERA** ☆ 3 🪧 4 🍷 1

This viewpoint is perched on top of cliffs along the GM1 road connecting Vallehermoso with Valle Gran Rey. The spot provides an amazing view over the western side of the island, with the canyons running towards Playa de Alojera and the silhouette of La Palma in the background.

17 **MIRADOR EL PALMAREJO & VALLE GRAN REY** ☆ 5 🪧 5 🍷 5

Nestled in the striking Valle Gran Rey, the Mirador el Palmarejo is one of the most picturesque spots in the west of the island. The viewpoint offers a spectacular bird's-eye view of the valley's sheer rock walls, terraced slopes, lush palm groves and traditional houses. This unique environment has been granted UNESCO Biosphere Reserve status.

The viewpoint is also sometimes known as the Mirador César Manrique, in honour of the renowned Canarian architect who designed it, blending modern architecture with nature. The gardens showcase a variety of indigenous plants from the valley, including Canary palm trees, famous for the exquisite palm honey derived from them. The mirador has a restaurant serving good local dishes as well as parking, information panels and a tourist information centre.

18 **BARRANCO DE ARURE** ☆ 4 🪧 2 🍷 2

This ravine close to Valle Gran Rey has a trail leading to the Arure waterfall. It's not a challenging trail, although care is needed as some sections are slippery.

The trail begins in traditional hamlet of Gura. The path leads to the ravine, where you can look up and see the three streams that converge into the famous waterfall.

ROQUE DE AGANDO

La Gomera
↳ To Stroll

A **SAN SEBASTIÁN DE LA GOMERA** ☆5 ↕4 🍷4

The capital of La Gomera boasts a vibrant yet relaxed atmosphere, packed with bars, restaurants, shops and charming squares. This city is historically significant as it was the last stopover for Christopher Columbus before he set out on his voyage to the Americas on 6 September 1492. Visitors can explore Casa Colón, the customs house Columbus frequented, or Casa de la Aguada, featuring an exhibit on Columbus's voyages.

Other attractions include the bustling Mercado Municipal, the historic Iglesia de Asunción, and the striking Torre del Conde – a medieval fortified tower linked to the story of the Castilian noblewoman Beatriz de Bobadilla, confidante of Isabella I – alongside traditional farmhouses such as La Laja, Vegaypala and Tejiade. It's the main entry point for most visitors, as it hosts the primary ferry port. Its lack of chain hotels and shopping centres, its rich history and tranquil ambiance mean that its ranks among La Gomera's top ten must-visit places.

The city's beaches, ranging from the wild and secluded to the more accessible, add to the city's allure, offering stunning natural beauty. The 18m-high statue of Christ on a 200m hill overlooking and protecting the city gives the capital of this exotic island a bit of a Río de Janeiro vibe.

B **PLAYA SANTIAGO** ☆5 ↕2 🍷3

Playa Santiago is a fishing town whose colourful houses are in striking contrast with its famous volcanic black sand beach, one of the prettiest on the island. Located on the southern end of the island, it offers a host of maritime excursions as marine life is abundant in these Atlantic waters, including dolphins, pilot whales, sperm whales, Bryde's whales and even sea turtles. Kayaking and diving are also popular. Whale-watching tours by Excursiones Tina depart from Playa de Santiago or Vueltas.

Playa Santiago is conveniently located next to the only golf course on the island and close to the airport.

C **HERMIGUA** ☆5 ↕3 🍷3

Situated in the north-east, Hermigua is home to the stunning Parque National de Garajonay, a UNESCO World Heritage Site. The municipality is known for its green valleys, with banana plantations, palm trees and laurel trees, and historical sites like the Convento de Santo Domingo, built in the 17th century.

Hermigua used to be the beating heart of the banana trade because of the many plantations and the proximity of El Pescante, the docking station for trade ships. Today the valley offers a good range of accommodation, often with views over the sea. With temperatures ranging between 18 and 27 °C, Hermigua has long been recognized as having the best climate in the world. Near Playa de Hermigua are Playa de la Caleta and Playa de Santa Catalina, the latter popular with surfers.

D **AGULO** ☆4 ↕2 🍷2

Just an hour's drive from San Sebastián, Agulo – often referred to as the 'Green Balcony of La Gomera' – is a picturesque village situated atop a hill, offering breathtaking views of the ocean and Tenerife's Mount Teide. Nestled in the northern part of the island, Agulo is enveloped in lush greenery, a result of the extensive banana plantations and the limited presence of buildings. As you wander through its streets, you'll find several information panels scattered around, which provide fascinating facts about the village and its history.

E **VALLEHERMOSO** ☆ 3 ↕ 3 🍷 3

Vallehermoso, located in the northern part of the island, is known for its natural beauty, including the impressive rock formation Roque Cano and the Encantadora Dam.

Vallehermoso offers a variety of hiking trails and is characterized by its lush vegetation and agricultural lands, with a rich history of trade. Its nearby beach, Playa de Vallehermoso, offers great sunbathing opportunities.

F **VALLE GRAN REY** ☆ 5 ↕ 3 🍷 4

Valle Gran Rey, a coastal town sitting at the end of a beautiful UNESCO-designated valley filled with palm groves, is a popular tourist destination, known for its beautiful beaches, relaxed atmosphere and stunning sunsets.

It's a versatile location, attracting photographers for its variety of dramatic landscapes – deep ravines, lush green valleys, towering cliffs, and picturesque beaches – and hikers for its trails through the ravines and along the coast.

The area boasts several beautiful beaches, such as Playa de Valle Gran Rey, Playa de Vueltas and Playa del Inglés, the last a legendary destination for hippies and other alternative types.

These beaches are known for their black volcanic sand and offer a perfect setting for sunbathing, swimming and enjoying stunning sunsets. Valle Gran Rey offers a range of accommodation, from luxury hotels to budget-friendly guesthouses.

The waters off the coast of Valle Gran Rey are a great place for whale and dolphin-watching. Various tour operators offer boat trips to see these magnificent creatures in their natural habitat.

G **CHIPUDE** ☆ 2 ↕ 2 🍷 3

Chipude is a small, traditional village, situated in the highlands of La Gomera, making it one of the highest villages on the island. This elevated position offers spectacular views of the surrounding landscapes and a great starting place of trails, with the GR131 passing by. The village is known for its rich cultural heritage, home to traditional Canarian architecture, with houses featuring typical stone construction and wooden balconies and famous for its proximity to La Fortaleza, a striking table mountain that is a significant natural landmark and considered a sacred place by the island's indigenous people, the Guanches.

H **ALAJERO** ☆ 2 ↕ 2 🍷 3

This town is a blend of coastal and mountain landscapes. The local church of El Salvador is a notable historical site, and the nearby Playa Santiago is a charming fishing village with a lovely beach.

↰ SAN SEBASTIÁN DE LA GOMERA, WITH EL TEIDE ON THE HORIZON

GR131 CROSSING GM-2
MIRADOR DEL MORRO DE AGANDO

A VIEW OF ALOJERA AND THE ISLAND OF LA PALMA FROM THE MIRADOR DE ALOJERA

GM-2, ROQUE AGANDO

ERMITA DE SAN ISIDRO, ALAJERO

GR131, MIRADOR RISQUILLOS DE CORGO

FORTALEZA DE CHIPUDE

ROQUES PEDRO Y PETRA, HERMIGUA

↰ AGULO, SEEN FROM THE MIRADOR LOS PASOS DE AGULO

PRESA DE LA ENCANTADORA ↴

↰ EL CASTILLO, PLAYA DE VALLEHERMOSO

PESCANTE DE HERMIGUA, PLAYA DE HERMIGUA ↴

GR131 ARRIVING AT
PLAYA DE VALLEHERMOSO

27.7277°
N

18.0141°
W

↱ Island 7 / 7
El Hierro

267km²
10,968 residents

7

→ CLIFF NEAR
HOTEL PUNTAGRANDE
27.79719° N / 17.99233° W

↳ Welcome to El Hierro, the least known, least populous and most westerly island of the archipelago. Dominated by the giant half circle of cliffs forming the El Golfo valley, the forgotten island was long considered the westernmost point of the world. The elements fight a constant battle with the landscape, through water and wind. Wheezing winds make trees bent on the El Sabinar plateau. The pull of gravity has created the valleys of El Golfo and Las Playas, and the desolate lava slopes of El Julan, which contrast greatly with the rolling green hills on the central highlands where you find a Mediterranean, Sicilian vibe. You can watch waves crashing on the rocks in the west, while you relax safely in the nearby natural pools. The calm waters in the south are a paradise for scuba diving.

El Hierro
La Isla Chiquita

Coastline: 90km
Highest point: 1,501m

La Isla Chiquita, the most pristine and westerly of the Canaries, with towering cliffs and natural pools.

↳ You can imagine the island as a giant L-shape, written by a 1,000m high ridge dominating the island. Impressive cliffs form the valleys of El Golfo and Las Playas. The biggest one, El Golfo in the north-west, features relaxing natural pools in the dark basalt rocks stopping the smashing waves. The Roques de Salmor mark the north of this fertile valley. On the other side of the long leg you find the Las Playas hollow, where you can find the longest beach of the island, the famous Roque de la Bonanza and the Parador de El Hierro. Both Las Playas and El Golfo are created by massive landslides millions of years ago. On the southern side, we find the desolate El Julan slopes ending in the west at the Orchilla point, the westernmost point of Spain and until 1492 considered to be the end of the world. On the highlands, pine forests and grass fields inhabit the rolling hills giving the highlands a rustic and relaxed feel with tiny villages such as Tiñor and San Andrés. Villa de Valverde, the island's capital, sits in the north close to Puerto de la Estaca, the port connecting El Hierro and Tenerife.

PARADOR DE EL HIERRO, LAS PLAYAS

El Hierro
↳ Introduction

HOW TO GET AROUND

El Hierro is the least accessible island, connected only to Tenerife, by plane or boat. Don't count on high frequency transits so plan your trip well. It's also probably best to rent your car on Tenerife and take it on the boat.

Roads are solid, with one long road connecting Valverde in the north-east with Orchilla in the south-west. El Golfo, the main valley, is accessible in three places, via Mirador de La Peña, Cruz de los Reyes or Arenas Blancas. It's a small island but due to the lack of real highway and the elevation travelling the relative short distances takes time.

WHERE TO STAY

The island features two iconic hotels: Parador de El Hierro in Las Playas and Hotel Puntagrande in El Golfo. The first one is a great pick if you want to get away from it all and enjoy luxury and space. The latter, once considered the smallest hotel in the world, is located on a pier with the roaring ocean as your background. Different vibe.

Most hotels are located either in La Frontera or El Golfo, which is a central location, well positioned to go anywhere, or a bit further north on the hills surrounding El Mocanal, where there are many casa rurals. Peace and quiet can also be found around Taibique, on a hill overlooking the ocean.

BEACHES

There are no beaches in the north-east but natural pools in La Caleta, Tamaduste, Charco Manso and Pozo de la Calcosas. At the El Golfo coast, you'll find a few beaches close to Roques de Salmor but the water is wild.

Alternatively, the El Golfo coast is scattered with beautiful natural pools, from north to south, La Maceta, Charco de los Sargos and Charco Azul. The larger beaches are in the west starting with Arenas Blancas, the closest one to El Golfo. In the west, close to Orchilla, you find Playa del Verodal, known for its red-ochre colours. Next to the Faro de Orchilla, there is the Muelle de Orchilla. It's not a beach but it's a great way to reach the Mar de las Calmas Marine Reserve and you can use the former docking place as a jumping platform. Further south, there is another red beach with Playa de Tacorón and ultimately you find the largest stretch of beach in Las Playas.

TWO-DAY STAY

Day 1
Arrive in the north-east at the airport or port. Shake yourself awake with a short plunge and visit to the authentic Pozo de las Calcosas, symbol of authencity of the island. Lunch at Mirador de la Peña for a stunning view on El Golfo. Take some time to enjoy a hike somewhere around the Toscany hills of San Andrès and Arbol Garoé, a beautiful and peaceful scenery. Towards the afternoon head towards Las Playas and check in in Parador de El Hierro. Keep enough time for a long aperitif on the terrace watching the sunset.

Day 2
Wake up early for scuba diving in La Restinga and the Mar de las Calmas, one of the best diving spots in the Canary Islands. Grab a seafood lunch in the port of La Restinga. Head towards the west to visit the El Sabinar fields and if you want to go a bit further check the Faro de Orchilla, the former most western point of the world. Spend the afternoon sunbathing, either on the beach Playa del Verodal or Arenas Blancas or in one of the natural pools of La Maceta or Charco Azul. Finish the day in Hotel Puntagrande or one of the surrounding bungalows.

EL HIERRO

EXPLORE / HIGHLIGHTS

1 Las Playas
2 Roque de la Bonanza
3 Parador de El Hierro
4 Mirador de Isora
5 Mirador de Las Playas
6 La Hoya del Morcillo
7 Arbol Garoé & The Water Route
8 Roques de Salmor
9 Mirador de la Peña
10 Hotel Puntagrande
11 La Maceta Natural Pools
12 Charco de los Sargos
13 Ecomuseo de Guinea
14 Charco Azul
15 Cruz de los Reyes
16 Pico de Malpaso
17 Parque Cultural de El Julan
18 Playa de Tacorón
19 Mar de las Calmas
20 Arenas Blancas
21 Playa del Verodal
22 El Sabinar
23 Meridian Zero Monument
24 Faro de Orchilla
25 Muelle de Orchilla

STROLL / HIGHLIGHTS

A Tamaduste
B Pozo de las Calcosas
C Villa de Valverde
D Tiñor
E San Andrés
F Las Puntas
G Taibique
H La Restinga

PUERTO DE LA ESTACA, START OF GR131

El Hierro
↳ Key Facts

WHEREABOUTS	Name	El Hierro
	Origin of name	The island name is not linked to the Spanish word 'iron', as many suspect. Some historians link the name to the Guanches word *esero*, 'strong', while others like Major link it to *herro*, 'cistern', which are constructed to save rainwater on the island
	Nickname	La Isla Chiquita, or 'the little island', is the most pristine and smallest island. It is also known as the Meridian Island, as El Hierro was used in parts of Europe for more than 500 years as the prime meridian
	Key towns and villages	Pozo de las Calcosas, Tiñor, San Andrés
DEMOGRAPHICS	Population	10,968 people, 1% of Canaries, 7th in rank
	Capital	Villa de Valverde - 5,000 people
	Biggest cities	Villa de Valverde, La Restinga
INFRASTRUCTURE	Commercial Airport	Aeropuerto de El Hierro (VDE), Valverde, east of Island – flights to Tenerife only
	Commercial Ports	Puerto de la Estaca, Valverde, east of Island – connection to Tenerife only
	Agriculture	Largest area of organic production of all Canary Islands, notably bananas
GEOGRAPHY	Size	267km^2, 7 in rank
	Highest point	1,501m, Pico de Malpaso
	Dimensions	Triangle / L-shaped. Heigth and width 20km. From north-east to south-west, 30km
	Coastline	90km, mostly rocky cliffs, 5km of beaches
	Origin (time)	Youngest of the archipelago, 1.2 million years old. Its present shape is derived from the erosion on its volcanic cone by three major landslides causing the El Golfo hollow, the Las Playas hollow and the El Julan slopes
HISTORY	15,000 years ago	El Golfo landslide, collapse of the northern flank of the island, formed the El Golfo valley and created a debris avalanche with a volume of 150–180km^3
	1405	Spanish conquest, carried out by Jean de Béthencourt, of the island and its inhabitants, the Bimbaches
	1793	Only one eruption has been recorded, but not confirmed, on the island – from the Volcán de Lomo Negro vent in 1793, lasting a month. A submarine eruption occurred, however, offshore La Restinga village in 2011/2012

El Hierro
↳ Where to Hike

OVERVIEW

The smallest of the seven islands is home to two stages. The GR131 moves from the east to the west, from the ferry port to the remote Muelle de Orchilla, which marks both the most western point of Europe as the end of the GR131. The trail climbs in the first half of Stage 31 to the high midlands. In Stage 32 the trail moves along the ridge of the El Golfo valley to Pico de Malpaso to drop along the pine trees of El Sabinar to the remote western side of the island.

TERRAIN

On El Hierro, slopes and gradients are relatively doable and gentle. Most of the trail is done on wider dirt roads offering relatively low technicality. The elevation looks impressive because of the smaller size of the island but the peak is considerably lower than the neighbouring peaks of La Palma and La Gomera.

Especially in the second part of Stage 31, gradients are low and roads wide, making it suitable for all kind of hikers. The surroundings vary from black volcanic sand with pine trees, to Mediterranean-looking fields, to plain lava rock when you reach the end in the west.

WHICH STAGE TO PICK

Stage 32 is definitely the most versatile with views on two of the three main flanks of the island, El Golfo in the east and El Julan in the west. The descent with views on El Sabinar's fields and the lighthouse in the middle of petrified lava is pretty dramatic. It's also more remote so prepare your journey well. For starting hikers or families, the Stage 31 between Tiñor and San Andrés is friendlier and closer to facilities.

ELEVATION MAP

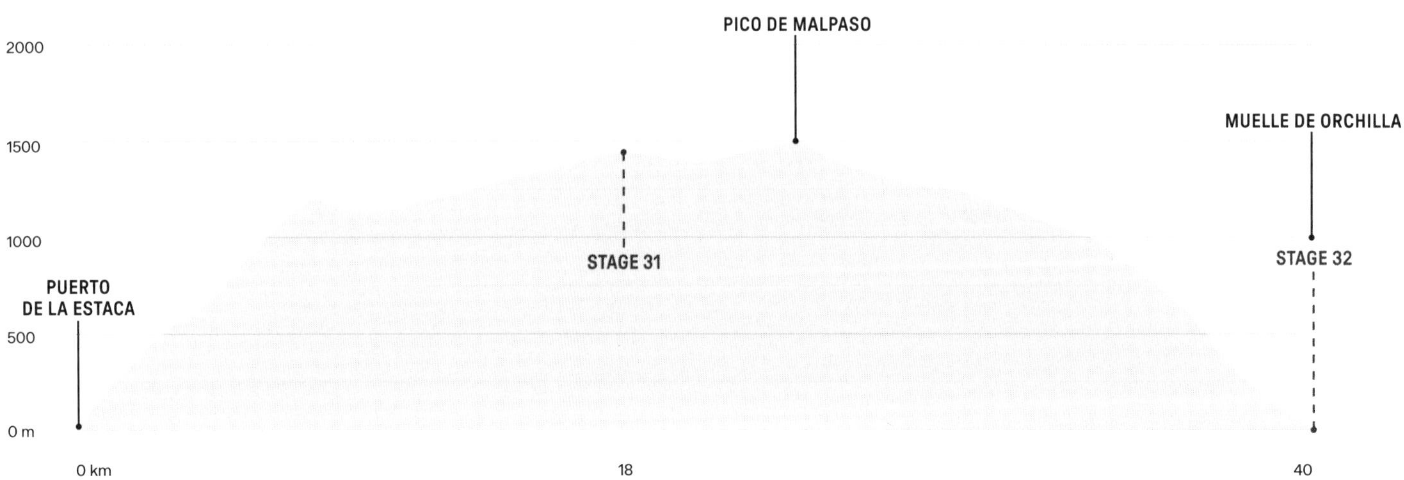

El Hierro
↳ Hikes Overview

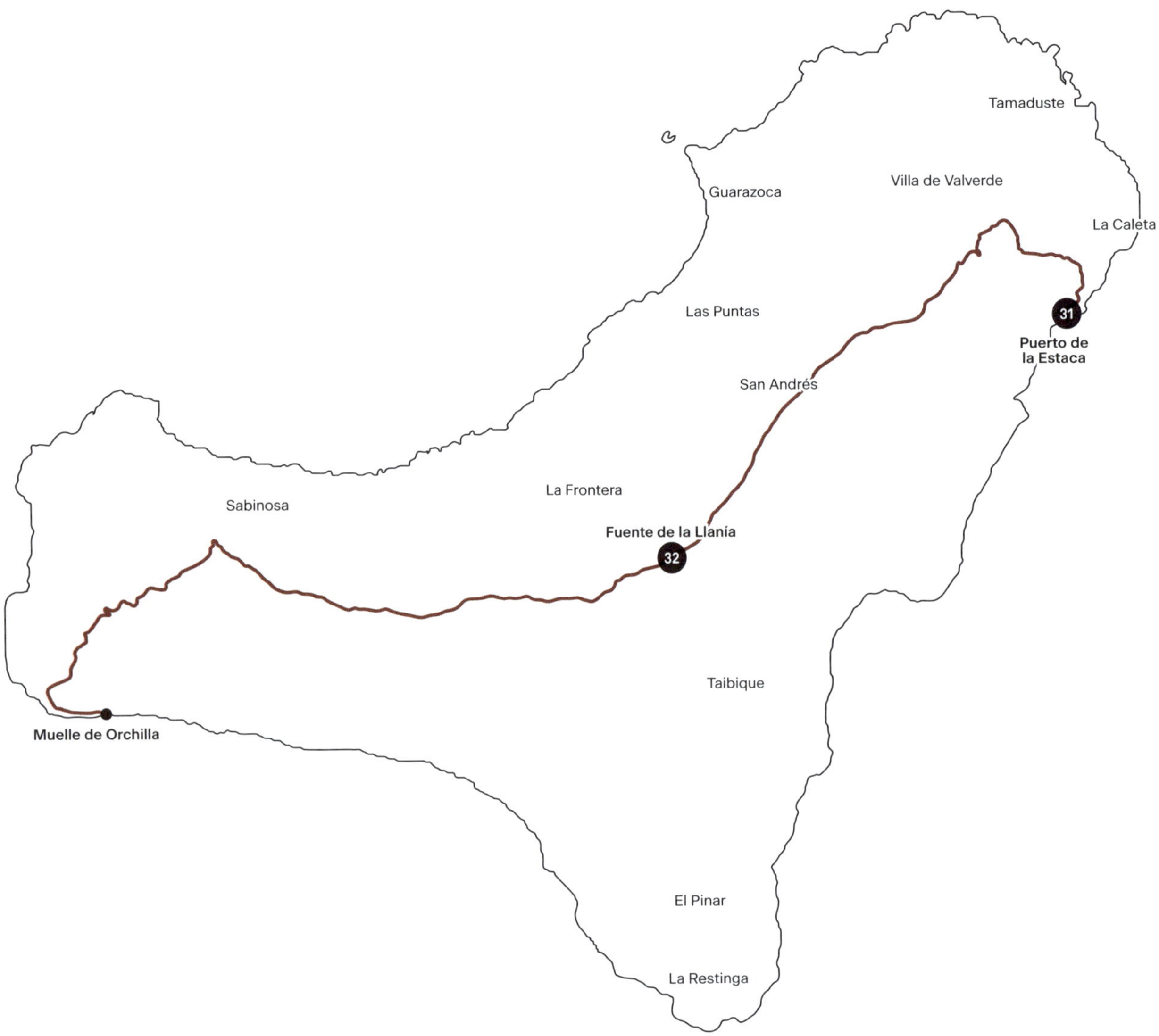

STAGE 31

PUERTO DE LA ESTACA TO FUENTE DE LA LLANÍA

Climb stage from the port via Villa de Valverde to the pleasant Mediterranean midlands.

Recommendation: 3 / 4
Technicality: 2 / 4
Facilities: 2 / 4
Type: GR131

Distance 18km **Ascent** 1,440m **Decent** 100m **Asphalt** 18%

The GR climbs from the port via a mix of asphalt road, dry single trails and garden routes to the town of Villa de Valverde. After the steepest parts in the first 5km, the terrain changes to wider views with a Mediterranean chill vibe through when we pass Tiñor. The second part is relaxed, rolling terrain.

STAGE 32

FUENTE DE LA LLANÍA TO MUELLE DE ORCHILLA

Spectacular stage linking the peak of the island with the most western point of Europe and the end of the GR131.

Recommendation: 3 / 4
Technicality: 2 / 4
Facilities: 1 / 4
Type: GR131

Distance 22km **Ascent** 240m **Decent** 1,580m **Asphalt** 27%

A spectacular stage with a wide variety of landscapes and terrain. The first 5km is a gradual climb on a broad dirt road towards Pico de Malpaso, the peak of the island, with views on El Golfo on the right when you look carefully. A long descent leads across the Sabinar and El Julan open flanks through black volcanics and, grasfields and later on petrified lavafields towards the lighthouse and the docking strip marking the finish line.

El Hierro
↳ To Explore

1 **LAS PLAYAS** ☆ 5 ⇨ 4 🍷 3

Las Playas is an impressive coastal valley surrounded by cliffs, formed by a massive landslide millions of years ago. The bay is dominated by the iconic Roque de La Bonanza, a symbol of the island. The coastline is made up of the island's largest beach, featuring a leisure area for picnics in its most sheltered spot. Nestled at the bay's end, you'll find the Parador de El Hierro.

2 **ROQUE DE LA BONANZA** ☆ 5 ⇨ 4 🍷 3

The Roque de la Bonanza is a tall, isolated, and distinctive rock formation rising from the sea at Playa de las Almorranas in Las Playas.

The rock, a result of volcanic activity like the rest of the island, is often featured in photographs, postcards, and tourism materials representing the island's natural beauty. The rock and its surrounding coastal area are part of a protected natural reserve.

3 **PARADOR DE EL HIERRO** ☆ 4 ⇨ 5 🍷 5

The Parador de El Hierro is a charming and unique hotel located in Las Playas, an ideal place for those seeking tranquility. Its remote location combined with the soothing sound of the ocean waves, offers a peaceful retreat. Paradores are a chain of luxury and historic hotels in Spain, often situated in historic buildings, monasteries or castles.

4 **MIRADOR DE ISORA** ☆ 5 ⇨ 5 🍷 2

In the town of Isora, near Valverde, there's an incredible lookout point atop a 1,000m-high cliff on the hollow of Las Playas, Roque de la Bonanza and the Atlantic Ocean, creating a natural amphitheatre of 4km in diameter. When the sun sets, you can gaze at the stars on the comfy benches. The area is accessible for people with reduced mobility.

5 **MIRADOR DE LAS PLAYAS** ☆ 5 ⇨ 5 🍷 2

Just 3km further south-west from Mirador de Isora, Mirador de las Playas features a similar viewpoint in the middle of the semicircular shape of Las Playas hollow.

6 **LA HOYA DEL MORCILLO** ☆ 3 ⇨ 3 🍷 2

Close to the town of El Pinar, La Hoya del Morcillo is the only recreational forest area on the island with a campsite and a picnic area, relevant for those who want to spend the night or lunch in the middle of nature. The area is in deep inside the Canary pine forest on the highest plateau on the island.

7 **ARBOL GAROÉ & THE WATER ROUTE** ☆ 4 ⇨ 4 🍷 4

The Garoé, also known as the Holy or Sacred Tree, is a key symbol in the history of El Hierro. Nestled in Tigulahe, now the town of San Andrés, this tree has been the subject of countless tales across centuries.

Its fame stems from its remarkable ability to save the Bimbaches—the island's original settlers—from perishing of thirst during their fight against the Castilian conquerors, through water that flowed from its leaves. In the 17th century, a devastating hurricane felled the original Garoé tree, but a lime tree was planted in its stead, continuing the legacy of this mystical symbol. Just 500m from the Garoé stands the Garoé Visitors Centre, offering insights into the native islanders' history and their ingenious methods of obtaining water, also unveiling the natural wonder of horizontal rain.

For those seeking to dig deeper into to the island's water heritage, the Water Route awaits. Stretching over 16km, this trail begins and ends in San Andrés, showcasing the vital importance of water in El Hierro's history.

8 ROQUES DE SALMOR ☆5 ⇨1 🍷2

The Rocks of Salmor is a serie of large and prominent rocky outcrops rising from the coastline, marking the northern part of the hollow and valley of El Golfo. They look like the beads of a giant necklace or the back of a dragon sleeping below the sea level and are natural refuge for seabirds or the endemic giant El Hierro lizard.

Because of their position in the ocean, you can't reach them but you can marvel at them from the coast of El Golfo or the Mirador de la Peña.

9 MIRADOR DE LA PENA ☆5 ⇨5 🍷5

This viewpoint in Guarazoca offers breathtaking views of El Golfo Valley and the dramatic Fuga de la Gorreta ridge, which shepherds once freely traversed.

From here, you can also admire the Salmor Rocks, vineyards, and fruit trees sloping down to the coast. Designed by Canary Islands architect César Manrique, the viewpoint pays homage to the land with lush greenery, large windows, and stone roofs.

Inside, the restaurant serves up Canary Islands gastronomy. This architectural gem stands at one of the island's highest points, around 1,200m above sea level.

10 HOTEL PUNTAGRANDE ☆5 ⇨5 🍷5

Nestled in the charming Las Puntas area of Frontera, you'll find the Hotel Puntagrande, once renowned as one of the world's tiniest hotels.

With a footprint of just 600m^2, this unique gem boasts four double rooms and one suite, each offering a glimpse of the magnificent environment, elevated above the roaring sea.

Constructed in 1884 as a customs post and warehouse, it welcomes guests with its rustic black stone walls and nautical decor, offering delectable local cuisine, spectacular sea views and even Wi-Fi throughout the property.

Las Puntas, a picturesque fishing village, showcases César Manrique's architectural influence with stone holiday homes. Hotel Puntagrande seamlessly integrates black basalt into its design, offering guests the privilege of visiting the breathtaking municipal swimming pool, Cascadas del Mar, another creation by César Manrique, practically at their doorstep for a small entry fee.

11 LA MACETA NATURAL POOLS ☆5 ⇨4 🍷5

La Maceta is the main bathing spot in El Golfo featuring natural swimming pools of different sizes and is a perfect stop for anyone, including families. While the surrounding open sea can be wild with smashing waves, the protected area remains calm and safe.

The lava squares surrounding the pools offer sunbathing space and stairs with metal railings, making the palace safe and accessible to get in and out the water. Nearby is a large parking area and a restaurant.

12 CHARCO DE LOS SARGOS ☆4 ⇨4 🍷3

A more remote and slightly wilder variant of La Maceta, only 300m away. A good alternative if you want to avoid the crowds, but less accessible and and with no drinking facilities.

13 ECOMUSEO DE GUINEA ☆3 ⇨4 🍷4

The village of Guinea is one of the island's earliest settlements, featuring the Guinea Ecomuseum offering a journey through fifteen centuries of history of pioneering inhabitants and subsequent colonists.

You'll also discover the Centre for Recovery of the El Hierro Giant Lizard, dedicated to the preservation of this highly endangered reptile, where you can get eye to eye with one being housed in the local lizardarium.

14 **CHARCO AZUL** ☆ 5 🪧 3 🍷 2

El Charco Azul is one of the most spectacular and cosiest natural pools, shaped naturally by the arches and hollows an ancient lava stream left behind. It invites visitors to a pleasant bath in the azure water, being protected from the impressive, crashing ocean waves.

It is easy to reach on foot. There is also a sun deck covered with a basalt arch and there are places where the biggest daredevils can dive from a couple of metres high.

15 **CRUZ DE LOS REYES (1,400M)** ☆ 2 🪧 4 🍷 1

This big wooden cross stands on an elevated plateau at 1,400m above sea level, intersected by the GR131 and the Camino de la Virgen trail. The latter path is renowned for hosting a festival known as the 'Descent of the Virgen of the Kings,' which occurs every four years on the first Saturday of July.

During the festival, a revered image of this holy figure is transported from its sanctuary in La Dehesa to Valverde, where it remains for a month. Halfway along this scenic route, a vibrant celebration unfolds. Communities from six local towns come together for traditional dances and festive family feasts, set upon elaborately adorned tablecloths. It's a joyous occasion that brings the island's communities closer and pays homage to their cherished patron saint.

16 **PICO DE MALPOSO (1,501M)** ☆ 3 🪧 4 🍷 1

El Hierro's highest peak at 1,501m with a viewpoint on El Golfo, accessible via the GR131 and a dirt road coming from another dirt road. Drive carefully, we got a flat tyre nearby.

17 **PARQUE CULTURA DE EL JULAN** ☆ 3 🪧 5 🍷 5

The Parque Cultural de El Julan is a remarkable archaeological site that offers a glimpse into the rich history of the Bimbaches, the island's original inhabitants. This cultural park is especially renowned for its extensive collection of petroglyphs left behind by these ancient people, known as 'Los Letreros de El Julan.' These petroglyphs are stone carvings and symbols that provide insights into the Bimbaches' beliefs and way of life.

The site also features remnants of an ancient gathering place known as a *tagoror*, shedding light on their communal traditions. Exploring the Parque Cultural de El Julan typically involves two parts: the first is the Visitors Centre, and the second involves a guided tour of the archaeological site itself. Visitors are advised to make reservations at least one day in advance for the guided tour.

18 **PLAYA DE TACORÓN** ☆ 5 🪧 3 🍷 4

Playa de Tacorón stands as one of the island's finest treasures, ranking among the best in the Canary Islands. Nestled near the Mar de Las Calmas, or the 'calm sea,' the beach offers remarkably tranquil waters year-round.

This small beach captivates with its unique colour palette – a seamless blend of the cerulean blue waters and the warm ochres and deep blacks of the volcanic sand. Conveniently, there is a small restaurant a few metres away.

A scenic road leads to the coastal village of La Restinga, renowned for serving up delicious fresh seafood, from its own harbour. From here, you can observe the El Julan slope, a testament to the island's volcanic history. Over 200,000 years ago, this slope witnessed the detachment of the south-western flank, a colossal event that saw the displacement of approximately 130km^3 of rocks.

Nearby, the Montaña de Los Cardillos rises with its vivid orange and reddish hues.

19 MAR DE LAS CALMAS ☆ 5 ⇨ 2 🍷 1

Mar de las Calmas is a remarkable and tranquil body of water throughout the year. The 'Sea of Tranquility', offers a sheltered location and a sense of tranquility that contrasts with the more turbulent waters found elsewhere. Its crystal-clear waters provide excellent visibility, making it a favorite spot for divers of all levels. Beneath the surface, a diverse underwater world awaits, with vibrant marine life, submerged volcanic formations, and even shipwrecks to explore, or underwater hot springs creating unique thermal vents with pockets of warm water. Home to a rich variety of marine species, including colourful fish, rays, sea turtles, and even occasional encounters with larger species like dolphins and whales, the area attracts marine biologists and researchers from around the world.

20 ARENAS BLANCAS ☆ 3 ⇨ 3 🍷 3

This beach offers a tranquil and uncrowded escape for those seeking solitude and relaxation. More uniquely it's the only beach on the island with white sand. Swimming here is a delight, with gentle waves and currents typically absent. It does not offer extensive facilities. If you desire a livelier atmosphere or additional amenities, El Verodal is located just under 3km away.

21 PLAYA DEL VERODAL ☆ 4 ⇨ 4 🍷 3

El Verodal Beach is situated near the iconic Orchilla Lighthouse and stands out because of its natural reddish-toned sand, a rarity on this island. It has a remarkable width, making it the broadest beach on El Hierro. While swimming at El Verodal may not always be advisable due to its powerful waves and currents, the beach remains a popular choice among visitors. While typical tourist services are not readily available here, there is ample parking facilities, with space for around 30 cars, ensure convenient access.

22 EL SABINAR ☆ 4 ⇨ 3 🍷 1

El Sabinar plateau, located in La Dehesa, is a remarkable natural area known for its unique Canarian juniper forest, (referred to as 'sabina' in Spanish), noteworthy for being one of the last remaining Canarian juniper woodlands, making it a precious ecological site. The juniper trees have been sculpted and twisted into bizarre and surreal shapes, a result of the powerful and persistent trade winds that sweep across the plateau. The trees appear as if they are frozen in time, creating a truly otherworldly landscape in a harsh and unforgiving world where the trees themselves stand as if engaged in a constant battle for survival against the relentless forces of nature.

23 MERIDIAN ZERO MONUMENT ☆ 4 ⇨ 3 🍷 1

A monument marks the most westerly point of the island, long considered the most westerly point of the world and used as Meridian Zero in many maps before Greenwich in 1884 was used as a global standard, with origins back to the era of Ptolemy.

24 FARO DE ORCHILLA ☆ 4 ⇨ 3 🍷 1

Punta de la Orchilla, standing a few meters from the archipelago's most westerly points, guides ships away from the dangerous basalt rocks.

The name 'Orchilla' is derived from the unique Orchil lichen that thrives on the rugged lava slopes of the region, including a prominent 238m peak.

The remote and isolated nature of Punta de la Orchilla makes it most probably Spain's 'most remote lighthouse', accessible via a 25km journey from Sabinosa on a partially paved path.

25 MUELLE DE ORCHILLA ☆ 4 ⇨ 3 🍷 1

This place marks the official end of the 650km long GR131 after a long descent passing El Sabinar. It's a small stone docking space built to ship materials for the construction of the Orchilla lighthouse, nowadays used to enjoy the water of the Mar de las Calmas.

El Hierro
↳ To Stroll

A **TAMADUSTE** ☆ 3 ↕ 2 🍷 3

Tamaduste is an old sailor town, very close to the airport on the Valverde coast with charming little streets.

Its large natural pool, with an almost perfect round shape provides an unforgettable bathing experience. It's also a great place for diving or paddle surfing, and there are solariums for a spot of sun-drenched relaxation as well.

B **POZO DE LAS CALCOSAS** ☆ 5 ↕ 1 🍷 2

Visit El Hierro's Pozo de las Calcosas in the north for a genuine experience. This village is distinguished by its unique *pajeras* houses with volcanic stone walls and rye straw thatched roofs, showcasing El Hierro's architectural heritage. The houses were originally built for summer use by fishermen.

Prized for their serenity and proximity, the natural pools here are a popular summer retreat for the residents of El Mocanal, who also enjoy the two local restaurants.

Descend the steep path to explore this well-preserved hamlet, resembling an open-air museum, and wander its quaint alleyways. Near the bathing area stands a unique statue of Neptune, crafted from recycled materials in 2007.

C **VILLA DE VALVERDE** ☆ 3 ↕ 3 🍷 4

Valverde in the north-east serves as the capital of the island with a population of 5,000 people, functioning as both the administrative and religious centre of El Hierro, since the island gained political independence in the 19th century.

There is a football field and you can find the bigger supermarkets on the island here. Most hotels however are located in El Golfo or further in El Mocanal.

Notable sites include the Church of Santa María de la Concepción, home to statues of the Christ at the Column and the Virgin, and the Town Hall, located directly opposite the church, a perfect example of traditional Canary Islands architecture.

Despite its inland location, the natural swimming pools at Tamaduste are conveniently nearby.

D **TIÑOR** ☆ 3 ↕ 1 🍷 0

The smallest village on the island is Tiñor, located in the north-east. Here you can find traditional houses, built out of volcanic rock, and sometimes featuring whitewashed wall that contrast with the surrounding landscapes.

The Bajada de la Virgen de Los Reyes (Descent of the Virgin of Kings) passes through the village every year in early July.

E **SAN ANDRÉS** ☆ 4 ↕ 2 🍷 2

San Andrés is a small village located on a plateau surrounded by beautiful rolling fields and fields. It is one of the oldest settlements on El Hierro, with roots tracing back to the early period of Spanish colonization and closely tied to the agricultural traditions of the island.

Known for traditional Canarian architecture, with characteristic features like stone houses with wooden balconies and tiled roofs, it serves a great starting place for hikes in the stunning natural surroundings. Its lush vegetation, terraced fields, and scenic views, make it a beautiful destination for nature lovers and photographers.

F **LAS PUNTAS** ☆4 ↕3 🍷3

The fishing town of Las Puntas is located at the north-eastern end of El Golfo, close to the Roques de Salmor. A small pier was built on one of its cliffs where we find the Hotel Puntagrande, which dates back to 1884, classified for many year as the smallest in the world. In the surrounding area there are numerous apartments and bungalows for rent, as well as a swimming pool, Cascadas del Mar, where visitors enjoy during the summer season.

G **TAIBIQUE** ☆3 ↕3 🍷3

This hilltop village overlooks the southern slopes of the island. A great place to stay if you like nature.

H **LA RESTINGA** ☆4 ↕2 🍷3

La Restinga is a small fishing village located at the southernmost tip of the island, known for its remote and tranquil setting. The local economy traditionally revolves around fishing and here you will find the best seafood on the island. It has gained popularity as a tourist destination, particularly for diving enthusiasts, because of the surrounding waters of the Mar de las Calmas Marine Reserve, known for their clear visibility, rich marine life, and unique underwater landscapes, making it one of the best diving spots in the Canary Islands. The village gained international attention in 2011 due to an underwater volcanic eruption nearby.

POZO DE LAS CALCOSAS

↰ PISCINA NATURAL LA MACETA

ROQUES DE SALMOR ↴

↰ GR131, VIEW ON EL GOLFO DURING THE CLIMB TO PICO DE MALPASO

HOTEL PUNTAGRANDE ↴

LA PALMA
ROQUES DE SALMOR
EL GOLFO
HOTEL PUNTAGRANDE

CAMINO DEL AGUA, TIÑOR & SAN ANDRÉS

EL SABINAR

LA DEHESA JUNIPER FOREST, EL SABINAR

DESCENT TO ORCHILLA

FARO DE ORCHILLA, SPAIN'S WESTERNMOST POINT

FINAL STRETCHES THE GR131, REACHING MUELLE DE ORCHILLA

Canary Islands
↳ Sources

SOURCES

barcelo.com
guidetocanaryislands.com
canaryforum.com
besidestheobvious.net
lanzaroteguidebook.com
golanzarote.org
hellocanaryislands.com
fcmanrique.org
mapcarta.com
solosophie.com
roughguides.com
salinasdejanubio.com
cactlanzarote.com
museodelapirateria.com
lageria.com
clublasanta.com
wonderfultenerife.com
centralreservas.tenerife.es
moonhoneytravel.com
webtenerife.nl
tenerifehost.com
dotravel.com
hikingtenerife.com
wikipedia.com
just-tenerife.com
ourwanders.com
dailytravelpill.com
aptosambassador.com
tenerife-costa-adeje.com
spain-tenerife.com
royaltenerife.nl
barrancodelinfierno.es
wandelenlangskusten.eu
triptenerife.com
mooistedorpjes.nl
vakantiehuizenspanje.nl
expedia.com
discover.hubpages.com
volcanoteide.com
karsteneig.no
summitpost.org
mountainsforeverybody.com
gigaplaces.com
novo-monde.com
overhere.eu
allesoverlanzarote.nl
zigzagonearth.com
spain-lanzarote.com
lanzarotegids.nl
ecotoerisme.eu
timeout.com
lanzarote.com
siebeninseln.de
amazinglanzarote.com
ferryhopper.com
thekitespot.com
rene-egli.com
lopesan.com
museosalinasdelcarmen.es
fuerteventuraenimagenes.com
pasaporteawonderland.com
royalfuerteventura.nl
blog.fuertecharter.com
gofuerteventura.com
fuerteventuraplayas.com
viagallica.com
visitafuerteventura.com
gran-canaria-info.com
swedishnomad.com
grancanaria.com
culturetrip.com
naturescanner.nl
peakvisor.com
spaingrancanaria.com
gran-canaria.traveltopper.eu
localguidegrancanaria.com
climbfinder.com
whileimyoung.com
climb-europe.com
traildino.com
denoorderzon.nl
wikivoyage.org
lanzarote3.com
coolturalanzarote.com
bowlandclimber.com
capturetheatlas.com
thenomadvisor.com
moganverde.es
yourtravelguide.nl
spanjevoorjou.com
visitcanaryislands.org
bajadaelhierro.com
elhierro.travel
tnttenerife.com
webairelibre.com
classic-collection.co.uk
royallagomera.nl
gomeralive.de
vallegranrey.es
etnograficolagomera.com
lagomera.travel
tripspoint.com
wikiloc.com
lapalma-oceaanzicht.nl
tui.be
etabroad.com
visitlapalma.es
lapalma-wandelen.nl
spanjevandaag.com
tenerife-wandelen.be
visit.tijarafe.com
fuerteventuraexplora.com
museosfuerteventura.com
lacasadeloscoroneles.org
otro-modo-surfschool.com
vakantiediscounter.nl
holaislascanarias.com
julychoo.com
gran-canaria.nl
klimgeiten.nl
visitagaete.com
gran-canaria.traveltopper.eu

COLOPHON

Texts: Charles Van Haverbeke
Images: Arthur Chambre
Copyediting: Léa Teuscher
Book design: Marcus Brown
Typesetting: Keppie & Keppie

D/2024/45/221 – Thema: WT, AJ
ISBN 978 94 014 9909 5
www.lannoo.com

↱ The Journey

625km
25,000m elevation
14 days
8 runners
2 support crew
1 photographer

8

RUNNERS, ACCOMPANIED BY A PHOTOGRAPHER AND SUPPORT CREW, CROSSED THE CANARY ISLANDS, FROM EAST TO WEST.

AIMING TO PUSH OUR LIMITS, EXPLORE THE UNKNOWN AND INSPIRE OTHERS, WE SPENT 14 DAYS IN THE WILD, FOLLOWING THE GR131.

THIS PART TELLS THE STORY OF THE JOURNEY OF OUR RUNNERS AND THE ADVENTURES AND CHALLENGES WE ENCOUNTERED ALONG THE WAY.

day	island	distance (km)	ascent (m)	descent (m)
01	Lanzarote	57	1,490	1,310
02	Lanzarote/Lobos/ Fuerteventura	48	710	672
03	Fuerteventura	52	1,260	1,280
04	Fuerteventura	42	1,040	1,190
05	Fuerteventura	37	683	731
06	Gran Canaria	46	2,450	940
07	Gran Canaria	28	802	2,311
08	Tenerife	53	2,730	2,310
09	Tenerife	43	2,740	1,600
10	Tenerife	66	2,534	4,570
11	La Palma	24	2,160	720
12	La Palma	45	1,984	3,421
13	La Gomera	45	2,384	2,382
14	El Hierro	40	1,683	1,681

OUR 'FOLLOW THE COAST' PROJECT

And then there was our notorious 'Follow The Coast' project. A lifelong adventure launched by Max and myself. We aim to run and explore the entire European coast through a series of 100km stages. Having measured and divided the entire coastline into pieces of 100km, we open a couple of dozen of them to the public every year. Anyone can register (www.followthecoast.com).

Our aim is to run and walk by every single inch of European coast. Having started a few years back in July 2019, every year we progress around between 2,500 and 3,000km on consecutive days. May 2023, we landed in Lisbon. In 2024 we are expecting to round Tarifa, the most southerly tip of Spain. And every 5,000km we publish a book, a virtual travel guide like the book you have in your hands.

The first book covered Knokke to San Sebastián, or the French west Coast. The second will cover San Sebastián to Tarifa, or the west of the Iberian peninsula. The third will explore Tarifa to Monaco. The fourth will be mostly Italian, Monaco to Trieste. And so forth. With 'Follow The Coast', we built a concept of exploration, of creating beautiful imagery and publications and a collective endurance challenge.

HOW THE SEEDS WERE PLANTED

When travelling, there is often this longing to understand the place. To wander through the landscape and gradually build up a know how of the mountains and valleys around. To not only see the map but understand the way the land flows, feel the texture of the land, grasp the shape of the region, to comprehend local customs and connect with the sheer size of it all.

Only when I have immersed myself to a certain degree, I feel less of a tourist and more worthy or grounded to the place. Trail running might be the activity that gets you closest to the soil. Road-tripping only gets you so far with the rubber and metal shielding you from our surroundings. With your feet rushing through the pebbles and dust and the ability to literally stand wherever you want, trail definitely is a ticket in.

I had set foot on Canarian soil before for various reasons. Lanzarote for triathlon, Fuerteventura for surfing and remote working, Gran Canaria for remote working again and trailing and finally Tenerife - surprisingly - for golfing. On each island, trails were explored, but only short strides, leaving a taste for more.

Talking to locals made me curious about local culture and about the hidden beauty that remained. There were talks about 'other islands'. Greener, more untouched, more pristine.

CROSSING THE CANARIES

So early 2022, the dots were connected. Wouldn't it be nice to explore the Canary Islands by foot, from east to west. What an epic challenge and journey it would be. What unique beauty we would find on our journey. Deserts, mountains, jungle, ridges, cliffs.

Komoot in hand, we started mapping trails by hand and were halfway Fuerteventura when we stumbled on the GR131. It didn't take long to realise that faith has crafted a trail that did exactly what we wanted. It crossed all the islands, exactly from east to west. Don't they say fortune favors the brave?

But wait, all the islands? Coast to coast? Not exactly. All but one. For some bizarre reason, the GR131 skipped the east and south part of Tenerife, notably the biggest and most visited island. Even stranger, it skipped the Anaga peninsula, which after a bit of research looked absolutely stunning. A rocky promontory covered with lush jungle, as if taken straight out of South America. So we connected the coast to the existing GR. The final verdict: 650km, 25,000 m elevation, 8 islands, 14 days.

THE DREAM TEAM

Some people like to go out alone on a challenge like this, but I felt the experience would be much richer with a group, bringing another dimension of energy. Travel and explorationare better working together as team. Kind people, curious people who were interesting and interested. To endure together and enjoy a campfire beer together. So yes, it would have to be a wolf pack, not a lone wolf.

It wasn't going to be an easy task, given the enormous challenge. Let's write it again: 650km, 25,000m elevation, 14 days, with some of the stages simply brutal. And to make things more interesting, we would have to climb and descent El Teide, Spain's highest summit at 3,718m high and face the decreased oxygen at high elevation. After nine days of trail. Each day would represent a fully blown trail challenge. 14 days in a row.

We needed seasoned trail runners. People who could endure physically and handle the technicality of the tracks, up and down. People who could handle adversity. Not simply athletes physically, also monks mentally. Team players who would put their ego aside for the group if needed. Comrades who would bring positivity and support to their fellows.

THE CREW

We needed a support crew. To move luggage from A to B and to hand carbs and water along the tracks. One or two people who could bear eight fatigued and demanding folks. A crew that could couple kindness with efficiency. A squad that was able to follow a tight schedule. We are lucky we found both angels and professionals in Maeve and Ben. We couldn't have found better.

We needed a world-class photographer. Luckily we knew a kind French gentleman, named Arthur. His masterpiece pictures were the ingredients for the first *Follow The Coast* book. We got him his own jeep, to roam freely across the islands, looking for spots to get close to the runners and the beauty.

Once the team was assembled, we needed a game plan. A schedule. And given the 14 days and the long distances, there was not a lot of room for margin. Imagine one being much slower than the group. The group could wait for delays, but reduced rest time would jeopardize our chances of completion. We could allow everyone to follow their pace. But then the gaps might become too wide, and the support crew would no longer be able to support all people. Even more pressing, we could miss a ferry, and then the whole plan would collapse. We needed military discipline.

We found eight runners. The first two were my loyal trail buddies Thomas (T) and Stephane. Colleagues once, now amazing friends and brothers in arms during many adventures. The GR20 in 7 days, the Tour du Mont Blanc in 4 days. We faced some challenges together, always with a beer and enjoying the local cuisine through great conversations. Later the second Thomas (VW) appeared, bringing along men of many wars Kasper, Matthias and - can you believe it - a third Thomas (VdW).

This squad brought a crazy trail resume along, stuffed with beasts like the Tor de Geants or 'TOR' (350k), one of the toughest challenges in the world. We felt like playing with the big boys. Arthur finally restored the gender balance, bringing his wife Amélie along, who had taken a few wins in shorter trails and was eager to join our party. What she lacked in experience she would make up in raw determination and willpower. Amélie & Arthur would bring Léo, their one-year-old son and Léo's grandma to support them. A different kind of family trip. Fifty per cent of the squad I had never met, but with eight seasoned runners, the team was complete and I believed that at least one of these folks would succeed in our mission impossible.

LE GRAND DÉPART

We started in Lanzarote. Often compared to extraterrestrial spaces like Mars or the Moon, the island features out-of-this-world black and red menus of stone and dust. Volcanoes, fields of petrified lava, deserts. Let's hope everyone was hungry, because the appetizer would be copious with 55km covering almost the entire island. We set up our camp close to Órzola, in a massive resort capable of housing more than a thousand beer-thirsty and sun-seeking tourists. The probability you would hear German or a thick British accent would be similar to finding water in the ocean.

In the midst of an atmosphere of holidays and abundance, we guarded our secret mission that was about to start. Beer didn't flow for most, water did. A few brave ones ordered 'only one'. Provocative masculinity? Or playful relaxation? Nervosity and careful planning filled the air anticipating 'Le Grand Départ' and slowly but surely the shape of some characters was taking form through jokes and conversation. But there would be plenty of time and space to discover more of each other personality. Hundreds of hours of road-tripping lay ahead.

At dawn, we departed from Órzola, a small hamlet in the north, the start of the GR131. No public, no arch of glory, just a 'let's go', followed by the sound of rubber on tarmac. The only cheering crowd was a bunch of plastic tables ready to host the few souls who would find their way to this part of town. Long dirt roads were the perfect scenery for getting to know one another.

Kasper marvelled at the local vegetation which was able to thrive in the windy, arid conditions. His 'veggie talk' would become a welcoming habit every time a crop met his eyes. His exploratory spirit might have caused him to forget about the key rules of ultra. Drinking, eating, sunscreen. He definitely missed the latter, because at the end of the day we had our first sunburned tomato. But he wasn't the only victim. Food poisoning forced one out of eight to stop without energy with the finish in sight. It's a miracle one can cover more than a marathon with no food since dawn.

The human mind is something remarkable, but a body without fuel has its limits. Harsh first principles. Some stayed behind to walk with the poor fellow until the last ounce of power had left his body. A beautiful sign of comradery. At the finish, we had lost and won. The first 54km was finished but we lost one man. What would the rest of this crazy journey bring?

DAY 2

The first next day. Sore legs will prompt you to stay in your relaxed position. Counterintuitively, you just have to overwrite your reflex. Because the reflex is a lie, optimizing your lazy state. Once you apply willpower to just start running, within a few minutes the pain will fade away and will leave the forefront of your mind. Beyond this point, there is a whole new world. It's classic trail textbook. Painful at first, a routine later.

A downhill of 15km through volcanic petrified fields was separating us from our first ferry. Armed with headlights we chased the night away and welcomed a glorious golden-red sunrise behind the volcanoes of Timanfaya, which one could mistake for a mighty eruption. As we started too late, we had to hurry up. Discipline and punctuality were skills that would need to be learned throughout the journey, and we learned it the hard way, when the curse of the ferry appeared in its bloody form.

A first victim fell on the single trail and got to know the unforgiving sharpness of lava rock. Luckily, no mortal wounds were counted and our first ferry was caught, leaving the Island of Fire. It was Léo's first cruise. After celebrating his first flight and his birthday, on the same day, it was one of many milestones he could tick off his bucket list.

The second day would be a weird day. It would be the only day to run on more than one island. As if two wasn't enough, the plan told us to run three islands. Lobos, a satellite island of Fuerteventura, with 2km diameter the size of a big nut, would be our next goal. We would have to take a ferry, then take a smaller boat to Lobos, stride through the island, popular for day tourists, to reach the lighthouse in the north and return.

Even at the slowest pace, we would have 2 hours to spare. So ironically, after the morning rush, in the middle of the day we lay down with our toes in the sand, took off our CamelBaks and try to get some tan on our still white-looking chest. On the other side lay Corralejo and the silhouettes of the volcanoes we would pass by later.

After the absurd stop-and-go and catching our third boat of the day, in the burning sun, we crossed the last asphalt of the day passing Corralejo's touristic paradise of quad rentals, umbrella cocktails and beats. Arid, ochre-coloured dirt roads led us towards the first volcano where we were met by Calderón Hondo's famous squirrels who approach you for their daily ration of nuts. A few hours later we strode through the dust on our first hill ending the day in La Oliva, where we would get a first taste of the local cuisine.

DAY 3 - GETTING INTO THE RHYTHM

Fuerteventura is a land of shadows and dust. Dirt roads, endless plains, rolling hills. A martian universe of brown and ochre. On Day 3, we would reach the mountainous midlands, for the first time ending the day with some serious climbs. I felt like a Tour de France climber eager to see the first Alps in sight. Hidden in a valley awaited the charming Betancuria where we would devour our lunch. Before that we would cross the bronze statues of Guise & Ayose, the last kings of Fuerteventura, after having conquered a single trail marked by stones patiently placed one next to the other over the total length of the mountain ridge climb. The first real climb let out the boys in the men with Thomas VW & myself heading on a little solo quest, pretending to be searching for the notorious 'escape of the day' in the Grand Tours of the cycling universe. Not long after the first duo reached the summit, Kasper lay his hand on the testicles of the former rulers, inspired by the many tourists touching Juliette's bronze breast in Verona, believing his touch would bring him luck and strength and eternal playfulness.

The support crew started to earn their five-star rating having prepared us a full-blown lunch, which came in handy before the two climbs that separated us from the finish at La Pared.

DAY 4 - LA PARED

Day 4 featured windy, bare dusty terrain literally in the middle of nowhere. After the forgotten town of La Pared post-lunch, which blends small resorts with surfer's town vibes, little by little we witnessed the grind below our feet faint to sand. The thinnest part of the island is the La Pared desert strip. Small on a map, but when you are standing in front of the path stretching out in nothingness, it feels like you are somewhere lost in Arizona or the Sahara. No wonder the famous Marathon des Sables chose Fuerteventura as a second destination of its famous franchise.

Kasper galloped away with a steady pace of 5min per km through the sand. After a cat-and-mouse game, we used the curvy grindy roads towards the finish of the day to prove that despite distance, age or place, boys will be boys. Is it smart to end the day with some 4 min-kms on day 4 / 14? Probably not, but oh god, is it fun. As majestic our end sprint was, so random was the finish line on some random roundabout with the sound of highway to cheer you up. After a fast stage, our Airbnb was a paradise of peace, hosting a garden full of local veggies and fruits (Kasper!). Mimicking the neighbours peacocks and enjoying a full blown dinner were the last feats prior to heading to bed.

bunch of hands (some bloody), checking off Day 5 with 237km of running done.

We felt invincible. Everyone felt strong and even crashes, burning sun, strong winds or daily marathons couldn't stop us. Ultrarunning teaches you that your body is an incredible instrument, its capacity matching to what you set your mind to and its natural state to move in nature.

FUERTEVENTURA TO GRAN CANARIA

Fuerteventura - Gran Canaria is the longest distance between any of the Canary Islands and we scattered on deck of a giant ferry lying in the sun, reading, napping or chatting. We docked in Las Palmas, the biggest city of the archipelago, but wouldn't have the time to pick up much of its charm, as the roadbook stipulated another hour's drive to Maspalomas, where we would start the first real mountain stage, with elevation topping 2,450m in ascent on a 46km course.

We started mentally preparing for another chapter. Excitement filled the air as we were about to embark on a different kind of mission. In the cafeteria of one of the many resorts in Maspalomas, Kasper told a story about an infamous sheep somewhere in southern Belgium that chased soldiers in the middle of the night during training practice.

LEAVING MASPALOMAS FOR THE HILLS

Maspalomas, with its vibrant nightlife full of ecstatic partygoers, contrasted sharply with our sport-focussed minds. In the midst of this madness, we got ready for the hills. The first two islands were a flat appetizer for what was waiting for us. With its steep canyons, this round island would be hosting our first mountain stages.
A different kind of challenge from the rolling running on the desert plains before and one that would demand more of our cardio, glutes and quads. Instead of arid plains, we would cross pine forests and gorges to reach the rocky midlands with the famous Roque Nublo as our northstar.

For the first time the group got splintered. Stéphane and I dropped immediately, held back by stomach problems. With a movie-inspired, 'cut the rope, save yourselves', we urged the rest of the crew not to wait. Also this is part of trail running and part of our adventure. For this mission to succeed, it was key for the group to get home in time to get the needed rest and to follow the milestones, with clear 'cut-off' times. If someone took too long, the support crew would not be able to attend the entire group and therefore jeopardize the 'mission'. Therefore, the strong would get priority on the weak.

HARDSHIP & ACCEPTANCE

Along the dried-out out riverbed marking Maspalomas, we saw the group lightly treading away out of sight. We would not see each other back before the finish at Cruz de Tejeda after a day in the blistering heat and through formidable mountain passes.

What would follow for Stéphane and I would be a grueling test of resilience, making the best of the cards that were dealt to us that morning. I didn't realize it in the moment or even the days after but ultra makes you not only a better athlete, it makes you a better person. It teaches you heads on that nothing is impossible and serves as a key lesson and metaphor for life that everything is fluid. Hardship will pass. Everyone got their stories.

Matthias fell on his hand on Day 5 gathering dust under his skin so we had to cut off the blisters and skin, cleaning off the blood while holding his hand. Afterwards he ran further like nothing happened with his typical energizing smile on his face. Thomas T fell on his head on Day 10 above the 3,000m line, cleaned up the streams of blood, urged his companions to continue and continued the rest of the day, another 50km, alone. He did so in a calm and confident fashion meticulously calculating when to arrive. He arrived, dead-tired but confidently only 30min before cut-off time.

Amélie went on this challenge with her baby. She took care of her child, in the morning and in the evening. She sacrificed the precious resting moments during the night. As a physiotherapist, she took care of the injured bodies of her fellow companions, including my own broken body, with a foot injury which miraculously disappeared after Day 7. Oh and on top of that, she ran a marathon in a day, with 1,800 elevation. While never having trained in the high mountains. Or never having done a multi-stage trail. If someone tells you life is over after kids, you gotta tell this story. If someone tells you something is impossible, read this again.

Personally, I got an inflammation on my foot on Day 2. So I learned a precious lesson that injuries can be cured during exercise. The increased blood flow accelerates the healing process. Prior to this experience, I thought an injury was somehow permanent and only rest would heal it back to completion. Knowing that injuries are not the end of the road and don't have to mean a sentence to rest, will broaden my world forever.

STOMACH PROBLEMS AND DIGGING DEEP

On Day 6, I got food poisoning in Gran Canaria. The cockroach passing on the floor at the entrance turned out to be a valid red flag. I spent every hour of the night sitting on the toilet, impatiently and worryingly hoping it would be cured by the morning.

Unable to take in any food, I swore by a Coke diet to cover the first very hilly 25km. My slow pace was a liability for the group so at the start I urged the peloton to stick to the schedule, running the flat paces, and leaving me behind. 'Luckily', Stéphane also suffered from stomach problems on the same day so we made our way towards and in the first mountains together.

Under the African sun, I was hot and cold. The 4th and then the 5th Coke turned my mouth into a fountain of stickiness, but Coke - the drink - was the only source of energy my stomach could take.

The finishline at Cruz de Tejeda was reached with lots of emotion, taking strength from the thoughts of family and friends. In the last rays of the sun, back against the famed cross in front of the parador, marking the midpoint of the island, I didn't even try to hide the tears welling up. Digging deep in a completely drained body is a different form of suffering than fighting the pain to go faster. This was a fight to keep going.

WE ARE CAPABLE OF ANYTHING WE SET OUR MIND TO

There are two kind of victories. There is the one of the victor, who finds 'the perfect race'. It's a journey of being lucid, being 100% in tune with one's body. Finding that perfect line to flirt with, getting you to a state of trance. It's an incredible kick to feel such an experience. And there is the victory of the loser. The so-called 'loser'. The self-stated loser. When you find yourself in a body you don't recognise. Both victories are worth a celebration. The latter marks a different kind of mental power. The power to accept your weaknesses. The power to accept an inferior version of yourself, and despite the poor cards, still carry on. It's a mental victory.

I learned that a human is capable of becoming sick, losing the normal version of itself and then returning from it, even during physical challenges. It's incredible to observe that a body can run and heal at the same time. This knowledge and confidence will stay with me forever. You are much more capable that you think. You are stronger than you think.

On Day 6, when the sun dropped, shivers appeared. The stunning sunset with the silhouette of the Roque Nublo against the golden canvas was one that I later saw on the pictures. Sweating as a pig, 39° C of fever forced me deep in the bunk beds.

The next day, the thermometer still showed 39° C when the start was given. I always swore to push until the end, but going in with a fever didn't seem responsible. Not to Dr. Google, nor the real doctors I consulted. With sadness but with a firm belief I did the right thing, I waved goodbye to the runners hiking up the first hill the next day. 45 minutes later I asked the thermometer for another chance: 37.5° C.

Cleared from all charges. Free as a bird. Feeling weak and light-headed, I turned to logic. A 28km stage, mostly downhill. Plenty of time before the ferry. No reason not to start. The beginning of a recovery journey of seven days. Slowly but surely, I got better, able to run again in the afternoon driven by adrenaline because of the massive hurdle I got the opportunity to overcome.

On Stage 8, Matthias joined me. On Stage 9, Thomas T was my companion at the tail of the group. On Stage 10, the monstrous Teide was conquered, the 4,000m downhill behind us and the longest stage in the bag.

DAY 7 - THE EASIEST DAY ON PAPER

My Gran Canaria journey didn't really reflect the group's, so it's hard to tell their stories. Everyone has had their fight. The one that made a lasting impression on me and on the group was Amélie's, who fought a battle in the back of the pack.

Arriving in Agaete, a small port town full of tourists enjoying their beer with not a worry on their minds, she collapsed on the ground while the rest was enjoying their pizzas. Grounded by cramps and fatigue, we were forced to let her get back to her senses, putting her legs up and refueling with coke and cold water on her forehead. Amélie had shown an enormous demonstration of willpower.

Day 7 was the easiest stage in the book and on paper: 28km with mostly descent through pine forest. But what a battlefield it had been for some.

What was lying ahead was about to get us truly tested. The madness of Tenerife. The main island with 3 days of 50k+ and almost 3,000m verticals per day. We better had something saved for this one. Ironically, some just had to dig deep to push through what felt like a hopeless situation. But unmistakingly and surprisingly, I felt I was getting better, little by little. The race would be conquered in bed.

ANAGA, THE FORGOTTEN JUNGLE

On the largest island, we would find the biggest variety in terrain. Jungle & cliffs on Day 8, never-ending pine on Day 9 and alpine terrain and the moon landscape of the Teide Natural Park on Day 10.

The first day was on an improvised trail. We had to connect the island extremities. If the GR didn't provide the route, we would carve one out. Not literally, as an existing trail network connected the mythical east of the island to the plains of San Cristóbal de la Laguna. The state of the trail wasn't always that great as few people travelled to these parts of the island. A real shame, as the landscape is gorgeous up there. Great rocks plunging in the ocean and surrounded by lush jungle. A small village near a black sand cove-shaped beach. A white lighthouse overlooking the bay as if wanting to spot ships transporting mysterious cargo. It felt like we were dropped on the set of an exotic movie in drug cartel territory.

The village near the sea could only be reached by a 3km-long single trail, impossible for car or bike to ride on. Televisions or sofas had to rely on the strong backs of donkeys or the propellers of helicopters. And yes, the tiny houses had inhabitants, as was confirmed by a friendly man waving us good morning while cleaning his porch.

YOU SHALL NOT PASS

This day counted almost 3,000 hm over a 55km course. An endless up and down through not well-maintained paths, often wondering whether they were a path at all. In order to stay on our track we had to pass a 'you shall not pass' sign warning us about the dangers of tumbling from cliffs and mortal drops.

With the confidence and stupidity of seasoned trail runners, we decided to 'at least check how bad it was' and unsurprisingly we continued our route. Luckily, everyone kept their feet dry and bodies intact.
Our reward: some of the best views you will find from a single trail, barely the width of your feet towering above the cliffs.

Dense jungle later on changed into the dark forests of the Bosque Encantado, which could have featured as decor for The Forbidden Forest in the Harry Potter movies. An hour later without encountering Hagrid we moved again into the famous plains of San Cristóbal de la Laguna, connecting to the high midlands of the island. A long and intense day, spent most of the day with Matthias, taking turns in babysitting on the back of the pack, grateful for this time of getting to know him better. Arthur got fined for using his drone. In front, Kasper and the Thomas'es raced on the boring but brutal asphalt strokes towards the finish line.

GETTING READY FOR D-DAY

Day 9 could not have been more different from Stage 8. The common trait was the lack of access. On a 50km course, there was only one point where we would meet a stretch of asphalt. The rest would be pine forest. We would start at 1,000 and end at 2,000. From this moment on, when the trees opened up, the Teide would not leave our side. The goal couldn't be more clear. Slowly but surely we gained altitude and got closer to the Teide National Park, a stretch of nature above the 2,000m line.

Day 10 would be the most anticipated day. The queen of all stages conquering the monstrous Teide. To do so, we would mount a long climb starting from 2,000m altitude to 3,700m. We had to go very early in the morning to be on time for the ferry and to avoid the fine you get when you linger on the summit after 9am without a permit. And if that wouldn't be enough, a 4,500m descent from 3,700m to sea level with a little peak in between awaited after the peak of all peaks. Leg day, to say the least.
We would start at 4.30am the next morning armed with pills against altitude sickness, named Diamox, and enough water to cover the 25km of trail with 1,700m up and down without and food stations.

EL TEIDE

Starting from the parador, the mythical hotel where cyclists stay to prepare their upcoming grand tours. A classy hotel with classic white table cloth was the decor of our silence before the storm. A few meters away Primož Roglič and Sepp Kuss were preparing their season. We didn't know it back then, but both would come out victorious in a Grand Tour later in the cycling season, respectively in the Giro d'Italia and Vuelta d'Espana. A sign of great fortune to dine in the presence of champions.

We were lucky indeed, because I spotted my only mistake in the logistics roadmap as our ferries of the next day were booked at 8am, an impossible deadline even if we would get up immediately. The gods of ferries smiled mercifully upon us and granted us new bookings at 6pm. We knew our deadline for tomorrow. After good pasta, beers for some, milk for others, we went to bed. A handful wanted to stay with the Olympic athletes on the neighbouring tables who were weighing their food and contemplating another day of training on their quest for glory.

ON TOP OF THE WORLD

The next day, in the dark, we started our disciplined ascent to the summit. Target to be on Spain's highest peak: 8.30am. Everyone was instructed to return back by cable car if the clock passed 9:00am and the peak was still in sight. Usually sensitive to high altitude, I took a Diamox and got sentenced to peeing literally every 20min. Luckily I felt strong and led the pack which felt liberating and free. Alone with the gods.

Thomas VW & I reached the summit at 8.18am, followed closely by Matthias, who had the day of his life. He would continue a blistering pace and finish first in Los Cristianos to await the group with a Corona in one hand, a burrito in the other. Freed by mastering the peak without accidents (we would only hear about Thomas T's dramatic crash later), the threesome dartelled down the long descent to the parador, where the crew would allow a tyre switch. Equipped for nightwalks on high altitude, we started to sweat in our long pants and jumpers as the sun was unmistakingly rising.

LA PALMA

Decompression would be an enemy to tackle. Day 11 was 'only' 24km, but fully uphill and the floor would be lava. Literally, as we walked over a crest of active volcanoes. No smoke or fire, but knowing that only a few years before one of these bad boys had erupted, was pretty special. We would marsh the whole day in a sea of black dust, fine like sugar, with bright green pine trees forming a unique spectactre. We marched on the Cumbre Vieja, the volcanic crest making a spine of the island allowing incredible views on the surrounding islands peering through the clouds which especially in La Palma form at lower altitude.

Kasper, the para who never stopped smiling, didn't seem to get tired. Playing in front of the group, moving back to talk to another and moving back again, he resembled a trail-running Obélix, having fallen in the cauldron of running potion, which made him unstoppable.

We ended the day early and made our way to Llos Llanos de Aridane, a mid-sized city surrounded by mountains in the midst of plains. For the first time in a week, time boxing was not needed and unimportant, so we took a little holiday from the rush, sitting under the trees and ordering local croquettes and sipping a beer, like there was no tomorrow.

With the finish in sight, we didn't make mistakes and the group digested the remaining 40km with relative ease. We made it. The feared Day 10, which had lingered on the back of our minds from Day 1, was behind us.

THE NEXT DAY

Luckily there was a tomorrow. We would march to the highest point of the island along the ridge of the curving Caldera de Taburiente, the eroded crater that dominated the island. Different to, but as majestic as our raid to the Teide, this stage would bring us to the summit at 2,612m, being surrounded by alien-looking telescopes, their eyes fixed towards the skies.

Then, the longest descent of the trip would await with a 2.6km drop over less than 18km. You don't have to be a rocket scientist to calculate that the average gradient is significantly more than 10%.

Another monster for our already molested quads.
With a grand finale, because less than 1km before the end, my Garmin watch was still marking 300 meters of altitude. Wondering if something was wrong and shaking the sports watch to force it back to reality, an S-curved goat path appeared before our feet.

Towering above the calm sea town of Tazacorte, the Mirador de la Punta is a viewpoint with dazzling sights offering a brutal downhill before we could plunge in the ocean and enjoy a vanilla ice cream on the black beach.

LA GOMERA, THE LAST TEST

A closer look at the roadbook would teach an observant reader that although the stages itself were less spectacular, the margin for error would be very small. Because the last islands are significantly smaller, we would need to take a ferry every day now in order to hop to the next day. We collectively decided to get out of bed earlier to reduce the chances of missing a ferry.
So, on the last days we started in the dark. We had gotten this close to the finish, we couldn't let this slip away because of longer napping time. This approach paid off. Largely on time for the ferry to La Gomera, we treated ourselves with chicken nuggets from the McDonald's next to the ferry port in La Palma. Rumor has it that god himself created it on the seventh day when everyone thought he was resting.

The next day, Day 13, felt like the last day. It was not the last day of running. But the true last day, Stage 14, was 'only' 40km, with 'only' 1,200 elevation, and most importantly, no time pressure. No ferry to catch.
Only barbecue and ocean view waiting for us. Therefore, the mental finish line was drawn at La Gomera. The day after would be a walk in the park. Smiles and waves. No pressure. Only champagne.

UNLEASHED

Day 13, we did have our last ferry to catch. Climbing towards the Garajonay midlands through jungle and forest, the sun started to rise painting the silhouette of El Teide in the orange sky. At Chipude, having left the summit behind, we had 15km to go and 5 hours left.
We would make it, even if we had to crawl with one hand tied around our back.

Powered by the espressos offered by the crew and the lack of pressure, our confidence and playfulness grew. Like young horses at the sight of the first spring rays, a herd of little boys and a joyful girl threw themselves into the deep, on the dusty single trail down to Vallehermoso, technical and dangerous, as if they hadn't run 600km before. A glorious race towards the beach at the end of the road, saluted by the ocean. Sport has the power to bring back the child in us. That descent, freed from the ties of the schedule, was sport in its essence. Comradery, rivalry, playfulness, freedom.

The roundabout at the end near the little beach bar was more epic than an Arc de Triomphe could ever be, with every finisher cheering for the next in line. The beach bar witnessed a never-ending flow of orders on everything we lay our eyes on. Fanta, espresso, beer, M&Ms, prawns, eggs, beer again, prawns again. We made it.

THE LAST DAY

Paris in the Tour de France. For old times sake, we stuck together for most of the day. The journey is about doing this together. Kasper brought back some vintage veggie talk and got so excited he walked into a bush with sharp thorns. Peloton talks, reminiscing about the past days and what meat we would throw on the barbecue tonight. The scenery accompanied the relaxed ambiance.

Mediterranean vibes with hints of Tuscany or Provence make El Hierro yet another landscape to taste among the endless treasures of the Canaries. But halfway through Kasper and I rolled up our sleeves for a little mid-stage battle inspired by 'peak fever' with the Pico de Malpaso in sight.

When a boy sees a hill, he wants to get to the summit. Having reached it, we threw ourselves into the descent, a non-technical and therefore a tough, fast one with Kasper raging like a bull one last time. A friendly bull. A powerful bull. At the last aid station, 7km from the end and the westernmost point of Europe, we waited in the shade, to regroup. For the last trails, we would form a single formation to conclude our formidable collective journey across the Canary Islands.

WHERE THE GR131 ENDS

It's incredible what you can do. You don't need to be a professional athlete to achieve the impossible. We just did it. Eight brave souls passed the lighthouse and made their way to the beach. Not a white sand, palm tree type of beach, but a concrete pier sticking out in the ocean.

But it looked like paradise to us.

Champagne, cool water and rest awaited. Eternal rest. Or at least for a while. Ecstasy filled the air as we touched the 'embarcadero'. Once built to construct the lighthouse, now our finish line.

Shoes were symbolically released from their duties. Our CamelBaks which so loyally had our backs for two weeks were destined to the cloakroom. The sound of high fives disrupted the peace and quiet that one lonely tourist was searching for at this end of the world.

We dove into blue water at the westernmost point of Europe.

Where the GR131 ends.

THE END

What an incredible challenge. The GR131. In 14 days.
625km, 25,000m elevation. More than 48km per day or 1,800m up per day. For 14 days in a row.
Our goals were to go beyond our comfort zone, to explore unknown territory and to create inspiring beauty.

We challenged ourselves.
I honestly gave myself a 50% chance of finishing this journey.
But then on a sunny day in April, we did it. The human body is made to be in motion. Once released in nature, you will be astonished by what it is capable of.
We survived crashes, sickness, ultramarathons and monstrous terrain.
And quite crazily, we did it as a group. What a supportive and positive attitude among people who barely knew each other and were pushed to their limits.
I'm honoured to get to know better some incredible, kind, brave and strong souls.

We explored unknown territory.
Eight islands. Desert and jungle. Mountains and endless plains.
Sunshine and rain. Not really, only sunshine.
The Canaries bring unmatched variety, a paradise for nature lovers, hikers and cyclists.

Last but not least, we created inspiring beauty.
With these last words, the last goal has been achieved.
Writing this book has been a collective journey with a little army of people spending hundreds of hours to get this done.
I'm grateful for everyone who believed in this little project and passionately pushed it to life.
Thank you for your running, supporting, kind words, copy, pictures, picture editing, design, belief...
Thank you.